3.09

25.

trout in Dirty Places

Theo Pike

50 rivers to fly-fish for trout and grayling in the UK's town and city centres

Merlin Unwin Books

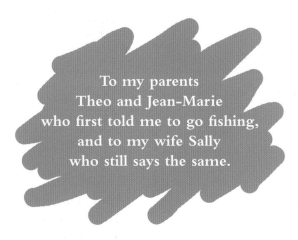

To my parents
Theo and Jean-Marie
who first told me to go fishing,
and to my wife Sally
who still says the same.

First published in Great Britain by Merlin Unwin Books, 2012
Text © Theo Pike, 2012

Merlin Unwin Books Ltd
Palmers House
7 Corve Street
Ludlow, Shropshire SY8 1DB
U.K.

www.merlinunwin.co.uk
email: books@merlinunwin.co.uk

The author asserts his moral right to be identified as the author of this work.
A CIP catalogue record for this book is available from the British Library.
ISBN 978-1-906122-42-3
Designed and set in Bembo by Merlin Unwin
Printed and bound by 1010 Printing International Limited

The author has made every effort to ensure that the information in this book is correct at the time of going to press. However, fishing seasons and other regulations may be subject to change: if in doubt, please check with your local Environment Agency office, Rivers Trust, or other fisheries managers.

CONTENTS

FOREWORD

Charles Rangeley-Wilson

I've thought a lot about why fishing for wild trout in a city should be so compelling. On one level there is the simple thrill of casting a line within sight of office blocks, planes overhead, trains rattling by: all that clatter and rush and you, the still point at its centre, tuning in to a slower, deeper rhythm of water and wild spaces.

Fishing brings you to a different place in more ways than one and if you can get there on the way home or in the lunch hour, then the pleasure, for being stolen or endlessly surprising – and the sight of a brown trout rising to mayflies in a city stream really is endlessly surprising – will be so much the richer. But underlying and resonating with this thrill is the wonder of finding something emblematic of wildness in the midst of its very opposite. There is Romance in that, in the thought that Nature can overcome, or at the very least co-exist. And if one way of accessing that Romance and the sense of hope that springs from it is with a fishing rod in hand, wet waders sploshing along a busy High Street, then why not?

As Theo's fascinating, celebratory book reveals, rivers and fish lost to generations of anglers – the once-wild rivers on the fringes of cities that have now grown to engulf them and the stunning, fabled trout that held on in spite of that encroachment until finally they gave in to tides of filthy water – are there again, for the first time in a century or more. Clean rivers and wild trout in the city!

City fishing for wild trout is – as well as being left-field, exotic on the doorstep, adventurous in the best sense, cheap and very cheerful – a wonderful affirmation of hope, a declaration that Nature can overcome and that we can build a world where there is room for both people and the wild.

Go to it.

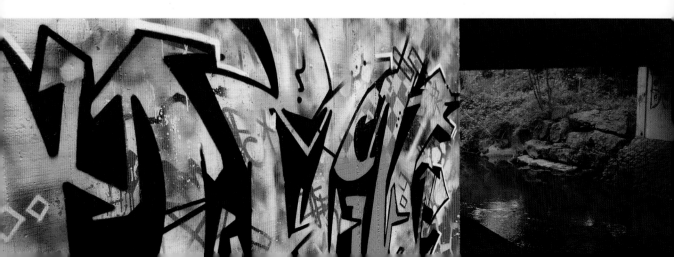

INTRODUCTION

Fly-fishing the urban wilderness

For adventurous fly-fishers at the start of the twenty-first century, it's easy to get the impression that there are no new waters left to discover.

Less than eighty years after Negley Farson fished his way across Chilean Patagonia with companions who thought the rivers were getting too crowded if another angler appeared within ten miles, Planet Earth already feels like a much smaller place. Cheap flights and plentiful leisure time have brought the world's furthest-flung waters within easy reach, and the new media revolution makes even the most exotic destinations feel familiar and a little too well trodden.

Steelhead in British Columbia? *Seen it on DVD.* Mahseer in the Himalayas? *All over the internet.* Taimen in Mongolia?

Wasn't somebody video-blogging that last week?

But as you're about to discover, fly-fishing's most fulfilling new frontier may be no further than the urban river at the end of your street. And there's nothing more inspiring and counterintuitive than casting a fly for iconic clean-water species like trout and grayling in the post-industrial surroundings of some of our most damaged riverscapes.

The world's first industrial revolution – and Britain's biggest conurbations – were powered by water flowing swiftly over Jurassic and Carboniferous geology, rich with deposits of coal, iron ore and limestone. Rivers naturally aggregate their catchments' features, so these steeply-falling streams paid the price for landscape-scale industrialisation: impounded and dewatered

5

for power and industrial processes, then converted into open drains to carry away every possible form of human and manufacturing effluent. Many rivers literally died at this point: scoured by floods of toxic waste, superheated by power stations and steel mills, hemmed in with vertical walls, even culverted completely when they overflowed with filth and became too much of a risk to human health.

Almost without exception, industrial rivers started out as their towns' defining features, but the economics of exploitation turned them into dangerously uncontrollable forces of nature that had to be subdued at almost any cost. Modern river restorationists recognise three distinct stages in our historic attitudes to urban waterways. From around 1850 to 1950, rivers were used for sanitation, waste disposal, and sometimes transport. Between 1950 and the 1990s, sewage treatment and pollution control improved dramatically thanks to the privatisation of the water companies, the creation of the National Rivers Authority, and finally the abrupt decline of Britain's heavy industries: a tragedy for many communities, but an unexpected blessing for the rivers.

Finally, in the early 1990s, a few radical thinkers returned to the realisation that waterways weren't just drains and sources of disease, but positive assets that could once again improve our lives and lift our spirits: the same pioneering philosophy that drives so many of the people and organisations you'll meet in these pages. (Today the upward trajectory of river restoration across Europe has been made legally binding by the EU's Water Framework Directive, complete with targets for the UK's Environment Agency to deliver in the form of river basin management plans by deadlines in 2015, 2021 and beyond. Classed as 'heavily modified water bodies', many of our urban rivers will probably be restricted to targets of 'good ecological potential' rather than the optimum 'good ecological status'… but it's a start).

All this time, relict populations of wild native trout and occasionally grayling had been holding out in headwaters and other refuges on the fringes of industry: now they started dropping downstream again, often as unnoticed as the recovering rivers themselves, to recolonise reaches that hadn't seen an adipose fin for generations.

Trout can stand small amounts of organic pollution, but grayling tolerate only the cleanest water, so their presence is an excellent indicator of the highest chemical and biological water quality. Like the knotgrass, docks and rosebay willowherb which reclaimed the barren stony landscapes left by the last Ice Age, salmonids of all species are natural early-adopters, and they're surreally suited to life amongst the decaying human infrastructure of post-industrial rivers. In these urban ecosystems, collapsing blockstone weirs provide oxygenation and pocket-water habitat. High walls and overhanging gantries give shade on the hottest days, and spawning can take place in plumes of gravel behind main-channel boulders, or on gravel ramps kicked up by the scour pools of major weirs if tributaries are blocked.

By the time urban trout reach maturity, they're hardened survivors, tender yet tough, streetwise to short-lived slugs of pollution, and capable of clinging onto life under the most adverse circumstances. In and around our towns and cities, I've gradually come to realise, there may very well be more water with trout than without.

But despite their recovery and fragile resilience, we shouldn't be in any doubt that urban trout and grayling still inhabit rivers on a knife edge. Chances are, between the time I finish writing this book and you start reading it, at least one of the fisheries I've selected as a snapshot of urban river restoration at the start of the twenty-first century will have been wiped out by pollution. Maybe this incident will be right in your face, a matter of public scandal like Thames Water's spillage of bleach into my own River Wandle in London, or Grosvenor Chemicals' fire on Slaithwaite's River Colne. But just as often, it may be as silent and insidious as the insecticides which leached from a wood yard at the top of the Rhymney River in the south Wales coalfield, killing fish-food invertebrates for miles downstream, undetectable without months of patient, determined detective work.

Besides the occasional catastrophe that headlines the national news, urban rivers face a whole suite of everyday problems, many of which you'll encounter as a fly-fisher exploring these ambivalent places. Every town offers countless sources of diffuse pollution, from dark grey fine-particulate road-dust that settles behind weirs and behaves more like water than ordinary mud, to iron-rich minewater seeping from long-abandoned tunnels and drainage adits. That ozone tang in the air probably suggests treated sewage effluent, contributed day and night by your fellow citizens, while rags trailing on brambles and low-hanging twigs betray sewer misconnections or Victorian-era combined sewage and stormwater outfalls which overflow in times of heavy rain. Sheet-steel revetments and concrete walls have often been installed as bunds to isolate the river from industrial waste permeating the soil and groundwater, and it's a rare dry-cleaning business that doesn't leave a legacy of land contami-

nated by chlorinated solvents. And then of course there's fly-tipping: in the words of Brian Clarke, 'anything that can be picked up, carried and dropped, you'll find it in an urban river'.

But as Stuart Crofts also points out whenever we're stalking grayling on his native River Don in Sheffield, salmonids love stability, and that's exactly what post-industrial rivers offer them: conditions which will undoubtedly have helped some populations improve even in the months since I visited and photographed their gritty urban environments. And the fact that these beautiful pollution-sensitive fish are here in the first place isn't always coincidental, or simply a citified variation on Christopher Camuto's whimsical compression that, 'roughly speaking, if you rub a mountain with cold, flowing water, you get a trout'.

All over Britain, soon after the benefits of better sewage treatment began to bite, people started regarding their local rivers in a fresh light. Inspired by forward-thinking organisations like the Wild Trout Trust and the Grayling Society, they looked for new frontiers in fishing and river restoration, and found them hiding in plain sight: under culverts, through industrial estates, and along the sprawling edges of big-box supermarket car parks where derelict mills recently stood.

Many of the people I've profiled got started in river restoration just like I did: driven by quixotic curiosity to follow ill-reputed urban streams wherever they led, slowly falling under the spell of their unloved currents, forming alliances with other wet-wellied pioneers, clearing decades of fly-tipped rubbish, and gradually taking responsibility for restoring water quality and habitat in whole river reaches and even catchments.

And inspiration flowed both ways. In 2008, enthused by the achievements of small voluntary groups on the Wandle and Colne Water in particular, the Wild Trout Trust launched its *Trout in the Town* programme: a support structure for anyone who wanted to see iconic wild trout making a comeback to their own part of the inner city. In various stages of development, *Trout in the Town* chapters already bracket Britain from London to Glasgow.

For all its international leadership in hands-on habitat improvement, I like to think the Wild Trout Trust does its best work by giving small groups of volunteers the expertise and confidence they need to champion positive views of unsung rivers to the statutory authorities and other more established wildlife organisations – some of which may never have considered the river as part of their conservation plans. Armed with knowledge and the right set of circumstances, these grassroots initiatives can grow all the way up to full-blown Rivers Trust status, officially recognised as project partners by government, its agencies and other third-sector bodies alike. (According to their own figures, Rivers Trusts are probably the fastest growing environmental movement in the world today, having expanded from five founding Trusts in 2004 to more than forty in 2011, covering more than eighty per cent of the UK's total acreage of land and water).

As Rivers Trusts, *Trout in the Town* chapters, independent local river care groups or angling clubs, all the voluntary organisations looking after our urban rivers are founded on deeply democratic and charitable principles, relying on voluntary involvement and consensual partnerships to generate surprising levels of social cohesion, and get local communities involved in caring for their rivers.

Over the last decade, river restoration in the UK has ridden a strong current of social and philosophical as well as environmental change, embodied in a deepening conviction that these unloved urban places, once heedlessly trampled in the rush to be elsewhere, have become the responsibility of everyone with the vision to appreciate their scarred and paradoxical beauty.

And why not? Recent studies in the field of ecosystem services have valued the health benefits of living close to green space in urban areas at £300 per year for the average person: probably more for anglers who don't just look at their surroundings but get actively immersed in them. Our new urban fisheries are a precious common resource, and from this angle it's logical to think of post-industrial river fishing as a positive ethical choice in challenging moral and economic times. Low cost, low carbon, low time commitment: this is where you can relax and get your fishing fix while your other half goes shopping, with no worries about lost rods, jet lag and all the paraphernalia and nagging guilt of high-flown destination angling. Crowds will probably stare and point from bridges, but you've already slipped through a portal into a parallel world, where shoals of grayling hover beside traffic cones and shopping trolleys, and trophy trout sip dry flies in the shadow of crumbling mill walls a hundred years older than America.

Naturally, there's a balance to strike. For months before starting to write this book, I thought long and hard about the dangers of hotspotting: the risks of exposing vulnerable recovering rivers to public atten-tion, and putting too much pressure on fragile populations of fish. But on the whole I believe it's better for an urban river to be known about and cared for – by the people and for the people – than overlooked, undervalued and repeatedly destroyed by pollution or simple ignorance. Then, if the worst does happen, we'll know what's been lost for a second time, and take savage steps to replace it properly.

So now it's over to you. Throughout these pages, I've tried to avoid giving too many detailed directions: partly to protect the rivers from too much casual pressure, partly to heighten your own sense of explo-ration and discovery in a post-industrial wilderness as unique as the hills of Assynt, Patagonia or the Kola Peninsula. This is truly a foreign country in your own backyard, a place where you can combine outstanding wild fishing with the deep satisfaction of getting involved in improving the ecosystem you live in. It's the cutting edge of twenty-first century fly-fishing, and the wild trout and grayling are closer than you think.

OKEHAMPTON

Rivers East and West Okement

The last week of August 1976 finally brought an end to England's hottest summer since records began. For 45 days, most of the south west had sweltered without a drop of rain: reservoirs were pans of baking mud, and people collected water from standpipes on the streets.

Finally, on the bank holiday weekend, the drought broke over north Dartmoor with a huge cloudburst and floods flashing down the faces of Meldon Quarry into an acre of rock chippings near the West Okement. A torrent of acid stone dust, magnesium, iron and arsenic rushed down the river towards Okehampton, killing almost every fish and insect as far as the Torridge: a distance of 14 miles. But the perfect storm that probably changed the Okement's trout fishery forever had already been brewing for years.

In 1970, four miles above Okehampton, construction started on the 132ft, 70-acre Meldon Dam: just one of several designed to take advantage of Dartmoor's self-generated microclimate and yearly rainfall of more than 80 inches. Two years later, the penstocks were closed, the reservoir started filling, and the compensation flow for the West Okement was fixed at 7.7 megalitres per day.

With its average flow reduced by three-quarters, the West Okement was already under serious stress by the time of the drought, and it's estimated that fish and invertebrates in this sort of naturally-acidic upland system would have taken at least seven years to recover from an incident like August 1976. But the likelihood is that they never got that chance – and ironically for all the best reasons. In 1981 a salmon pass was opened on the weir at Monkoke-hampton, and that winter's record run took full advantage: 'Fish up every ditch', wrote Poet Laureate Ted Hughes for Anne Voss Bark's anthology *West Country Fly Fishing*, '*and salmon seen spawning within the town of Okehampton, probably for the first time in hundreds of years*'.

This may have been the final twist for the trout of the Okement, previously numerous enough to be recorded in catch reports of four to eight dozen, including occasional trophies up to a pound. Recent observations by the Riverfly Partnership's Dai Roberts on the Rhymney suggest that if invertebrate populations are weakened by other factors, voracious salmon parr can send a river's ecosystem into a negative feedback loop that never allows it to recover: without significant caddis predation on salmon eggs,

Urban fishing starts here: on the edge of Okehampton, the West Okement tumbles over a series of natural rock weirs

At East Bridge, high walls and old mill buildings reflect the river's industrial history

more eggs survive, and more salmon fry and parr predate in turn on the remaining invertebrates. Much research still needs to be done, but it's a narrative that seems to fit the Okement perfectly.

"Of course the river's changed," says another local angler gloomily, peering over the West Bridge as a passing shower spatters on the windscreens of passing cars and flecks the beery surface of the pool below us. "Now the weir's gone down at Monkokehampton, it's full of migratory fish. I had a five-pound trout taken to the taxidermist forty years ago, it was nothing to catch fifty trout of ten or twelve inches each. Old Ted Walsh the barber – he'd have a hundred a day on the wet fly. You couldn't do that now."

But the East and West Okements still carve quietly down through the town in parallel sandstone clefts to converge in a sprawl of supermarket car parks, and it's cheering to see that even massive abstraction, quarry pollution and the town's own

history of industry and fishing pressure can't eradicate the trout that splash in the foam lines. Domesday Book listed just one mill at Okehampton: in 1894 the *Comprehensive Gazetteer of England and Wales* recorded joinery works, three flour mills and a large cattle market that fed a noxious complex of tanneries, boot factories, and bone-crushing plants on both branches of the river. Until its pipe broke, the chemical fertiliser works on the East Okement pumped sulphuric acid up the hill to the station, and the Old Mill still stands empty, awaiting redevelopment, with a little wild brownie loitering under its concrete footbridge.

It's also cheering to chat to my guide for the day, and hear how these rivers are being cherished again. Paul Cole is a local fisherman, farmer and volunteer for the Okement Rivers Improvement Group: a small, highly-motivated charity founded by the Mayor of Okehampton before she moved on to even higher office as chair of Devon County Council. On this last

Saturday morning of the month, Christine Marsh is back in her element, organising more than 15 volunteers to clear litter and generally make the river more appealing and accessible for Okehampton residents.

As Paul and I watch chainsaw gangs coppicing trees on a near-vertical slope above ancient mine drainage adits, I'm starting to understand how the area's most ancient rock formations are still influencing the river. "Here in Okehampton," he explains, "we're on the very edge of Dartmoor, which is really one vast bulge of volcanic rock that took three million years to solidify. The granite was capped before it could cool completely, so metals like tin, copper and lead were deposited according to how long they took to crystallise in fissures and hydrothermal vents.

"That's why you find tin mines on seams in the middle of the moor, copper

Catch 'em young: Ethan Drewe collects litter during an Okement Rivers Improvement Group river clean-up

a bit further out, and lead out here on the edges. The heat of the magma also cooked some of the older surrounding rocks, which gave Meldon Quarry its amazing mixture of metamorphic deposits. Overall, it's a very acid geology: the river naturally comes off the moor at a low pH, and we often get minewater flowing out of the old adits in wet winters."

Watching for a rise: Alan Biggs' bronze statue of a little boy fishing at West Bridge

13

OKEHAMPTON

Caddis crazy: a wild trout from the West Okement

Since 2000, when the ORIG's first major initiative rebuilt a public footbridge washed away in 1952, Christine and her team have successfully completely several other landmark schemes along the rivers. From a fisherman's point of view, their work at West Bridge is most striking: repairing the weir and fish pass, filling in a derelict leat, clearing Japanese knotweed, and finally commissioning local sculptor Alan Biggs to create a statue of a little boy fishing, to draw the eye away from a big black sewage pipe. A few hundred yards downstream, at the confluence of the rivers behind those supermarket car parks, another long-term project culminated in May 2010 with the ceremonial opening of a wooden viewing platform backed with symbolic Y-shaped picnic benches carved from local cedar, and a bronze deer and fawn nestling in the undergrowth.

At the time of writing, ORIG has raised more than £80,000 from a combination of Natural England's Aggregate Levy Sustainability Fund linked to Knowle and Meldon quarries, together with match funding and community grants from the District Council and other partners. "Our latest funders have been the Big Lottery under their Groundworks umbrella," Christine tells me, "but they're not so easy to deal with, lots of paperwork and hoops to jump through.

"The hard part is finding a funder for environmental work: then you hold onto them and try to keep them on board while you get Environment Agency permissions and other match funding in place. But because of our success rate and contacts, when the end of year budgets come near,

it's also in some partners' interests to get rid of that odd one or two thousand pounds of underspend, or it will be reflected in their own allocation grant for the coming year. A little voluntary group like ours can always use that little bit of money to make a path, plant or coppice a tree, or hire a contractor at short notice. Job done!"

No way down: the West Okement from Okehampton's supermarket car park

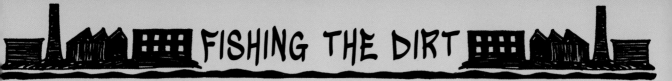
Okehampton: Rivers East and West Okement

Who's looking after the rivers?

The Okement Rivers Improvement Group was founded in 2000 to protect and enhance Okehampton's rivers and riverside environment for the benefit of the local community and visitors.

Registered as a charity in 2006, the group organises rubbish clearances on the last Saturday of every month, and raises funds for future enhancement projects. For the latest information, search online for the Okement Rivers Improvement Group.

Getting there

Okehampton lost its regular passenger trains in 1972, but a summer Sunday service returned in 1997 and may be extended in future. There are several supermarket car parks adjacent to the East and West Okement confluence, with parking for Old Town Park near Okehampton Castle, EX20 1JA.

Maps of Okehampton are available from the Tourist Information Centre in the Okehampton Museum Yard: OS Explorer 113 is also recommended.

Seasons and permits

Brown trout season runs from 15 March to 30 September; salmon from 1 March to 30 Sept.

Trout can be seen rising through the town, and locals do fish for them, but despite the statue of the little boy fishing at West Bridge, Okehampton Town Council isn't keen to promote fishing in the deeply-incised river gorges for health and safety reasons.

Instead, West Devon Borough Council allows fishing on the West Okement in Old Town Park opposite Okehampton Castle with a valid EA rod licence: about a quarter of a mile from the first white cottage on Castle Lane up to the Okehampton golf course fence. Please leave your details at the West Devon Borough Council Okehampton Customer Services Centre on St James Street, EX20 1DH in return for a free permit.

Fishing tips

Today's Okement wild trout are small but feisty, measuring from 4 to 10 inches.

A rod of 7 to 8 ft is ideal, rated for a 1 to 4 weight line. Local fly-fishers like Paul Cole use very small nymphs in early season, switch to shrimp imitations until the end of May, and then often fish dry flies until the end of September. Black Gnats are essential, with extra hackle for reliable flotation, and small Klinkhamers imitate a wide range of sedges and other naturals.

Mike Weaver's Sparkle Caddis was originally tied for the Teign, but proves equally useful on many other Devon rivers: a classic modern fly pattern from a local master (and founding father of the Wild Trout Trust).

Don't miss

● The Okement Rivers Improvement Group's viewing platform at the confluence of the East and West Okement

● English Heritage's Okehampton Castle: a romantic ruin painted by JMW Turner

● Meldon Dam: 4 miles above Okehampton, free moorland stillwater fishing with a valid EA rod licence

TAUNTON

River Tone

Fifteen miles from its steeply wooded headwaters on the slates and shales above Clatworthy reservoir, the Tone in Taunton is probably as pure a post-industrial fly-fishing experience as you'll find in south-west England. The river's big-skied, big-scaled urban middle-reaches feel a world away from the deep coombs of Exmoor and the Brendon Hills. But even under the Obridge viaduct, with construction lorries shuttling overhead to the aggregates plant, and inter-city trains hissing along the opposite bank, the wild trout and grayling are here.

Taunton grew up as a hub of the wool trade. Three watermills appear in Domesday Book, the Bishop of Winchester owned a fulling mill from 1224, and its markets extended as far as Africa by the end of the fifteenth century. Silk-weaving reached the town in 1788, followed by machined lace, shirt-collar making, brewing and iron foundries. Upstream, Wellington's Tonedale Mills became the largest integrated wool-milling complex in the West Country, employing 4,500 workers and assuming national importance by developing the first khaki dye for military uniforms during the Boer War. (Production at Tonedale ceased in the late 1990s, but not before dieldrin mothproofing fluid, used as an alternative to DDT, reportedly killed invertebrates,

fish, and a pair of otters as it biomagnified up the food chain after a spill in 1972).

As well as pollution, the Tone has suffered from significant re-engineering. At the top of the town water, French Weir dates from 1587 at least, and marks the traditional head of navigation between Taunton and the tidal River Parrett at Burrowbridge. Until the Bridgwater and Taunton canal opened in 1827 to offer a more direct transport link, milling and navigation interests continually collided on the mainstem of the river – with mills, lock gates and regular dredging at Firepool, Obridge, and Bathpool all designed to solve the bargees' nightmare-combination of steady gradient and shifting sandy substrate.

But the Tone's real problems probably began in October 1960. After ten inches of rain over the Somerset Levels, the river burst its banks, and several hundred Taunton homes and businesses disappeared under 3ft of water. Estimated costs of £1.7 million ruled out a flood relief channel based on the canal, and made way for a cheaper but far more environmentally damaging option: an aggressive programme of river straightening known as the Tone Valley Scheme. Between 1965 and 1967, old pictures show how the narrow, meandering channel below Taunton was dredged into

In Taunton's eastern edgelands, the Obridge viaduct carries heavy traffic high over the Tone

Even a shopping trolley can create a vital pocket of slower-water habitat in highly-modified rivers like the Tone at Firepool Weir

improve the health of the Tone by installing low sandstone boulder weirs and chutes at strategic points along the sterile Obridge to Bathpool straight, creating slightly deeper pools upstream of the weirs, and pools and riffles below – a diversity of habitat niches for different insects, fish and plants.

Today, ranunculus has taken hold in 'the fast stretch' (as locals call it), the river is quietly dropping its own willow sweepers into the not-quite-straightened half mile above the viaduct, and fly life is slowly recovering to levels that even George Dewar might have recognised when he wrote *The South Country Trout Streams* in 1899: 'May-fly, March brown, February red, blue uprights and duns'. Members of Taunton Fly Fishing Club have been kick-sampling the Tone and Yarty since 2006 as part of the Riverfly Partnership's *Anglers' Monitoring Initiative*, and although the river is still suffering from siltation problems due to run-off from shallow-rooted maize crops sown on sandy soil, co-ordinator John Woods confirms that invertebrate counts seem to be improving in the Bathpool area, thanks to recent upgrades at Taunton's sewage treatment works.

Certainly my own cursory rock-turning reveals baetis and blue-winged olive nymphs as well as pollution-sensitive rhyacophila caddis. It's a match-the-hatch situation which is vindicated when a grayling grabs my tungsten beadhead nymph in the scour below one of the boulder chutes: real evidence of water and localised habitat quality, though I might not have risked a multi-fly rig so freely if I'd seen the crusted layers of shopping trolleys in the depths of the pool before casting.

a featureless drain, including a mile-long straight shot from Obridge to the Bathpool meander already cut off by Isambard Kingdom Brunel for his Bristol to Exeter railway in 1824.

And so the river remained – until the Environment Agency was created in 1991 to bring a newly integrated approach to statutory flood defence, environmental protection, conservation and fisheries. The earlier National Rivers Authority had already persuaded late-1980s housing developers to pay for extra flood water storage in new wetlands at Hankridge Water Park. Now, in 2006, the EA saw no harm in trying to

Messing about in boats: locals still paddle on the historic Tone Navigation

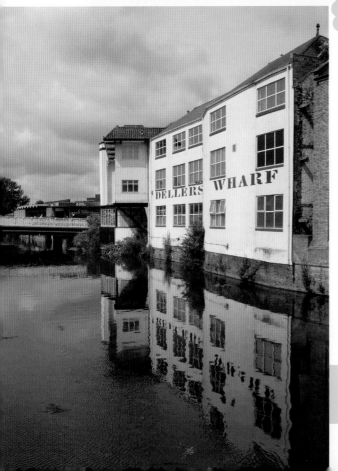

In low flows year round, Wessex Water guarantees minimum compensation of 4.54 megalitres per day from Clatworthy reservoir, and fish of all species stack up in the oxygenated water below the river's weirs. Walking up through the town centre past the Somerset county cricket ground, the right angle of light slicing into water 8 or 9ft deep reveals trophy-sized chub, roach, dace, carp and bream. Small numbers of salmon are also known to migrate up from the Parrett, and when the river's not too coloured, gravel shallows at French Weir make wading and sight-fishing for all species a real possibility. "You'll almost certainly catch trout and grayling up there,"

The ponding effect from Firepool Weir reaches far upstream into central Taunton.

says Kevin Gregson, chairman of Taunton Angling Association. "Some of the trout will have been stocked by the fly-fishing club, but there are wild ones as well."

So what does the future hold for Taunton and the Tone?

When Blackthorn's cider-making operation moved away to Shepton Mallet around the turn of the century, and the livestock market closed after eighty years at Priory Bridge Road, the town seemed directionless, marooned in a tangle of ring-roads, with dereliction at its heart. But as the bulldozers shuffle endless piles of rubble, and the lorries rumble over the viaduct, urban regeneration is coming to Taunton. Better still, it looks likely to benefit the Tone.

Beside Firepool Weir, at the junction of the river and the canal, the seventeen-acre site of the former livestock market is slowly being reborn as a 'commercially viable net zero carbon development'. Over a period of ten years, Project Taunton plans to build 14,000 new homes, 2,500,000sq.ft of office and retail space, and create 11,000 new jobs.

Developers have been briefed to incorporate sustainable urban drainage systems including grass swales, storm-water run-off attenuation ponds and reedbeds, and the buildings are required to have green or brown roofs as well as roosting and nesting areas for birds.

The Tone has been recognised as a major wildlife corridor from Exmoor all the way to the Somerset Levels, with bio-engineering recommended to restore diversity along its banks, low-intensity lighting for the benefit of bats and otters,

A healthy grayling from the Obridge stretch indicates great water quality ...but beware of shopping trolleys!

and 'significant blocks of undisturbed natural habitat'. After many hundreds of years, big business may finally be about to bring Taunton's river the improvements it deserves.

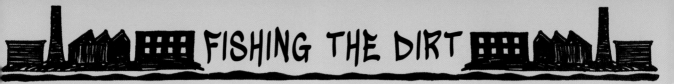

Taunton: River Tone

Who's looking after the river?

Taunton Fly Fishing Club has been monitoring the Tone's invertebrates since 1996, and the benefits of habitat work on the club's beats upstream (such as installing large woody debris and influencing landowners to fence livestock out of the river) will eventually be felt on a catchment scale.

The upper Tone has been identified by the Environment Agency as a key catchment for river restoration to meet the standards of the Water Framework Directive, and the EA will also be closely involved in biodiversity enhancements linked to Project Taunton.

For the latest information, visit:
www.tauntonflyfishing.co.uk
www.environment-agency.gov.uk

Getting there

The Tone Navigation is 5 minutes' walk from Taunton station: from here, it's about 10 minutes upstream to French Weir. The Obridge and Bathpool stretches require longer walks downstream.

Maps of Taunton are available from the Tourist Information Centre on Paul Street, TA1 3XZ: OS Explorer 128 is also recommended.

Seasons and permits

On the town water, brown trout season runs from 1 April to 15 October. Below Firepool Weir, Taunton Angling Association permits fishing for all species during the coarse fishing season only: 16 June to 14 March.

Taunton Council allows free fishing with a valid EA rod licence through the centre of town from Firepool Weir to French Weir. Taunton Angling Association controls 6 miles of water from Firepool Weir downstream through Obridge and Bathpool to Newbridge.

For a full list of day and season ticket outlets, visit www.taunton-angling.co.uk

Fishing tips

The Tone is classified as a cyprinid fishery below Bishops Hull, so a full mix of species can be expected: chub to 6lbs, brown trout and perch to 2lbs, grayling to 1½ lb, plus roach, rudd, carp, bream and tench. Salmon to around 5lbs have very occasionally been caught at French Weir.

A rod of 9 to 10 ft, rated for a 3 to 5 weight line, will help you to land the larger residents. The Tone's grayling tend to shoal with chub, and local lore suggests drifting small weighted Hare's Ear or Pheasant Tail nymphs between the weed beds, or matching the hatch when fish start rising.

Don't miss

- Clatworthy reservoir: hidden in the Brendon Hills, with fishing available via Wessex Water
- Massed winter flocks of starlings in the big skies at Obridge
- Creative local graffiti on many walls and bridge piers

3

TAVISTOCK

River Tavy

If stark granite tors and high moorland blanket bogs are the modern visual and ecological riches of North Dartmoor's Special Site of Scientific Interest, the deeper veins of copper, lead and tin under Britain's largest area of granite have provided the region with more immediately bankable wealth for more than 4,000 years.

From the start of the Bronze Age, when early metallurgists discovered that adding a small proportion of tin to molten copper created a harder and more useful alloy, tin became a key commodity of the international economy. Phoenician sailors extended their trade routes west of the Mediterranean to discover new supplies, and almost certainly reached the shores of Cornwall and Devon where the first local tinning operations were working surface veins and alluvial deposits in the gravels of fast-flowing upland rivers like the Taw, Dart, Okement and Tavy.

By all accounts the valley of the Tavy has always felt isolated by the wide expanses of Dartmoor, and the 22-mile river still runs clear, rocky and slightly acidic down its western flank to meet the Tamar estuary in the drowned river valley of the Hamoaze, a natural harbour off Plymouth Sound. Tavistock is situated at a point where the river once widened and shallowed, and the surrounding area is scattered with archaeo-

logical remains from the Bronze and Iron Ages. As early as 1305, residents shared the distinction of stannary duties – weighing, stamping and assessing mined metal for taxation – with Ashburton, Chagford and Plympton, and more than eighty mines are recorded in the immediate area. But wealth also came from the woollen trade. By 1500 there were at least 15 fulling or tucking mills within a two-mile radius of the town, damming leats and tributaries of the main river to power hammers that beat raw woven wool into felt and produced rough cloth known as 'tavistocks' and 'kerseys'.

When the West Country's woollen industry went into its late eighteenth century recession, tin mining saved Tavistock from becoming a backwater of the early Industrial Revolution, and the town was transformed after Devon Great Consols copper mine opened in 1844 near Blanchdown.

Four large foundries wrought and cast the ironwork for the mines and built metal-plated barges for the Tavistock Canal, dug by French prisoners of war. These barges transported copper ore down to the navigable River Tamar at Morwellham Quay. The town's population soared, and the profits from producing half the world's copper paid for almost total urban reconstruction according to plans drawn up by

Tavistock's Abbey Weir provides a staging-point for sea-trout and salmon smolts on their way down to the Hamoaze estuary

Tied by Tim James: a local selection of quill-bodied dry flies for the Tavy

the seventh Duke of Bedford, whose crest can still be seen on many buildings.

With the Tavy's water already being exploited for power and cooling, it wasn't difficult to imagine total re-engineering, so the Duke obtained an Act of Parliament to move the river fifty yards sideways to make room for the now-famous Pannier Market. Spilling under an ancient packhorse bridge, the resulting pool is probably the best dry fly water in town: a beautiful long glide with the stone solidity of former foundries and warehouses at its head, and the Abbey Weir below. In early summer, you can watch

salmon smolts moving down the river in great silver shoals, circling between the fish pass and the Abbey Bridge, sometimes skittering across the surface in excitement as they feel the pull of the sea and the next big spate.

In the past, both these smolts and the river's resident trout risked getting drawn down the intake to the Tavy canal and the Morwellham hydro-electric power plant, but an automated Environment Agency screen now keeps the river's migratory fish populations out of trouble.

On either side of the mid-town re-engineering, the Tavy rapidly rediscovers its natural deep-pool and riffle character, with general water quality immeasurably improved since the boom years of the mines and foundries in the 1860s.

Today the catchment is mainly rural and free from intensive agriculture, and there are few pollution problems from either farming or industry. "Occasionally someone puts something down their drains in Tavistock, but we keep an eye on that and jump on it pretty quickly," says recently-retired EA bailiff Dave French, who stood down from duty in 2010 after 35

Tiny but jewel-like, a Tavistock trout comes briefly to hand

Looking downstream from Tavistock's packhorse bridge: a perfect place to spot early-season trout rising to large dark olives

years in post. As a result, fly life is prolific, with plentiful baetis, stonefly nymphs up to an inch and a half long, and caseless caddis that can often be seen pulling themselves back upstream on silk threads.

Many of the Tavy's sea trout smolts return as seven-pounders among salmon twice that size, and even the resident browns run large for a West Country river. Environmental consultant Dave Brown puts this down to a combination of water chemistry and pool structure: on its course down from Dartmoor, the Tavy benefits from a varied, slightly-richer-than-average Lower Carboniferous geology including deposits of sandstone and limestone, and its steep gradient cuts deep, impregnable gorge pools with plenty of cover for trout to get big, avoid predation, and finally turn predatory themselves.

Local guide Tim James confirms this theory of large trout moving around the river. "In mid-November, most of the larger fish migrate up the weir in the town centre to the upper reaches on the moor, where you can see them spawning amongst the salmon – they move back down into the middle river by mid-May. But they're cyclical too, so when there are too many pound-plus fish in the river, most will migrate to sea, and there may be fewer large fish in the town water the next year."

As the UK's first ever amputee instructor, Tim is a fishing guide with a difference. Invalided out of the army after an accident, he spent years wearing a leg brace, enduring years of morphine and repeated surgery. Finally he made the doctors' decision for them, opted for amputation, and picked up a camo-pattern prosthetic

leg left over from a Royal Marine's own rehabilitation. He's now involved in *Help for Heroes*, coaching amputee commandos from Plymouth, running summer casting courses, and planning to be fully mobile again for the 2012 season.

Fishing the Tavistock town water in early May, the big wild trout haven't yet made it back from the moor, but the smaller ones are a perfect match for Tim's description: "very pretty, very spooky, and always lying where you'd least expect them in the shallow reaches, tucked into the eddy of a boulder ready to dash out and intercept food."

As far as fly patterns are concerned, local experts' views on flies balance nicely: Dave draws on a lifetime of experience to recommend time-tested West Country patterns including Blue Uprights, Gold Ribbed Hare's Ears for coloured water, and Alexandras or Wake Flies for sea trout. Meanwhile, Tim reinterprets more modern classics like Peacock Nymphs and Beacon Beiges with barbless hooks, dyed-quill bodies and paraloop hackles.

"When you're tying the paraloop, wind the hackle around a foam post so that it sits at the right height in the surface film but doesn't sink," he suggests, "with a tiny head over the eye for extra buoyancy in rough water. The Tavy often runs very clear, so stalking fish under cover of a broken surface will often give you a far better chance of success."

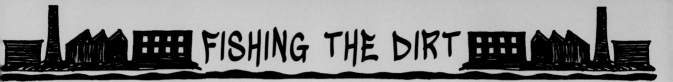

Tavistock: River Tavy

Who's looking after the river?

The Environment Agency took over the roles and responsibilities of the National Rivers Authority in 1996, regulating pollution, reducing flood risk and improving the environment where possible.

As the angling regulator in England and Wales, it sells over a million rod licences a year, and uses the proceeds to maintain and improve the quality of fisheries like the Tavy by tightening pollution controls and restoring habitats.

For the latest information, visit: www.environment-agency.gov.uk

Getting there

Tavistock station closed in 1968 as a result of the Beeching Report, so the nearest station is now 5 miles away at Gunnislake. The river is easily accessible from large car parks in the town, some within the old Abbey walls.

Maps of Tavistock are available from the Tourist Information Centre on Bedford Square, PL19 0AE: OS Explorer 108 is also recommended.

Seasons and permits

Brown trout season runs from 15 March to 30 September; sea trout from 3 March to 30 September; salmon from 1 March to 14 October.

Tavistock Council used to sell very inexpensive tickets, but now don't bother due to administrative costs, so fishing is effectively free with a valid EA rod licence. The lower limit of the fishery is the A386 Plymouth Road

Bridge, with fishing all the way up to the ancient packhorse bridge at Vigo Street: up to three quarters of a mile.

Fishing tips

Wild trout in the Tavy average around half a pound, but you may encounter larger residents up to 2 or 3lbs, and sea trout up to 7lbs.

A rod of 8 to 9 feet is ideal, rated for a 3 to 5 weight line. For resident trout, flies recommended by Dave French and Tim James range from traditional Devon patterns like Blue Uprights to more general Greenwell's Glories, March Browns and dyed-quill Beacon Beiges. Gold Ribbed Hare's Ears work well in slightly coloured water when the gold can show through. Start with very small imitative nymphs in early season, with pheasant tail and peacock herl for texture and bugginess.

Don't miss

● Tavistock Pannier Market, for which the river was moved in the 1850s

● Devon cream teas: reputedly served by local monks as refreshments for workers restoring Tavistock's Benedictine Abbey, sacked by Vikings in 997 AD

4

TIVERTON

. . . .

Rivers Exe and Lowman

Ian Cook, director of the River Exe Foundation, is adamant. "Money dictates all pollution policies, so if you can translate pollution into money, that turns it into an insurance problem for the company concerned. And when you decide to bring a case to court, hit it hard, because your opponents will hit it hard from the other side too!"

After more than a decade of funding habitat work across the Exe catchment with the profits from his private prosecutions against polluting companies, Ian's reputation as a litigant precedes him, and Broad Oak Toiletries must have known what was coming as soon as they polluted at least a mile of the little River Lowman with more than 110lbs of detergent.

In August 2009, a delivery lorry overfilled a 30,000-litre storage tank at Broad Oak's own-label cosmetics factory with sodium lauryl ethyl sulphate, a commonly-used foaming agent. The company's containment procedures mopped up a lot of the spillage, but heavy rain next day flushed the rest off the site and into the river via surface water drains and a containment tank. At least 28 local residents called the Environment Agency to report a chemical smell from the Lowman, and EA officers arrived to discover that more than a

thousand trout, salmon parr, bullheads and minnows had been suffocated by the effect of the detergent on their gills.

Volunteers from the River Exe and Tributaries Association spent days taking statements and gathering evidence on behalf of the EA, whose prosecution resulted in a fine of £8,000 plus £4,196 costs under the Water Resources Act. But this wasn't enough for Ian. The fine was far less than the maximum possible £20,000 for a Category 1 pollution incident, and none of the money would ever come back to compensate the river, where more than four years' work by RETA to restore the populations of juvenile salmon and trout had been abruptly destroyed.

As a riparian owner whose fishery on the Exe had implicitly suffered damage, he costed the total impact of the spill, including time spent on evidence gathering, hatchery work and resources for restoring the Lowman to its previous state, before presenting Broad Oak with a bill for £30,000. Faced with Ian's record in the courts – a perfect eleven out of eleven cases won, including the first-ever successful prosecution of the EA for a pollution offence in 2006 – and knowing they'd lose the case and be hit even harder, the company agreed to an out-of-court settlement in five figures.

Fish on! The author hooks a wild trout in Tiverton's Amory Park

29

TIVERTON

"It's an unusual model for funding river restoration," Ian agrees, "but it means we don't have to ask anyone else for money, and the Foundation can finance a lot of very important habitat work. I always prosecute on the basic principle of common law that I have a right of action against anyone higher up the catchment whose actions damage my fishing downstream.

"Standard pricing for a salmon fishery is £5,000 to £10,000 for each salmon caught, so you can see how the figures mount up. As a result of cases like this, we were able to grant about £30,000 for work on the Exe in the first half of 2011 alone: eighty per cent of the costs of RETA's hatchery which stocks the Lowman and the Little Exe with salmon parr at the end of the summer, £10,000 for buying out the nets in the Exe estuary, and a study into native white-clawed crayfish. Part of our annual contribution to RETA's project officer pays for catchment-sensitive farming initiatives on the upper Lowman to reduce siltation and diffuse pollution. And we give a lot of

Heavily canalised: the Lowman in Tiverton

money generally to farmers who want to fence cattle out of the rivers: it's one of the very best things you can do to help natural banks capture silt and regenerate. The *River Exe Project* has now spent around £500,000 on restoring the Exe, and we've played a major part in that."

Less than two years after the Broad Oak spill, the lower Lowman is visibly recovering. Although the pollution killed hundreds of trout and salmon parr, the river's invertebrates seemed to escape long-term harm: today, shrimp, caddis and hepta-genids swarm away from the light when I turn over large rocks in Amory Park for fellow fishing writer Dominic Garnett to photograph, and we find good-sized trout rising eagerly to a hatch of olives.

Half a mile from Tiverton's town centre, the artificially-straightened channel is interrupted by little blockstone weirs, with rocky revetments and marginal plant-

A wild trout from the Lowman

ings providing plenty of cover at the edges of deep-scoured pools. According to local researchers, the cluster of weirs suggests that several fulling mills once stood on these playing fields, helping to establish Tiverton's seventeenth-century reputation as the industrial focus of the south west, with a total of 56 water-powered fulling operations and many other mills besides. But this town's biography often reads as a tale of boom and bust, and the late 1700s were a period of decline. Local serges and kerseys fell out of fashion: starved of export opportunities by the Napoleonic Wars, and out-competed by a new state-of-the-art factory on the Tone at Wellington, Tiverton was only rescued in 1815 by the arrival of industrialist John Heathcoat from Loughborough.

In the heartland of the Industrial Revolution, his lace-making factory had been attacked by Luddites, prompting him to relocate the entire business to a derelict cotton mill on the west bank of the Exe. By 1861 the site employed almost 2,000 workers and boasted a gasworks, the first factory school in the West Country, and a foundry: a combined thread of engineering and texile making which continued unbroken through twentieth-century wartime production of shells, aircraft components and parachutes to the modern company's range of technical and military fabrics.

Although Heathcoat's colony of workers' terraces finally brought prosperity to the other side of the Exe, conditions around the smaller river lagged far behind.

Mind that bike: planning a tactical side-cast under the ring-road at the top of Amory Park

In *Tiverton and the Exe Valley*, Mary de la Mahotière describes the Elmore slum area as *'a rough quarter on the west bank of the Lowman, with a reputation for lawlessness, drunkenness, dog-fighting, cock-fighting and badger-baiting'*, and railway passengers complained about the gestures from children bathing in what had become a public sewer. Drainage invariably took the shortest route downhill: by 1875, nearly half the town's cases of scarletina were linked to the Lowman, and many drinking-water wells were contaminated. The problem was finally solved in 1887, with interceptor sewers and a treatment works replacing the older solution of piping the contents of the river out to Collipriest Marshes for the landowner to profit from the water's *'extremely fertilising qualities'*.

Today, most of Tiverton's industrial heritage has disappeared as completely as Heathcoat's prototytpe steam plough which sank overnight into a Scottish peat bog, but it's still possible to find clues along the Lowman if you know where to look.

On the Foundry estate, chain-link compounds full of modern agricultural machinery line the edges of a savagely sterile concrete channel that's only matched by the Exe's own 1960s vertical walls, and there's a suspicion that those flood defences cut both ways: keeping the river out of Tesco at the same time as protecting the river from contaminated land left by the gasworks which recently occupied the site. This Monday afternoon, motorists glare as we march across the petrol station forecourt, fully wadered-up with rods, nets and rucksacks, but revenge is waiting for us upstream, where the river dives into a shadowy pool between the skatepark and the graffiti-covered underpass.

"You won't catch nothin' there, mate!" shriek a couple of girls from the footpath.

"Oh yeah?" replies Dominic, turning to face them with a perfect little trout he's just played to hand. "So how's this for a townie brownie?"

A deep bend pool on the Lowman, complete with riprap revetments, concrete maintenance slipway, and the inevitable shopping trolley

Same difference: with its massive trapezoidal channel, the Exe displays even larger-scale re-engineering for flood defence

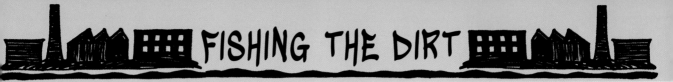

Tiverton: Rivers Exe and Lowman

Who's looking after the rivers?

In a grassroots partnership with the River Exe Foundation and the Westcountry Rivers Trust, the River Exe and Tributaries Association's *River Exe Project* aims to double the river's salmon population between 2004 and 2018. At the time of writing, more than £500,000 has been invested in catchment-wide habitat improvements.

Gravel improvement, riverfly monitoring, hatchery work and educational programmes like *Salmon in the Classroom* will also benefit trout, grayling and many other species. The River Lowman's productivity as a nursery area was seriously damaged by pollution in 2007, but is now recovering thanks to these and other catchment-sensitive farming initiatives.

For the latest information, visit: www.fishtheexe.co.uk, www.wrt.org.uk http://dgfishtales.blogspot.com

Getting there

Since 1964 the nearest station has been Tiverton Parkway, about 7 miles east of Tiverton, but the Exe and Lowman are both easily accessible from several car parks in and around the town.

Maps of Tiverton are available from the Tourist Information Centre on Phoenix Lane, EX16 6LU: OS Explorer 114 is also recommended.

Seasons and permits

Brown trout and sea trout seasons run from 15 March to 30 September; salmon from 14 February to 30 September (trial extension to 14 October).

Fishing on the urban Exe is mainly controlled by Tiverton Fly Fishing Association, with additional day tickets available from Exe Valley Angling for about a mile of water downstream of Head Weir. Mid Devon District Council allows free fishing on the Lowman in Tiverton with a valid EA rod licence. For more information, visit: www.fishtheexe.co.uk

Fishing tips

The middle Exe holds good trout and grayling in addition to its runs of salmon and sea trout. On the Lowman, salmonid populations are recovering, with trout up to 11 inches and rumours of grayling returning from the Exe.

The Exe at Tiverton is a large river, so you'll need a long rod of 9 to 10ft, rated for a 3 to 5 weight line, or correspondingly heavier if you're targeting sea trout. For stalking smaller fish in canalised areas of the Lowman, choose a shorter rod of 6 to 7ft, rated for a 1 to 4 weight line.

Classic Devon sea trout flies include silvery Butchers, Invictas and Alexandras. For dry fly action, Dominic Garnett suggests starting with Beacon Beiges, Klinkhamers, or Partridge and Hare's Lug spiders: alternatively, give the fish a choice with the duo method, a small nymph suspended off the point of a buoyant floating fly.

Don't miss

- Heathcoat's Mill: complete with original gate lodges, factory school building and leat from the Exe
- The National Trust's Knightshayes Court: the Heathcoat family's flamboyant Gothic Revival mansion, overlooking the town and mill from a nearby hillside

5

FARNHAM

River North Wey

From the headwaters of the Itchen around Alresford, the busy A31 trunk road climbs steadily north-east to the crest of the chalk ridge.

The top of the aquifer is flat, and the road runs straight and featureless through linear villages, but the gradient gradually dips away towards Alton, and you suddenly realise you're in a new catchment. Further down the valley, only a fringe of alders gives the river away where it cuts deep curves under the fast grey line of the road, and the four lanes of the Farnham bypass cross it twice without a tremor: once above the town, once below.

Running rapidly from chalk onto greensand on its northern branch, and straight out of greensand on its southern arm, the Wey seems to have missed most of the razzmatazz of fly-fishing history.

In *Chalk Stream Studies*, Charles Kingsley mentions targeting large trout *'in the rich meads of Wey'* with his favourite monstrous black and brown alder fly imitations, but Farnham's industrial past tells a story of its own. Halfway between London and Winchester, the town evolved at a hub of roads on a natural ford: from 1086 there were already at least four milling sites on the main river, with two more on nearby tributaries, and the Wey's reliable year-round corn-

grinding power helped Farnham become one of the great grain markets of southern England. The river's mills switched production according to market forces, processing flour, animal feed, woollen cloth, paper, leather and gunpowder. Above the town, Willey Mill could produce a ton of wheat from a single pair of stones in an eight-hour day, while Farnham Hatch Mill served as a dairy, firewood processing plant, laundry, civil defence centre, motor oil depot and rehearsal studio, before becoming part of a complex of retirement homes.

From the seventeenth to nineteenth centuries, large areas of local farmland were also dedicated to growing hops for Farnham's other main industry, brewing. The red brick Farnham Maltings in the centre of town started out as a tannery, then changed to brewing and barley-malting until Courage moved away in 1956. Twelve years later, a public appeal raised £28,000 for one final conversion into a riverside arts and community centre, which still stands above the river on a brutalist concrete plinth: a legacy of flood alleviation schemes in the 1930s and 1970s which probably did more damage to the Wey than all the previous centuries of modification for milling.

With a catchment area of almost 400 square miles but a fall of less than 100ft,

Straightened and dredged... but the north branch of the Wey holds good wild trout

35

An audience gathers on the Maltings' footbridge

"This was your classic take-no-prisoners two-stage flood defence channel," he recalls. "Everything straightened, all the marginal cover taken out, just a closely-mown berm with lots of walkers in a public space. Very neat and tidy, so all the fish dropped down to Snail's Lynch below the bypass, but by the 1980s there were a few trout and chub working their way up through the town again. I caught some good ones with electricity!

"But then again," he muses, "maybe I shouldn't have been so surprised. In 1999 there was an incident when an ice-cream factory in Alton lost a lot of refrigerant down a surface water drain whilst decommissioning freezer units, and caused a huge fish kill down 13 miles of river. One of my colleagues saw a dead trout of ten pounds, and I personally saw six to at least five pounds… also lots of minnows, bullheads and dace. No-one knew the trout were

the whole Wey system has a tendency to flood – especially on the upper north branch between Alton and Farnham. But Wild Trout Trust conservation officer Andy Thomas still winces as he remembers the effect of the flood defence works inflicted on the river during his time as a fisheries specialist with the National Rivers Authority and then the Environment Agency.

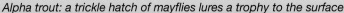

Alpha trout: a trickle hatch of mayflies lures a trophy to the surface

Not just for fishing: the Wey also hosts Farnham Rotary Club's annual charity duck race

there, including me, and they must have just been munching through the smaller fish undisturbed!"

Those red brick flood walls and closely-mown trapezoidal banks are still very much in evidence through the central parklands of Farnham today, contrasting strangely with ornate ironwork bridges and planters overflowing with pansies and civic pride. But the outlook gets wilder up and downstream, where houses give way to water meadows, and swathes of nettles invade the berms by mayfly time. And in these areas too, local people are taking more and more notice of their subtle little river and its environment.

Farnham's water meadows have formed the heart of the town ever since Saxon settlers crossed the river at '*fearne-hamme*' – meadow of ferns. The floodplain was probably used for travelling fairs and circuses in the Middle Ages, and a defen-sive ditch and rampart were built across it during in the Civil War. In 2009, eighty years of single-family ownership suddenly came to an end with the possibility of sale to a property developer, and the Bishop's Meadow Trust was swiftly formed to campaign against this unforeseen threat. At the eleventh hour, *Farnham Herald* owner Sir Ray Tindle stepped in with £200,000 of his own funds, promising to re-sell the meadows to the Trust when the same amount could be raised by public appeal. The Trust is now fundraising with active support from many other local groups, and a management plan is being developed for the meadows and river.

Around the same time, Grayshott Angling Club approached Farnham Town Council offering to restore the river upstream of Farnham alongside Coxbridge roundabout. "You could tell this stretch was unloved – it needed looking after,"

Summer sun: the banks of the river are a magnet for families on weekend afternoons

says Andy, and volunteers like Grayshott's Stephen Frye are now working with the EA and Wild Trout Trust to maintain flow velocity by installing large woody debris and pulling burr reed back from the centre of the river to the margins where it belongs. As part of the *Anglers' Riverfly Monitoring Initiative*, the club is also sampling fly-life at two sites between Alton and Farnham every month.

Here above the bypass you can still see how this whole river must once have looked: undredged, unmodified, with deep ranunculus-filled gravel runs and bend pools holding Kingsley's *'great trout'* as well as mayfly, olive, caddis and midge nymphs. But the bugs and trout parr have come back since the 1999 ammonia kill, partly as a result of radically reduced abstraction, and as I'm walking back downstream to the station, I put a final cast over the last naturalised pool in Gostrey Park's geometrical two-stage channel.

The mayfly disappears in a shower of spray, the one-weight jags over, and the little reel whimpers as I steer a much bigger fish out of perfect natural woody snags at both ends of the pool. Lifting this trout for the camera, I'm riveted by the pattern of shining spots on golden flanks, and I hold it in the current for a long time while we both recover. I can miss a train any day of the week, but I've travelled a lot further for wild trout of Farnham's quality.

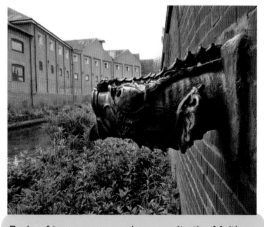

Drain of terror: a gargoyle opposite the Maltings

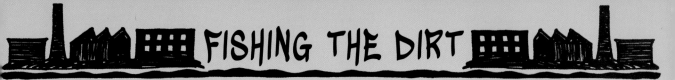

Farnham: River North Wey

Who's looking after the river?

Founded in 2009, the Bishop's Meadow Trust is a registered charity which aims to acquire, manage and maintain Farnham's historic water meadows, and the adjacent river, for the benefits of residents and visitors.

The Wey's invertebrates between Alton and Farnham are monitored monthly by Grayshott Angling Club, and the Wey Fisheries Action Plan, created by the Environment Agency and the Wey Valley Fisheries Consultative, will help direct many future aspects of river restoration work.

For the latest information, visit:
www.bishopsmeadowtrust.org.uk
http://home.btconnect.com/grayshottanglingclub

Getting there

The River North Wey is 5 minutes' walk downhill from Farnham station.

Maps of Farnham are available from the Tourist Information Centre on South Street, GU9 7RN: OS Explorer 145 is also recommended.

Seasons and permits

Brown trout season runs from 1 April to 30 September.

Farnham Town Council permits free fishing with a valid EA rod licence through the town, with each end of the fishery marked by the Farnham bypass: about a mile and half of fishable water.

Fishing tips

The North Wey's brown trout run to at least 2lbs, and the Farnham stretch also holds healthy populations of dace, roach, gudgeon, chub, carp and pike. Minnows are present, but grayling only appear further downstream at the confluence of the north and south branches of the river where they were stocked in the 1980s.

For the trout, a rod of 7 to 8ft is ideal, rated for a 1 to 4 weight line. Important hatches to match include olives (particularly small pale wateries), black gnats, hawthorn flies, mayflies and sedges. Weighted shrimp patterns will also help you plumb weir pools and the deeper water at the downstream end of the fishery. Charles Kingsley's traditional Alder Flies, March Browns and Red Hackles may also be worth a cast.

Don't miss

● The Watercress Line heritage railway between Alton and Alresford: once an major transport link for watercress production on the Wey and Itchen

● Sir Ray Tindle's renovated gipsy caravan on Bishop's Meadow

● Farnham Castle: a stronghold and administrative centre of the Bishops of Winchester for 800 years

6

NEWBURY

....

River Lambourn

Slanting down to its confluence with the Kennet through tight-knit housing estates and office parks on the edge of Newbury, the sightlines around the Lambourn are short, and you can easily forget that almost six thousand people live within a single council ward along two miles of the river.

The ancient wool town of Newbury has sprawled across this valley since the 1960s, burying water meadows and wet woodland under red brick, concrete and tarmac, wrapping the Lambourn ever tighter in urbanisation and a token tunnel of trees. Since 1995, the river's whole 16 miles have been designated as a Special Site of Scientific Interest and Special Area of Conservation for their chalkstream characteristics. But by the end of the last century the contrast between the lower Lambourn's actual condition and its official conservation status was more than embarrassing: it was also politically problematic.

"Deep, dredged, straight, silty, uniform, heavily shaded... yes, this was a really nasty old stretch," recollects Paul St Pierre, the Environment Agency project manager responsible for radical recent improvements to the river. "You couldn't imagine more of a difference between Newbury and the expensive beats up towards Lambourn where Hugh Tempest Sheringham and Howard Marshall used to fish. For years we'd spoken about getting it into good shape, but we could never afford to do anything until funding finally arrived through PSA, the government's public service agreement to return 95 per cent of SSSI areas to favourable or recovering condition by 2010."

Given this opportunity, Paul's team acted quickly. After extensive hydrological modelling and consultation with residents and local anglers, the first physical phase of the project involved lowering three weirs at the Lambourn-Kennet confluence, in the grounds of the Newbury Manor hotel, which together had obstructed fish passage for more than a century.

This wasn't a small job. "Starting in January 2009, we budgeted three months for each stage of the project, but it was quite a trick keeping the hotel onside," admits Paul as we squelch along the banks in thick October drizzle.

"The old penstocks didn't work anyway, so the grounds flooded every time it rained, but we had to dig a new relief channel to rebuild the structures. Of course that trashed the lawn, and so did all the heavy machinery. Then there were floods, and the whole site was still under water by mid-February. And when we started

A river reborn: above the A4 road bridge, the Environment Agency has created a showpiece of chalkstream restoration

installing a pool-and-traverse fish pass on the overflow channel of the old mill system, we found that the original structure had been built directly onto the gravel substrate, and the whole lot started collapsing inwards as soon as we touched it. Fortunately there was a lot of underspend in the flood defence budget that year, which was able to provide an extra £150,000 on top of the original £300,000 from the PSA, but it got pretty hairy for a while!"

Despite these unexpected difficulties, the team's hydrological calculations proved correct. Within two days, trout were running the lower Larinier fish pass, and as soon as the weirs were dropped, the river started pulling through, dispersing centuries of silt and scouring down to a clean gravel bottom. And there's a real glint in Paul's eye as he starts telling me how he and his team went about the second phase of recreating a river.

"Overall, we wanted to be as adventurous as possible with large woody debris. The river was very shaded, so we took out sixty per cent of the trees before moving upstream, introducing 4,000 tonnes of gravel to a depth of 400 millimetres over a one-kilometre reach, and recycling the timber as flow deflectors and brushwood mattresses at the same time.

"We sourced good angular Kennet gravels from a local pit, spreading the larger stones first and overlaying those with smaller 20-60mm gravel. For the lower reach, the excavator sat in the river and moved the gravel around once a dumper had dumped it down the banks. Above the big timber footbridge, we actually had large tracked dumpers bringing the gravel up the bed of the river for the excavator to distribute it. As the gravel extended further upstream, the dumpers ran along this like a new road, to minimise disturbance of silt.

"Once we'd reached the upstream end of the works, the excavator moved back downstream, roughing up the gravel for topographic diversity. So now we have pools and riffles, woody revetments to squeeze the river up, and staked large woody debris to provide the heterogeneity and diversity of habitats that trout and grayling require throughout their different

Autumn leaves: it's grayling time

Lambourn grayling are notoriously difficult to tempt, but this perfect specimen took a lightly-weighted shrimp pattern among the EA's new large woody debris structures

life stages. And these structures also help to hold up low flows exacerbated by abstraction in summer."

Fishing up the reconstructed river behind Newbury Business Park, less than a year later, the deep flint gravels shift loosely and luxuriously underfoot. Watercress has colonised the brushwood mattresses, gravel-loving ranunculus is taking root, and the new, shallower gravel-toed banks may be helping to engineer out invasive signal crayfish. It's easy to see how this textbook example of river restoration has successfully achieved its target of 'unfavourable recovering' status for the lower Lambourn, and the EA's early efforts to consult and educate local people on flood risk and the future of the river have also paid dividends.

In 2010, West Berkshire District Council and the Farming and Wildlife Advisory Group's *Pang, Kennet and Lambourn Valleys Countryside Project* won a Heritage

Lottery Fund grant to follow the restoration work by promoting the river as a community resource. With additional funding from the Council, the EA and Natural England over three years, the £380,000

Community engagement: a laminated poster announces RENEWAL's next event

43

Shaw Mill: first built before 1086

RENEWAL community project aims to involve local residents in learning about the river's history and wildlife, and actively working to conserve and improve it.

Project manager Vicky Pudner launched a comprehensive programme of events by the end of 2010 including pond dipping, river clean-ups, tree coppicing and meadow management, and even a Great Aurochs Hunt to introduce children to the ancient cattle whose bones were found near the Lambourn during building work. And the idea of local care for a recovering river may already have started to reap rewards. "Before this project started," Vicky smiles under her long fringe of extrovert pink-purple hair, "FWAG's annual river clean-ups always used to fill at least two skips with rubbish, but there's been far less ever since."

RENEWAL is making the most of local support, inspiring volunteers to identify and monitor trout spawning sites along the project's two-mile length of the lower Lambourn. "It's already given us excellent records for the river," says Vicky, "and part of the project funding has allowed us to purchase Wildkey software to run on smart phones, which we can use to train young people to identify plants and animals, and upload all their records to a database and map.

"We're also promoting wildlife-friendly gardening practices to people whose gardens run down to the Lambourn, and we're planning riverfly monitoring and kids' fishing workshops, as well as a *Trout in the Classroom* programme with five schools, and two river clean-ups a year. By the time our funding finishes, I'm aiming to have recruited a permanent team of volunteer river watchers to keep up the good work – looking after the river should be something that just carries on!"

Pool and traverse: the fish pass in the grounds of the Newbury Manor hotel now connects the Lambourn and Kennet for the first time in hundreds of years

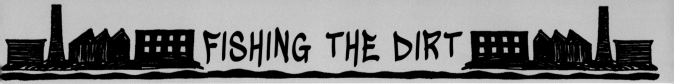

Newbury: River Lambourn

Who's looking after the river?

Between 2006 and 2010, the Environment Agency spent £902,000 restoring around a mile of the lower Lambourn, plus £600,000 further upstream at Hunts Green.

Following this work, the Farming and Wildlife Advisory Group launched the three-year *RE-NEWAL (REstoration in NEWbury Along the river Lambourn)* community project, which aims to get local people more involved with the river through heritage, wildlife, fishing and volunteering activities.

For the latest information, visit:
www.environment-agency.gov.uk
www.renewalproject.org.uk

Getting there

From Newbury station, it's about 15 minutes' walk to the Lambourn at Shaw, or 20 minutes to Newbury Business Park.

Maps of Newbury are available from the Tourist Information Centre on the Wharf, RG14 5AS: OS Explorer 158 is also recommended.

Seasons and permits

Brown trout season runs from 1 April to 30 September; grayling season from 16 June to 14 March.

From the A4 London Road bridge upstream to Walton Way, the south bank of the river is owned by Newbury Business Park, then by Newbury Town Council: both allow free fishing with a valid EA rod licence. Similarly, West Berkshire Council allows free fishing on the south bank of the river from the Shaw House footbridge to the gauging weir at the top of Shaw Recreation Ground. In total, about a mile and a half of water is fishable.

Fishing tips

Since the installation of fish passes at the confluence with the Kennet, numbers of wild brown trout have started improving. Grayling catches have also increased, and fish up to 14 or 16 inches can be expected.

According to Howard Marshall in *Reflections on a River*, and *The Book of the Piscatorial Society 1836-1936*, there was a population of breeding Shasta-strain rainbow trout in the 1960s, but these now seem to have disappeared.

A rod of 8 to 9ft, rated for a 3 to 5 weight line, will help you make the most of this small river. The water is usually crystal clear, so extreme stealth is necessary. Local fly-tyer Cecil Terry created his Terry's Terror for the Kennet and Lambourn: today, many modern mayfly and shimp imitations work well for delicate sight-fishing.

Don't miss

● Shaw House: a key strategic location in the Second Battle of Newbury in 1644 during the English Civil War (soldiers' skeletons have been found in the Lambourn nearby)

● Lambourn gallops: high on the springy turf of the chalk downs, a training area for more than 2,000 race horses

7

RICKMANSWORTH

River Chess

'Gaily into Ruislip Gardens runs the red electric train'…

Like the clatter and sway of the antiquated carriages themselves, the lines of John Betjeman's hymn to 1950s suburbia rattle and swoop in my head as the tube train gathers speed, barrelling north-west up the fast track of the Metropolitan line.

Apart from London and Glasgow, there aren't many cities where you can fish an urban river from the underground network, and the uncompromising view from the window puts the keenest possible edge on my anticipation. Past the cloud-grey hoop of Wembley Stadium, the glass and concrete bulk of Northwick Park hospital, the delicate spike of Harrow-on-the-Hill, then sudden woodlands and golf courses around Moor Park. Exactly 33 minutes out of Baker Street, the train squeals to a stop at Rickmansworth. I swing my rucksack, net and rod tube off the opposite seat, and make tracks of my own into Metroland.

Rickmansworth's first railway arrived in 1862 as a spur from the main line at Watford, but it wasn't until 1889 that the Metropolitan line created a direct connection from Chesham into London. Speculators began buying and developing the farms and fields, and the population of Rickmansworth doubled between the World Wars as low interest rates tempted city-dwellers to stake their claim as landowning commuters in the Chilterns' new Arcadia.

The gentle valley of the Chess falls 200ft in 11 miles from the river's source at Chesham to the main River Colne at Rickmansworth, combining with the Colne, Ver, Gade, Bulbourne and Misbourne to form a catchment 400 miles square. All the Colne's tributaries flow south towards the Thames from the chalky northern edge of the London basin, a vast but temperamental aquifer whose seasonal cycles of winter recharge and summer depletion dictate water levels in the rivers' upper reaches – and as Metroland boomed, so did the public need for water in this fragile landscape.

Today, Veolia Water operates close to the limits of its abstraction licence to satisfy demand in an area with higher average household consumption than almost anywhere else in Europe: 176 litres per person per day in Chesham compared to the average of 148 litres across the rest of the UK. The Environment Agency classifies the entire Colne catchment as over-abstracted, and long stretches of the Chess suffer from damagingly low flows for at least 65 per cent of the year. Yet water demand only looks set to increase, with 2,500 new homes planned

Catching the bug: a budding entomologist inspects his kick-sampling net on the Chess above Scotsbridge Mill

in Chiltern District Council's 2010 core strategy, and an obligation on the water company to provide water for every one of them.

Under such stress from over-abstraction, the Chess almost matches the Wandle in its dependence on treated sewage effluent to retain at least a memory of a river. Allen Beechey now works as chalkstreams project officer for the Chilterns Area of Outstanding Natural Beauty, but he was born in Chesham, spent his childhood fishing the upper river, and understands its

current problems better than most.

When the headwater springs fail, Thames Water's sewage treatment works in Chesham can sometimes provide almost 75 per cent of summer flow, returning water to an ecosystem in desperate need of every drop. "It's true that we get some of the water back again eventually," Allen concedes, "but the majority of abstraction occurs in the upper valleys well above Chesham and the discharge from the works. The net result is that the upper Chess and its tributaries don't benefit at all, and are less able to tolerate drier years. In fact, the river regularly dries down about two miles below its recognised winterbourne source."

The River Chess Association was formed in 2009 as a direct response to local suspicions about increasingly frequent discharges of untreated sewage and storm water from 2003 onwards. Like many treatment works, Chesham receives consent from the EA to overflow its storm tanks on a certain number of occasions each year. The system is designed only to discharge after heavy rain when river levels should also be high and able to dilute the input of sewage, but chalk streams often respond more

Travelling light: kit for the Chess

Rickmansworth station: gateway to Metroland

To avoid dog-walkers, it's best to fish the Chess early, late... or in the foulest weather you can find

of future water quality and quantity issues. "Whatever the outcome of these studies," the Association's chairman Paul Jennings tells me, "there's always a high degree of shock whenever I mention the black water discharges to other residents for the first time – they're not aware it happens, and it changes their view of the river completely!"

In 2010 five monitors were trained by the Riverfly Partnership to sample seven locations along the river, and Paul himself takes responsibility for the stretch in Rickmansworth, where Scotsbridge Mill is a typical relic of the town's industrial past. After centuries of service as a corn and fulling mill, the building was converted to paper-making in 1746, helping Rickmansworth's domination of Hertfordshire's paper industry throughout the Industrial Revolution, and even becoming famous for supplying printing stock to the *Illustrated London News*, before it was finally refurbished as a riverside pub and restaurant in 1989.

Upstream, the Chess still bears the telltale scars of industrial history: culverted under a car park, gone feral in a thicket behind the playing fields' chain link fence where Charles Rangeley-Wilson filmed part of *The Accidental Angler* television series, then unnaturally straightened, shallow and featureless for several hundred yards upstream.

As I scan the placid surface, artificially perched above its floodplain to channel steady power to long-departed industries, a sequence of river-mending ideas flashes through my mind, always returning to large woody debris to kick the current about, size-sort those golden gravels, and

slowly than rain-fed rivers, and several of Chesham's discharges seemed to be occurring when river levels were very low.

Despite supporting UK Biodiversity Action Plan priority species such as brown trout, water voles and reed bunting in the Chilterns AONB, the Chess is undesignated in conservation terms, and there's no statutory pressure to improve storm flow retention in the works. But regular visitors remarked on significantly-reduced fly-life over the time of the increased discharges, and one of the River Chess Association's first priorities was launching a riverfly monitoring scheme to verify long-term trends and short-term impacts

provide fish with refuge from splashing kids and dogs. Later, Paul confirms he's thinking along similar lines, earmarking a demonstration site where the public can be shown what a healthy river looks like, and trout fry from the River Chess Association's *Trout in the Classroom* programme can be safely released, far enough downstream from Chesham for organic pollution to have broken down and dispersed.

He's also keen to assemble an archive on the legendary breeding rainbows of the Chess, introduced with less-successful brook trout in the nineteenth century, but now thought to have succumbed to recent pressures on the river. "It's a subject we always get asked about, and we have no evidence that they're still around, but it would be fun to reintroduce them if the habitat is suitable. If they were anything like the Derbyshire Wye strain which hit you like a train, strip off yards of line, clear the water three or four times and fight all the way to the net – they'd be fun to bring back to a small rivers in the Chilterns!"

And grayling? Just as I start writing this chapter, I run into one of Paul's colleagues at an evening of fishing-themed readings in a pub by Tower Bridge.

"Oh yes," laughs Stephen Webster as he hands me a pint, "there've always been grayling at Rickmansworth. The EA stocked some from Calverton a few years ago, but right back in the 1940s, the British record was two three-pounders in one day from that stretch. Reckon we'll manage it again sometime?"

Fisherman's rest: once part of Rickmansworth's paper-making industry, Scotsbridge Mill enjoys a new lease of life as a convenient gastropub

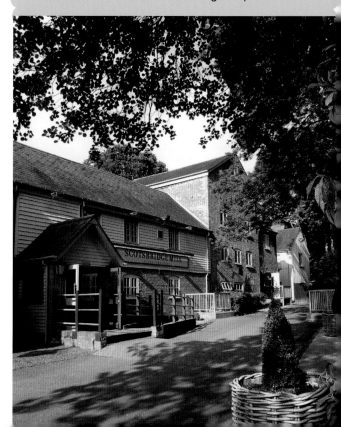

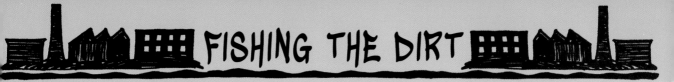

Rickmansworth: River Chess

Who's looking after the river?

The River Chess Association was formed in 2009 in response to growing concerns about environmental pressures on the river, and is now developing projects in many areas including protecting the river, raising public awareness, exchanging ideas and expertise, and lobbying.

Riverfly monitoring takes place every month, habitat work is planned with the Wild Trout Trust and Three Rivers District Council, and a *Trout in the Classroom* educational programme has been established through the Chilterns Conservation Board's *Chilterns Chalk Streams Project*, with support from the Wandle Trust. In Chesham, vegetation management and rubbish removal is also co-ordinated by Chesham Town Council's *Impress the Chess* volunteer programme.

For the latest information, visit:
www.riverchessassociation.co.uk
www.chilternsaonb.org

Getting there

The Chess at Scotsbridge is 15 minutes' walk from Rickmansworth station. There is a public car park beside the playing fields.

Maps of Rickmansworth are available from the Tourist Information Point on Northway, WD3 1RL: OS Exploer 172 is also recommended.

Seasons and permits

Brown trout season runs from 1 April to 30 September; grayling season from 16 June to 14 March.

Three Rivers District Council allows free fishing with a valid EA rod licence along the playing fields and public footpath above Scotsbridge: up to half a mile of fishing.

Fishing tips

As I write this, the Rickmansworth stretch of the Chess still seems to hold more chub up to 2lbs than trout or grayling, but both salmonid species are rebounding. The river's famous self-sustaining strain of breeding rainbow trout appears to have died out.

For this small, open chalkstream, a rod of 7 to 8ft is ideal, rated for a 1 to 4 weight line. The whole length of the fishery is popular for dog-walking, but the fish recover quickly from being spooked. Mayfly hatches on the Chess always seem to have been variable, with olives offering more consistent sport, and traditional fly patterns including Blue Duns and Red Spinners.

Modern fly-fishers like Paul Jennings and Allen Beechey report success with updated equivalents such as Oliver Edwards-style Poly May Duns and one-feather CDC olive emergers, in addition to shrimp imitations and a range of bead-head nymphs.

Don't miss

● Scotsbridge Mill: complete with antique prints of flies and internal windows overlooking a fish pass in the mill's old wheel pit

8

ROMSEY

• •

River Test

Longparish, Leckford, Stockbridge, Mottisfont, Timsbury, Broadlands: follow a map of the Test from its source in a meadow near Ashe down to the sea at Southampton Water, and the places you pass read like a roll of honour of chalkstream history.

Maybe more than any river, England's longest chalkstream has shaped the literature and defined the conventions of fly-fishing. Throughout the nineteenth and twentieth centuries, Frederic Halford, John Waller Hills, Harry Plunket Greene and countless other writers conjured a rural idyll of upstream-only dry fly sport that still fuels the fantasies of fishermen worldwide.

By the time the Test reaches Romsey, it's less a stream than a surging chalk river that runs fast and deep even when divided into carriers and back-channels, with an average flow measured by the Environment Agency at just under 12 cubic metres per second.

The river's whole length is designated as a Special Site of Scientific Interest, and the statistics are awe-inspiring: 40 miles long in a catchment 500 miles square, with eight species of stoneflies, 22 of olives and mayflies, 38 of caddis, and 70 other kinds of invertebrates living amongst more than a hundred species of emergent and marginal flowering plants, mosses and liverworts.

All this rich biodiversity is underpinned by the 65 million-year-old chalk geology of the Hampshire downs, releasing fertile, alkaline, calcium-loaded water year round at constant levels and temperatures – which also proved ideal for driving mills and drowning water meadows. As a result, like most chalkstream SSSIs, the Test has been so heavily modified over the centuries that hardly a yard now flows in its untouched, original bed: a fact reflected in Natural England's assessment of the river as 'unfavourable' and even 'unfavourable declining' when compared to ideal chalkstream conditions.

In 2006 the Test at Romsey was missing its targets on chemical water quality, naturalness of macrophytes, and aspects of habitat within the channel and on the banks, with particular problems arising from siltation, pollution from agricultural run-off, and all those weirs and other structures. Anecdotally, many river keepers complain that water quality has declined. But there's lots of willingness to solve these problems, as NE conservation advisor Alison Graham-Smith explains.

Investment by the local water companies has already seen phosphate strippers installed on all discharges of treated effluent into the river, which should reduce nutrient

Fishing on the dark side: Romsey's industrial estates contrast dramatically with the usual clichés of chalkstream fly-fishing

Weed-beds full of grayling: the Test in Romsey's War Memorial Park

'shaggy management' of the river banks at Mottisfont have already demonstrated how it's possible to balance the needs of a functioning commercial fishery with good invertebrate and wild fish numbers. Alison is also developing a project to restore some of the smaller, non-SSSI river channels in Romsey itself.

"Many of these channels are very hardened and canalised, without much surrounding space to break them out. But urban projects in places like Winchester have shown that you can use coir rolls to soften the edges if there's something in the channel to key them into. We're also considering issues like division of flow – is it better to send more flow down a channel with more potential for quality habitat? Then there's the question of all those historic structures that you can still use to control the flow – do you remove them completely, modify them, or just leave them as they are?"

And the Test does have a lot of structures. Located on the strategic river crossing between Salisbury, Winchester, Stockbridge and the wool staple port of Southampton, Romsey was ideally situated for fulling, dyeing and other cloth-finishing processes, and some of the river's earliest mills were already working here in 1086. Water-powered fulling mills revolutionised cloth-making from the late twelfth century, and wool was a staple of the local economy until the 1700s, when many milling sites converted to tanning and paper and leather board-making. Brewing also became a dominant Romsey industry, with several smaller breweries combining under the Strong label which remained in

levels in the long term. Catchment sensitive farming projects are also underway, and a joint EA/NE project has identified many opportunities for catchment-wide river restoration, with future funding linked to the Water Framework Directive from Defra and Higher Level Stewardship Schemes. "We're not going for European funding in this case," says Alison, "but a lot of low cost, high value options were explored under the Avon *LIFE* project, which can definitely help to offset the expense of river restoration."

Some of these are surprisingly simple and cost-effective: the National Trust's

the town as Whitbreads until the 1990s. Romsey Council's guidebook cheerfully states that *'streams carried away the troublesome effluents from the great brewery complex'*, and behind the heritage centre in King John's House on Church Street you can still see the Holbrook Stream flushing in and out of the holes below a block of Victorian privies.

These days, the brewery site is slowly being redeveloped as dormitory housing for Southampton, and many of the town's waterways are lined with 1980s retirement terraces, updating Hampshire's cottage vernacular with bow windows, plastic soffits and twitching net curtains. Under their gaze at the edge of the War Memorial Park, the Test's biggest carrier flows deep and swift behind municipal green railings, the back-eddies of its main pool churning with 4lb stocked brown trout which a local coarse angler is popping out like peas from a pod. But the rich ranunculus beds are full of wild grayling as I work down past the bandstand and playground to the junction with the main river, ignoring the yells of local teenagers who've cracked the combination code on the gate, and are now bombing the swimming-hole just vacated by my brother of the angle. And I'm also remembering the stretch of river I'd explored earlier in the day...

Priced out of the centre of town, Romsey's modern businesses have mostly relocated to the northern perimeter, where the Fishlake carrier leaves its SSSI water meadows, and sluices sideways into a culvert and the heart of the Greatbridge industrial estate. Rimmed with concrete and hard-revetted sides that look suspiciously like corrugated asbestos, this is a perfect working

Urban splendour: a spectacular grayling comes to hand. Research from Sweden's post-industrial logging rivers suggests that grayling may do better than trout in highly-modified channels with uniform flow and little cover

From SSSI to concrete corset: the Fishlake carrier enters Romsey's industrial landscape

bit of the river changes from year to year," he tells me. "One year you'll have big ghost carp and commons, the next it's trout – big ones from the farms upstream, the kids get most of those – as well as little ones and grayling. Dunno why it changes so much, but it does."

Just downstream, under cover of a railway arch, I drop a nymph into a double-barrelled culvert and hook one of those little wild trout. Dirty urban fishing at its finest, even on the Test.

Hard-revetted banks make Romsey's carriers a prime candidate for softening with coir rolls and brash bundles

model of an 'unfavourable'-status urban chalkstream. There's a stench of industrial solvents from a bin behind a rigid-raider powerboat workshop, spiritual successor to Romsey's nineteenth century collaps-ible lifeboat-building Reverend Berthon, and IT staff from a tech company eye me incuriously as they drift in and out on cigarette breaks. But small pollution-sensi-tive grayling swoop above a sandy bottom, and an eel as long and thick as my arm sidles back into a luxuriant starwort bed.

Clutching his coffee cup, a transport foreman wanders up to the opposite bank to see what I'm doing, and we start talking about fish. "It don't look like much, but this

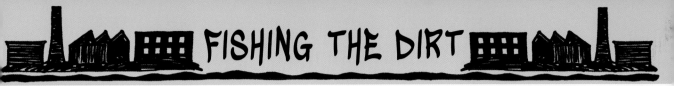

Romsey: River Test

Who's looking after the river?

Natural England and the Environment Agency are working with many partners to improve the Test's SSSI status and restore its ecological connectivity. Projects in the Romsey area involve the Wessex Chalk Stream and Rivers Trust, the Test and Itchen Association, the Romsey and District Society, Hampshire Wildlife Trust and Test Valley Borough Council.

The Romsey and District Society organises annual stream cleans in the town's carriers and tributary channels, and the Wessex Chalk Stream and Rivers Trust is planning fish passage improvements at Sadler's Mill.

For the latest information, visit:
www.romseynet.org.uk
www.wcrst.org.uk
www.hwt.org.uk

Getting there

Romsey War Memorial Park is 15 minutes' walk from Romsey station, via the Test Valley Borough Council offices on Duttons Road, SO51 8XG.

Maps of Romsey are available from the Tourist Information Centre on Latimer Street, SO51 8DF: OS Explorer 131 is also recommended.

Seasons and permits

Brown trout season runs from 3 April to 31 October; grayling season from 16 June to 14 March. For conservation reasons, no fishing for salmon or sea trout is allowed in the War Memorial Park.

Test Valley Borough Council sells two tickets per day for around 200 metres of fishing in the Park. For full details, contact the council via www.testvalley.gov.uk

On most industrial estates, fishing is controlled by the riparian owners: explore at your own risk and discretion.

Fishing tips

The lower Test is well-known as an excellent mixed fishery. Stocked brown and rainbow trout up to 4lbs or more outnumber wild trout of smaller average size, but grayling reach 2lbs, perhaps because they're less frequently killed. The river also holds good roach, chub and carp, and salmon are slowly returning.

A rod of 9 to 10ft is ideal, rated for a 4 to 6 weight line. To match the river's hatches of olives, blue-winged olives and caddis, time-tested flies include Lunn's Particular, Leckford Professor, Houghton Ruby and Caperer. Midge and shrimp patterns are also useful, and mayfly imitations are indispensable in season.

Don't miss

● Broadlands house and estate: former homes of Lord Palmerston and Lord Mountbatten of Burma

● The Japanese 150mm field gun in the War Memorial Park: presented to Lord Mountbatten upon the Japanese surrender at the end of the Second World War

● Romsey Abbey: saved from demolition by Romsey residents during the Dissolution of the Monasteries in 1539

9

SALISBURY

· ·

Rivers Avon and Nadder

If solitude is what you seek in your fishing, Salisbury city centre on a summer Saturday afternoon may not be your place. Flying columns of kids spin past on pimped-up bikes, armed to the teeth with float rods. Supermarket security guards eyeball you grimly, and harassed shoppers stare at your long rod and inscrutable polaroids as they hustle past, nervously suppressing their kids' enquiries: "Mum, what's he doing in the riv-eer? Dad, why's he fishing? Gran, whyyyyyyy...?"

But you can meet kindred fly-fishing spirits, too, in this town of retired colonels on the edge of Salisbury plain. "There's a trout a yard along here," nods a knowing member of the local angling club as we hang over a bridge that used to carry the railway line across what's now Sainsbury's car park. "And if you look a bit further downstream, past the library, you'll see one that's four pounds if he's an ounce!"

Within two miles of the city, six rivers converge to form one of the finest chalk systems in the world – and Salisbury's modern location is no coincidence. Relocated in 1220 from Old Sarum's high, dry hilltop a few miles to the north, the new riverside settlement attracted the region's main concentration of wool-dyers who profited from the fourteenth-century craze for dressing household servants in matching liveries. The drapers specialised in 'Salisbury rays': brightly-striped cloths in tones of red, blue and green which were marketed as far away as London. Much of the dyeing industry was probably based in Castle Street, backing directly onto the Avon, and the medieval city's numerous tan-yards and leather-works also exploited the river to carry away noxious concentrations of lime, urine, and scourings from the hides.

But the Avon survived this cluster of industry at the mid-point of its catchment, and still provides habitat for more species of fish than any other British river. With greensand headwaters in the Vale of Pewsey, and the Nadder, Wylye, Ebble and Bourne all contributing their own different characteristics and chalkstream water chemistries, the whole system is classified both as a Special Site of Scientific Interest and as a Special Area of Conservation under the European Habitats Directive.

In common with the Test and Itchen, the Avon is struggling to meet conservation targets, particularly on recovering its runs of salmon, but its status has also spawned several international-standard river restoration programmes. From 2005, with funding worth £1 million from the European

Below their confluence in Queen Elizabeth Park, the combined Avon and Nadder form the southern perimeter of Salisbury's cathedral close

Commission's *LIFE Nature* programme, the *STREAM* project addressed the need to integrate whole-catchment management strategies in order to reconnect the river and its valley, ending in 2009 with a knowledge-sharing conference for experts across Europe. Meanwhile, between 2006 and 2010, the *Living River* project worked on community engagement with partners including Natural England, Wildlife Trusts and local councils, to increase appreciation of the Avon and its tributaries.

Alongside these wider programmes, the Environment Agency and local residents have also been noticeably busy in the heart of Salisbury. The city's industrial past had left the river hostile to wildlife: heavily engineered and straightened, walled with brick, concrete and sheet piling, lacking both marginal vegetation and healthy in-river habitat. Now, as part of the Millennium Festival initiative, EA river restorer Allan Frake negotiated funds and designed a scheme to soften the banks between Fisherton Street and the old head of navigation at Crane Bridge Road, with greened-up edges designed to bring wildlife back into the city.

"We learned stuff at every stage of that project," reflects Allan more than a decade later. "For instance, we had one particular group of residents, living in flats overlooking the river, who actually liked the neatness and nice clean lines of concrete riprap and sheet piling, and couldn't see why we'd want to mess it up with all this untidy green stuff. It taught me one of the most important lessons I always try to pass on: not everyone will like your ideas for re-greening the river, and their opinions

can be just as valid as your own. Eventually all we could do was ask them to sort it out amongst themselves, and fortunately they did!"

"In the fullness of time," he continues, "we completed over a hundred yards of work on both banks: mostly willow weave soft revetments backfilled with earth from wheelbarrows, planted with pot-grown chalkstream plants. And it was all a great success for about three years as the purple loosestrife sprouted and the other plants came up: we won at least three awards for it, and we all patted ourselves on the back!"

But the lessons weren't done yet. "By year four or five, it was clear that all these enhancements were actually deteriorating quite badly, mainly because of

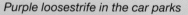

Purple loosestrife in the car parks

In the net: 16 inches of Nadder trout from the Churchfields industrial estate

ranunculus in the channel. Narrowing the channel had increased the water's velocity, and luxuriant beds of weed were forcing all the flow into the banks, causing erosion even at low summer levels. And the water voles liked their new habitat so much, they burrowed into the artificial banks and deconstructed them even faster. Today we know willow weave only lasts about five years, but Salisbury was where we learnt all that: unless you get the roots of the plants binding everything together really properly, you need geotextile in the design as well."

At this point, Allan approached Agenda 21, a local community catalyst group, and started to talk about retro-fitting. "We took a good hard look at every-thing, and almost started again. Lots of new geotextile, as well as gravel to raise the river bed, and extra netting to keep some of the birds off." The new phase of the project involved more than a hundred volunteers from local businesses, the EA and NE, the British Trust for Conservation Volunteers, and Salisbury and District Angling Club. "It worried me a bit when we had this line of one-tonne gravel bags craned off the lorry by the bridge – how were we going to move them into the channel? But when you get a load of volunteers with buckets who like throwing stones in rivers, it's pretty quick and easy!"

Passers-by loved the look of the work, and the spontaneous idea of 'sponsor a plant for a quid' raised almost £700. Work had already been done on the Summerlock mill stream, and the *Living River* project later extended Allan's enhancements more than three hundred yards upriver, with post-monitoring entrusted to Southampton University. At least three or four pairs of salmon are now seen spawning in the centre of Salisbury every year, and salmon parr are common here and on the Nadder behind the Churchfields industrial estate, where a boulder flume installed in the late 1990s has scoured out a huge plume of well-aerated gravel from a new deep-water refuge.

Back in the bustling shopping centre, trophy trout barge between Avon-signature flocks of swans for the bread that showers down from the crowds on the walkways, Allan looks back on his favourite project with satisfaction – and a final lesson from forty years of river mending.

"Whatever restoration works you do," he cautions, "make them sustainable and low maintenance. The hardest thing is working out who'll take up the cudgels to look after it afterwards, and there's still no benchmark for quality of maintenance. It's something else for us all to learn as we go on."

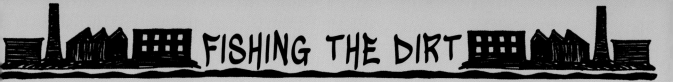

Salisbury: Rivers Avon and Nadder

Who's looking after the rivers?

The Environment Agency took over the roles and responsibilities of the National Rivers Authority in 1996, regulating pollution, reducing flood risk and improving the environment where possible. In Salisbury and elsewhere, EA officers work with local groups to maximise the effectiveness of projects and funding.

The Avon's invertebrates are also monitored by Wiltshire Wildlife Trust through its *Wessex Chalk Streams Project* (affiliated to the Riverfly Partnership). Salisbury and District Angling Club performs keepering duties on its urban fisheries, and is working with Cyril Bennett on a blue-winged olive ranching project.

For the latest information, visit:
www.environment-agency.gov.uk
www.wiltshirewildlife.org
www.salisburydistrictac.co.uk

Getting there

The Avon and Nadder are no more than 10 minutes' walk from Salisbury station.

Maps of Salisbury are available from the Tourist Information Centre on Fish Row, SP1 1EJ: OS Explorer 130 is also recommended.

Seasons and permits

Brown trout season runs from 1 April to 15 October; grayling season from 16 June to 14 March.

Salisbury and District Angling Club controls around 5 miles of water on the Avon and Nadder above and below Salisbury town centre, and around the edge of the Churchfields industrial estate.

For full details and a list of day ticket outlets, visit www.salisburydistrictac.co.uk

Fishing tips

The Avon holds more varieties of fish than any other British river, and its wild trout and grayling commonly reach at least a pound, with some trout much larger. Specimen dace, perch, roach, pike, chub and gudgeon are also present in the Avon's urban reaches.

Most local fly-fishers rely on a rod of 8 to 10ft, rated for a 2 to 5 weight line. Frank Sawyer's fly patterns have been regarded as iconic since the 1950s: the Killer Bug to imitate freshwater shrimp, the Grey Goose to suggest hatching pale wateries, and the Pheasant Tail nymph for all other olives. Grannom and mayfly hatches can be spectacular on both the Avon and Nadder, and Pheasant Tail Spinners are almost always useful.

Don't miss

● Salisbury Cathedral cloisters: the final resting place of George Selwyn Marryat, Frederic Halford's early collaborator, marked with a simple marble memorial stone

● Constable's view of Salisbury Cathedral across Harnham water meadows

Softer focus: luxuriant marginal plants provide superb bankside cover for insects, birds and fish in the centre of Salisbury

10

SOUTH LONDON

River Wandle

"You wouldn't believe what was happening on this river even twenty years ago," Environment Agency flood risk manager Dick Kew confides as we lean over a bridge in Carshalton, planning the next phase of the Wandle Trust's works to restore spawning gravels and large woody debris around a weir we've recently demolished.

"All winter long, the National Rivers Authority had a team of fourteen men who had to be kept occupied, so they'd set them to toeboarding and shoaling: literally driving bulldozers into the river and scraping all the pools and riffles flat to produce a nice clean, square channel, optimised for flood conveyance.

"I stopped that when I got here, mind you, but you've also got to remember that those practices dated from earlier times when far worse stuff was being done to the Wandle. For instance, the Croydon power stations used to abstract water via boreholes, then run it into the river through concrete cooling channels across Beddington farmlands. But around 1975, as my colleague Peter Ehmann will tell you, someone measured the temperature of the water at the point of discharge into the Wandle at 75 degrees centigrade. Add urban run-off and industrial waste, as well as sewage liquor pouring out of every treat-

ment works along the banks from Colliers Wood down to the Thames, and you've got a stack of problems for one little river!"

Today, the only traces of Croydon's power stations are the twin chimneys still towering over IKEA's superstore and the lines of pylons striding down the valley, and it's sometimes hard to believe that the Wandle's fortunes ever sank so low. Until the end of the nineteenth century, the river maintained its reputation as one of the great trout streams of fly-fishing history: praised by Sir Humphrey Davy's *Salmonia* as *'the best and clearest stream near London'*, boasting Victorian-era fishing rights so desirable that even the editor of *The Field* couldn't be sure of an invitation, and spawning a technique of upstream dry fly fishing known as the 'Carshalton Dodge', which Frederic Halford learned from the locals before advertising it to the world as a gentlemanly sporting code.

But when Halford spent his last summer on the Wandle in 1881, the graffiti was already on the wall. Falling steeply at 14ft per mile from a string of spring-line villages on the North Downs, the river's 11-mile course to the Thames at Wandsworth had been industrialised since Domesday, powering at least 13 flour and malting mills. Fulling and metalworking arrived in the 1300s, and Huguenot refugees

Urban angler: Andrew Farr fishes the Wandle near Merton bus garage

brought calico bleaching to the middle river. The Wandle drove London's own Industrial Revolution during the eighteenth century: by 1805 James Malcolm described it as *'the hardest worked river for its size in the world'*, powering more than 90 mills which tanned leather, stitched boots, dyed fabrics, rolled copper and paper, bored cannons, mixed paints and varnishes, and ground snuff, gunpowder, dyewood and opium from the poppies which flourished in the valley's market gardens.

The same year that Halford left the river, Arts and Crafts supremo William Morris arrived, leasing a mill in the old precinct of Merton Priory just downstream from the factory which supplied Liberty's department store with printed silks and chintzes. Despite Arthur Lasenby Liberty's competitive jibe that *'we send all our dirty water down to Morris'*, Wandle water proved ideal for the indigo discharge dyeing process, and Morris' complex of workshops also created tapestries, carpets, wallpapers, stained glass and decorative tilework until the luxury goods market collapsed in 1940.

As suburbia sprawled south along the Wandle, proper sewage treatment for the valley's growing population turned urgent. In the early 1870s, horticulturalist Alfred Smee fought a landmark case against the Croydon Board of Health for polluting the upper river, and Beddington farmlands became an early sewage farm. In hot weather the sewage-soaked fields were sprayed with a toxic odour-suppressing compound of gas tar and quicklime known as McDougall's Fluid: many mill-owners thought this killed more fish than it saved, but such drastic measures probably

protected the Wandle from being culverted like many other London rivers, even when it was officially classified as a public open sewer in the 1960s.

Treated sewage effluent from 28 square miles of south London now provides at least 80 per cent of the river's average flow below Goat Bridge, where a unique water recirculation system pumps water back up to Carshalton Ponds to compensate for over-abstraction from the aquifer – and the Wandle's ecological status is still inextricably linked with the performance of Beddington sewage treatment works. From

Chalkstream idyll: ranunculus, starwort and clean-scoured gravels at Wandle Bank

Once heavily polluted by the Morris and Liberty print works, this stretch of the Wandle now holds good populations of fish

the early 1980s, water quality improved enough for the National Rivers Authority to stock with chub, dace, roach, barbel, and even a few experimental grayling and trout. But a slug of cyanide knocked out the works' biological function in 1995, and the river ran with raw sewage for several days, motivating Mitcham angler Alan Suttie to form a local educational and environmental charity which soon evolved into the Wandle Trust.

Twelve years later, Beddington struck for a second time when contractors cleaning tertiary screens mistakenly released 1,600 litres of sodium hypochlorite into the recovering river, bleaching more than three miles of the channel, and killing at least 7,000 fish of all species. In negotiations led by the Angling Trust, Thames Water quickly admitted responsibility, and the Wandle Trust was nominated as lead partner in the *Living Wandle* project: a programme of river restoration and habitat improvement worth £500,000 to the catchment over five years. (The water company's initial fine of £125,000 was reduced on appeal to £50,000, a clear indication that the judge recognised the magnitude of the directors' efforts to repair the damage with the river's stakeholders).

Bracketed by these catastrophes, the growth of the Wandle Trust was a true phenomenon of our interconnected digital age: a virtual community of interest coalescing to take direct environmental action in the real world. From the first time Richard Baker and I started to discuss the Wandle on the UK's *Fly Fishing Forums*, anglers we'd never met offline began converging from all over London and south-east England, inspired to help pull centuries of rubbish out of an historic chalk stream. As the project developed, web communications helped us to multiply our numbers of clean-up volunteers from five or six irregulars to an average of fifty or sixty every month, and the Trust now uses email updates and a sector-leading charity blogsite to recruit more and more supporters from surrounding communities and thank them for their hard work. It's a dramatic demonstration of the power of localism on the world wide web, and a significant signpost for the rest of the river restoration movement.

Thanks to Thames Water's settlement after the second Beddington disaster, the Trust was able to recruit Bella Davies, a passionate PhD-level aquatic biologist, to guide the river's recovery on a basis of sound science, strong partnerships, and a Ballinderry-style community-driven catchment plan. "For urban rivers like the Wandle, there's no other way forward," she maintains.

"Long-term sustainability depends on reconnecting the population with their river, giving them that sense of ownership and realisation that it's not a flowing rubbish dump but a resource to be valued. And when all 800,000 people in the catchment are looking out for the Wandle, and every inch of its habitat is in a perfect condition, we'll have happily worked ourselves out of a job!"

South London: River Wandle

Getting stuck in: clean-up volunteers, and the Wandle Trust's director Bella Davies

Who's looking after the river?

Founded in 2000, the Wandle Trust is an environmental charity dedicated to restoring the health of the Wandle and its catchment, rotating monthly river clean-ups through Wandsworth, Merton and Sutton, and educating up to 9,000 kids every year with its *Trout in the Classroom* programme.

As one of the pioneering *Trout in the Town* chapters, the Trust works with many partners including the Environment Agency, local councils, London Wildlife Trust and the Wild Trout Trust. Future projects will focus on reducing diffuse urban pollution, eradicating invasive non-native species, restoring the river's roughness and connectivity, and re-establishing a breeding population of wild trout. Since 2007, the Wandle's invertebrates have been monitored by the Trust's spin-off angling club, the Wandle Piscators, on 12 sites as part of the Riverfly Partnership's *Anglers' Monitoring Initiative*.

For the latest information, visit:
www.wandletrust.org
www.wandlepiscators.net

Getting there

The Merton Abbey stretch of the Wandle is 5 minutes' walk from Colliers Wood underground station. The Wandle Trail runs the full length of the river, and many areas can easily be reached from train, tram and tube stations.

A map of the Wandle Trail is available to download from www.wandletrust.org: OS Explorer 161 is also recommended.

Seasons and permits

Brown trout season runs from 1 April to 30 September; grayling season from 16 June to 14 March.

During the river's years as an open sewer, the majority of fishing rights vested in the boroughs of Sutton, Merton and Wandsworth, which mostly allow free fishing with a valid EA rod licence. Only members of Morden Hall Park Angling Club can fish in Morden Hall Park and the Watermeads nature reserve.

For full details, visit:
www.wandlepiscators.net
www.mordenhallparkanglingclub.co.uk

Fishing tips

The Wandle has been classified as a cyprinid fishery since the 1980s, with 10lb barbel, 5lb chub, and 2lb roach as well as carp, dace, and perch originally stocked by William Morris. Grayling are very rare, but trout reintroduced by the *Trout in the Classroom* programme are now reaching maturity at 3lbs or more, and the river's first wild-spawned trout fry in more than 80 years was discovered during riverfly monitoring in 2010.

Ranging from narrow and deep to wide and shallow, the Wandle's heavily-modified course suits a wide variety of tackle, but most local fly-fishers rely on rods from 7 to 9ft, rated for a 2 to 5 weight line. Traditional dry flies include the Carshalton Cocktail and Dun, while William Tall (winner of the Thames Rivers Restoration Trust's John S Hills Memorial Award in 2009 for co-ordinating riverfly monitoring on the Wandle) recommends small modern Black Gnats, JG Emergers, CDC and Elks, and shrimp imitations to match the river's vast biomass of freshwater shrimp.

Don't miss

● The National Trust's Morden Hall Park and Liberty's old Merton Abbey Mills: historic milling sites complete with working water wheels

● Merton Priory's chapter house foundations: preserved under the Merantun Way flyover, open at least 3 weekends per year

● Nelson, Victory, Hardy and Hamilton Roads near Colliers Wood: commemorating local hero Horatio Nelson, who reputedly fished the Wandle before his death at Trafalgar in 1805

Smiles all round: Adrian Grose-Hodge cradles a very special Wandle trout

11

WIMBORNE MINSTER

River Allen

In American river restoration circles, there's a saying that sums up the whole-catchment approach: *'Because we all live downstream'*. It's an aphorism that applies particularly strongly to the tiny, limpid River Allen, which rises in gentle chalk downs between Wimborne St Giles and Monkton Up Wimborne, twelve miles above the Dorset market town of Wimborne Minster.

By the time the Allen joins the Stour, the catchment's geology has shifted to tertiary deposits of silt and gravel, but the smaller river flows over chalk for almost all its length. By contrast with the high, steep-sided downland sources of other chalkstreams like the Avon, the Allen's low, rolling aquifer fills and depletes quickly, producing natural boom-bust cycles of high and low flows, with additional peaks of run-off when the saturated downs can't absorb any more rainfall.

Historically, as human populations grew in the chalk valleys, the productivity of the natural riverside water meadows was maximised with high-level carriers, lower-level drains, and elaborate timetables of immersion that provided professional 'drowners' with full-time employment, raising and lowering water levels to fertilise the meadows and protect them from frost.

On main river channels, weirs, hatches and leats powered corn, fulling and paper mills, fragmenting natural habitats whilst producing the illusory benefit of deeper-water impoundments which could then be stocked with fish.

On the Allen, as demand increased for public water supplies and sanitation, large-scale abstraction began from a borehole close to the river at Stanbridge Mill, about two-thirds of the way down its course. By 1989, under the terms of a licence that permitted Bournemouth Water to abstract almost the equivalent of the river's total summer flow of 25,000 cubic metres every day, water levels had dropped so severely that the Allen was identified as one of the twenty most critical low-flow sites in England and Wales.

Meanwhile, the river was also losing most of its water meadows. Natural or engineered, these had always provided an extra buffer of flood storage capacity at times of high water, as well as reservoirs of seepage in summer droughts. But the last 22 were all given up between 1949 and 1994, and even as Wimborne Minster's own Crown and Mill Meads disappeared under valuable 1980s red brick shopping centres and long-stay retail car parks, town-centre

Hemmed in by bridges and shopping precincts, the urban Allen still provides a haven for trout, grayling, salmon, otters and native crayfish

Delicate presentation reaps rewards: a wild trout from a corner pool between supermarket car parks

finally brought a full fifty per cent reduction of Bournemouth Water's unsustainable abstraction licence, as well as ongoing stream support at Stanbridge Mill, Gussage All Saints, Long Crichel and Wyke Down. The whole of the Allen is now classified as a priority habitat under the UK Biodiversity Action Plan, with protected species such as water voles and otters moving up and down the river through Wimborne itself on an almost nightly basis.

Remarkably, the river has also retained a stable population of the nationally threatened white-clawed crayfish: one of only four watercourses in Dorset where this native species hasn't been ousted by non-native American signal crayfish and the crayfish plague they carry.

In terms of its fly-life, the river's reputation has always been non-committal: *'scarce'* and *'always somewhat sparse'* agreed George Dewar and John Ashley-Cooper in *The South Country Trout Streams* and *A Ring of Wessex Waters* respectively. But it's easy to find olives, blue-winged olives, stoneflies and caddis in the clean river gravels and tufa, and Malcolm Anderson of the Wessex Chalk Stream and Rivers Trust reports the most prolific mayfly hatch he's ever seen.

Reeds, sedges, watercress, forget-me-not and water mint have also drifted downstream from the dredged sections around Walford Mill into the town centre, where two philosophies of urban design are facing off across the no man's land of the river. On the west bank, there's the red brick and vertical concrete retaining walls of the 1978 shopping precinct. Meanwhile, to the east, snuggled in grass swales and soft landscaping, a gleaming new-millennium

flooding became a problem. In November 1995, Councillor Diann March unveiled a proud little plaque in the Allen View car park to commemorate the Wimborne Flood Defence Scheme. Fifteen years later, from the shining tarmac of what was once Mill Mead, it's still impossible to reach the river without climbing a flood berm or scaling an engineering-brick wall. The urban Allen's disconnection from its natural landscape and ecological processes looks unarguably complete.

Yet even the healthiest chalkstreams are often profoundly artificial – and by these standards the river may be getting its balance back. In May 2003, a complex study originally commissioned by the National Rivers Authority in the mid 1980s

supermarket of glass and steel rises from Wimborne's former cricket ground.

Under the *quid pro quo* of section 106 of the Town and Country Planning Act, developers often get consent for planning applications by paying for other local-priority regeneration projects: sports facilities, children's playgrounds, and environmental improvements. In the case of Wimborne's new Waitrose, section 106 funds were used for relocating the town's cricket pitch.

"The council didn't think it was important to enhance the BAP-listed chalkstream around the edge of the development," says Sarah Williams, Dorset Wildlife Trust's co-ordinator for the *Dorset Wild Rivers* programme. "Also, Waitrose probably didn't want to imply that they needed to mitigate for their development up front, but they're still the kind of company that wants to be seen to be helping the local community. We've written them a joint proposal with the Environment Agency for putting rocks into the river as crayfish habitat, as well as quite a lot of soft bank engineering. The river is trying to narrow itself in some places, so it's easy to formalise that by adding brushwood bundles. Lots of consents need to be in place before the work starts – we've got almost every possible protected species moving through – so it didn't happen in autumn 2010, but I'm hoping it won't take too much longer."

Consistent with healthier fly life, Wild Trout Trust founder Charles Rangeley-Wilson confirms there are now many more fish than he remembers from the early 1990s, and the Allen's trout, grayling and cyprinid stocks seem strong enough

to attract a constant flow of fishermen (not all observing strict catch and release, as I deduce from frantic thrashing and a heavy flash of gold inside a plastic shopping bag). Under the midday sun, the fish look confident and streetwise, happy to move between habitat pockets under bridges and trailing swags of ivy, enjoying easy pickings of bread and chips of ice cream cone from the riverside cafés and craft shops that now occupy the old milling quarter.

Under high brick walls, cushions of watercress help to hold up water levels when flows drop in late summer

It's a good place for a dawn raid: in and out of the braided carriers before the supermarkets open and the paths fill up with trolleys and screaming kids. But the shopping centres empty again in the evening, clearing the concrete catwalks over the river, leaving the scene to the urban angler, the trout and the grayling. As I'm finally rehydrating, de-rigging and checking my photos by the car, a girl in a blue-patterned uniform and retail-issue heels comes clicking across the tarmac, heading home after her own long shift.

"Didn't I see you here this morning – you've been fishing here all day?"

"I have… exploring up and down-stream… couldn't think of a better way to spend it."

"Must have been nice!" She smiles, flicks her hair, and walks on.

Balanced ecosystem: wild trout and grayling co-exist happily in Wimborne's old milling channels

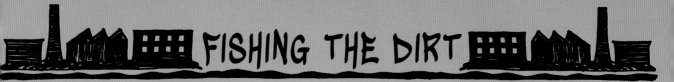

Wimborne Minster: River Allen

Who's looking after the river?

In partnership with the Environment Agency, Natural England and the Farming and Wildlife Advisory Group, Dorset Wildlife Trust is running the *Dorset Wild Rivers* restoration project for five years from 2010 to 2015.

With major funding from Wessex Water, the partnership is working with the Wild Trout Trust, local councils, other landowners and local communities to restore Dorset's rivers for the benefit of fish and invertebrates, reducing agricultural run-off into chalk-streams like the Allen, and creating wetland habitat in the floodplains.

For the latest information, visit: www.dorsetwildlifetrust.org.uk

Getting there

As a result of the Beeching Axe, Wimborne Minster's last passenger train ran in 1964, but there are plenty of car parks in and around the town.

Maps of Wimborne are available from the Tourist Information Centre on the High Street, BH21 1HR: OS Explorer 118 is also recommended.

Seasons and permits

Brown trout season runs from 1 April to 15 October; grayling season from 16 June to 14 March.

According to the EA, fishing rights through the town belong to East Dorset and District Council. Free fishing with a valid EA rod licence is allowed from the bridge by the Rising Sun pub upstream to Walford Bridge: at least half a mile of river and carriers.

Fishing tips

The urban lower Allen is a good mixed chalkstream fishery. Wild trout average up to half a pound, and larger triploid stocked fish up to 3 or 4lbs may also appear; grayling are present up to about a pound, as well as dace and chub. The river is an increasingly important salmon spawning site.

A rod of 6 to 8 ft, rated for a 1 to 4 weight line, will allow you to make the most of the tight casting and mainly small fish.

Traditional flies for the Allen include Olive and Iron Blue Duns, Red Palmers, and Pheasant Tails: local experts like Jon Petterssen and Malcolm Anderson also suggest small CDC and Elk patterns, Griffiths Gnats and Copper John nymphs.

In low, clear water conditions, stealth is necessary. Avoid bright coloured fly lines, use the lightest tippet possible, and degrease it often.

Don't miss

- Wimborne Minster itself, complete with chained library, astronomical clock and…
- The Quarter Jack: the painted figure of a grenadier which strikes the quarters every hour on the Minster's west tower
- Wimborne Model Town: a 1:10 scale mode of the town centre as it looked in the 1950s

12

WINCHESTER

. . . .

River Itchen

When the hawthorn berries are darkening to burgundy on Twyford Down, and other chalk rivers have sunk almost into their gravels, the Itchen in Winchester still feels fast and powerful. Just below ground level from Alresford to Eastleigh, the river's great aquifer slopes gently from north to south, absorbing and redirecting rainfall so efficiently that only a few right-angled tributaries remain above the surface to meet the Itchen's mainstem through the hottest summers and driest autumns.

The groundwater seeps into the city's consciousness in other seasons too. While Salisbury's masons carefully balanced their cathedral's shallow faggot-bundle founda-tions on the stable gravel terraces of the Avon, Winchester Cathedral's architects chose their own flat space beside the Itchen, and found themselves building on a bog. Undeterred, they felled a nearby forest for a floating platform: green oak trunks pile-driven vertically into the peat, beeches laid horizontally on top. Teetering on this slowly-rotting raft as the water table rose and fell, parts of the heavy limestone struc-ture collapsed and had to be rebuilt on several occasions. The aquifer still floods the crypt in winter, even as the year's flows peak in the river outside the Roman walls.

But Winchester's powerful river and wilful aquifer tell only half the story, and the Itchen as a whole suffers seriously from abstraction. At Otterbourne, three miles below Winchester, a hundred-year-old borehole is licensed to pump 58 megalitres of water per day from the chalk, while 46 megalitres can be taken directly from the river. In total, the Itchen provides a public water supply for 300,000 homes in the south Hampshire urban corridor, equivalent to the population of Winchester, South-ampton and Eastleigh, with another 30,000 new dwellings proposed by 2026.

The river's upper river reaches around Itchen Stoke can be boosted when necessary by deep-aquifer stream support via the Candover Brook – but when low flows and over-abstraction converge below a threshold of 237 megalitres per day, salmon have difficulty migrating upstream to spawn, and populations of shrimp and mayfly can be damaged. In view of this threat to the river's status as a Special Area of Conservation and Special Site of Scien-tific Interest, international conservation charity WWF-UK identified the Itchen in 2009 as the flagship for its UK-focused Rivers on the Edge programme. Fronted with a consumer-friendly film by Charles

Winter warmer: Jez Mallinson and Richard Baker dissect a favourite pool below Winchester's ancient City Mill

Rangeley-Wilson, and funded for five years through the HSBC Climate Partnership, the campaign aims to show policy-makers and the public alike the real impact their everyday decisions can make on the chalk-streams.

"Of all our case studies," says WWF-UK freshwater policy officer Rose Timlett, "including the Kennet and upper Lee, the Itchen has probably been most successful so far. *Rivers on the Edge* uses the chalkstreams to tell a compelling story – taking one or two issues, really trying to understand them, and suggesting solutions. As a result of this work, abstraction from the Itchen is now being reviewed, South West Water have proposed universal metering for their area by 2015, and the government and OFWAT are talking about sorting out abstraction licences on a national scale. If we can continue to perform this valuable role as an extra thinking resource for high-level policy-makers, the whole river will certainly benefit, and we'll try to roll out the results of the *Itchen Initiative* to other catchments as well."

With WWF-UK fighting for the Itchen's future at policy level, other groups are working in the river itself. Since 2006, Environment Agency regional fisheries strategist Lawrence Talks has brought his day job home with him to the Nun's Stream in the Hyde suburb of Winchester, inspiring more than 25 other residents to restore 200 yards of canalised stream along-side Saxon Road as part of celebrating the 900th anniversary of Alfred the Great's burial in Hyde Abbey.

In November 2007, volunteers ranging in age from under ten to over sixty moved ten tonnes of gravel by wheelbarrow to repair eroded banks and concentrate flows back into mid-channel. Trout started spawning again in the stream in January 2009, and subsequent years have seen gravel berms and flow deflectors installed to recreate a lost sequence of pools and riffles. New bankside plants including yellow iris and purple loosestrife have encouraged kingfishers and grey wagtails to return to what was recently a concrete ditch. "It's fantastic to see the enthusiasm of local people getting involved in looking after their stream," grins Lawrence as he lays out plans for a pollution prevention project, visual interpretation and future phases of planting.

Nearby, on Winnal Moors and the historic Abbots Barton fishery just above the old Durngate milling site, Hampshire Wildlife Trust has reversed years of dredging and siltation on the Park Stream and other carriers by raising the bed with sacks of chalk, adding layers of loose chalk and gravel, and recreating

A grayling from the Itchen

nursery habitat for trout, grayling and salmon fry. Management of this sustainable wild trout fishery has now been handed to the Piscatorial Society, with stipulations including catch and release, dry flies and lightly weighted nymphs on barbless hooks, and a no-stocking clause that can only benefit the balance of the river's ecology.

Such duties of care, some might say, are long overdue to the urban Itchen. Along Water Lane, hard concrete edges and wooden toe-boarding still recall the drainage programmes begun by the Romans and continued by King Alfred, who cut new channels through Winchester to attract trade and industry into his capital city. His investment paid off: brewers used the cleanest water at the northern end of Alfred's Brooks, as they became known, and fullers, dyers, shoemakers and butchers set up shop further downstream.

Many of these businesses can still be distinguished by the rules designed to regulate their waste disposal. Butchers were apparently banned from throwing '*intrayles or other vile things in the river of the Cytie... but onlie in the place called abbies bridge and there nother but where the same intrailes and other vile things be cutt iiii inches longe*', though records confirm that trout could grow fat on this largesse when other forms of pollution weren't too damaging.

By 1208 there were 22 mills between Hyde Abbey and St Cross, and public latrines were also built over the network of channels, in addition to the Benedictine monastery's 46-hole '*necessarium*' in what is now the Dean's garden. From 1554 the Brooks had to be dried for ten days in May every year for cleansing, with the threat of

Richard Baker wades deep at Durngate to present his signature three-nymph indicator rig

prison for riparian owners who failed to address their own stretches.

Even centuries later, despite regular cholera epidemics and life expectancy in the Brooks-side slums of just 42 years compared to 1850's national average of 58, there was determined local resistance to the idea of a better drainage system. But public sewerage finally arrived in 1875, and by the early 1880s, when Frederic Halford joined Francis Francis, William Senior and George Selwyn Marryat for their annual Mayfly Mess on the Old Barge beat of the Itchen Navigation, both Winchester and the Itchen were already cleaner and greener, evolving towards their modern status as a leafy little cathedral city in the smart chalk country.

These days, treated sewage effluent is filtered back into the fine-grained aquifer for final purification, and you can watch wild trout spawning in Alfred's Brooks at the turn of the year. And as you walk the banks through this capital of chalkstream angling, one poignant thought might make you pause: here on the Itchen, at that singular point in history, Frederic Halford was a post-industrial urban fly-fisher too.

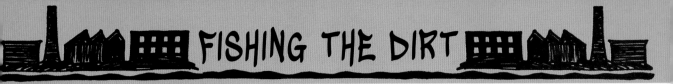

Winchester: River Itchen

Who's looking after the river?

WWF-UK is working with policy-makers to restore sustainable abstraction to the whole Itchen as part of the *Rivers on the Edge* campaign and *Itchen Initiative*. Partnership projects by Hyde900, Hampshire Wildlife Trust and the Piscatorial Society are gradually enhancing carriers and tributaries above the city, and the Environment Agency is also restoring spawning gravels lost through historic dredging.

For the latest information, visit:
www.wwf.org.uk/riversontheedge
www.hyde900.org.uk
www.hwt.org.uk

Getting there

The Itchen is no more than 15 minutes' walk from Winchester station, downhill through the centre of the city. There are public car parks at Durngate and St Catherine's Hill.

Maps of Winchester are available from the Tourist Information Centre at Winchester Guildhall, SO23 9GH: OS Explorer 132 is also recommended.

Seasons and permits

Brown trout season runs from 3 April to 31 October; grayling season from 16 June to 14 March; sea trout season from 1 May to 31 October.

By long tradition, Winchester City Council permits free fishing with a valid EA rod licence at the Weirs from Wharf Mill (Segrim's Mill) to City Mill, and upstream along Water Lane to Durngate Bridge. Free fishing is also allowed on the Old Barge (Itchen Navigation) from St Catherine's Hill to the rowing club and official head of navigation at Black Bridge. In total, at least a mile of fishing is available.

Fishing tips

With the great clean-up of Winchester's waters, wild trout now average more natural sizes than the 8-pounders once caught below the fish smokery in Eastgate Street, or the 16-pounder caught at Durngate in 1888 by a local angler with a hazel rod and minnow bait. Grayling were introduced to the Itchen in the mid-1800s, and provide some of the most reliable sport: average sizes fluctuate from ¾ lb to more than 2lbs according to natural cycles.

A rod of 9 to 10 feet, rated for a 4 to 5 weight line, will cover most eventualities. Except at the height of the mayfly hatch, it's rare to see a rising fish on the Winchester town water, and shrimp or caddis patterns on heavy modern nymph rigs are often most effective. However, mayflies also hatch sporadically through the summer, so it's worth carrying imitations just in case.

Don't miss

● Winchester Cathedral: Izaak Walton's tomb and stained glass in Prior Silkstede's chapel, restored in 1914 with donations from fishermen across Britain and the USA

● Winchester Cathedral: the bust commemorating the diver William Walker, who saved the cathedral from collapse by working in total darkness for 6 hours a day, 6 days a week to reinforce rotting wooden foundations with stone, concrete and steel rods between 1906 and 1912

● The National Trust's City Mill: complete with night-vision otter camera

Lovingly restored by local volunteers, the Nun's Stream now offers ideal spawning gravels for trout, grayling and even salmon

13

DURHAM

··

River Wear

A nagging little easterly wind whistles through the bushes behind me, scattering bright hawthorn and cherry leaves in a flurry round my strike indicator on the slowly dancing surface of the Wear. Distant cathedral bell-notes burst away in snatches on the breeze, and the sun drops sharply behind the viaduct by the station.

It's the end of October in Durham: a bright, squally afternoon is fading into Hallowe'en, and I've yet to encounter one of the river's elusive grayling. Chub, yes, and maybe a wriggle from an angry little brownie, but of *Thymallus thymallus* there's not a sign. A shout of laughter goes up from the huddle of teenage hoodies under the willow on the corner: a dented beer-can smacks into the river, bobs past as sluggishly as my team of heavy tungsten nymphs, and suddenly I know this outing is over. Half a lifetime ago I'd have been racking my oars after a hard sculling session on the Wear, wiping down the boat, thinking of hot tea and doughnuts from Greggs on the way back up to college. Twenty years later, why should this afternoon feel any different?

Still, things do change, and sometimes with surprising speed. Salmon and sea trout were already known to be running the Wear in my rowing days, and water quality was improving all the time: racing on the Tyne left oily black smears on splashtops and boats, but I got away with nothing worse than gastroenteritis from my one full-body immersion in the Wear at a boat club party. Even more recently, the river has come into the care of the Wear Rivers Trust, a rapidly-expanding charity that's part of the Rivers Trust network, itself perhaps the fastest-evolving environmental movement in the UK today.

"Yes, we've been able to develop pretty quickly," agrees Ivan Dunn, the Trust's education and community engagement officer, when I call to ask him about the river's future prospects. "Partly thanks to the National Lottery, partly as a result of support from the Community Foundation for Tyne and Wear, we've grown from one project officer to a team of four people in less than a year, and there's plenty of work to be done on water quality, invasive species and general awareness.

"Like a lot of other Rivers Trusts, we're very much involved in helping the Environment Agency to deliver the requirements of the Water Framework Directive: that's still mainly focused on fish passage, with projects like our rock ramp on the Cong Burn near Chester-le-Street, to

The Wear at Ferens Park, dominated by long, luxurious pools and riffles

Rowers under Kingsgate Bridge

Gill, just downstream from Durham."

On its 65-mile course from the eastern Pennines to the sea at Sunderland, the Wear cuts steep, narrow gullies through moorland and granite bedrock before breaking out into wider plains incised with deeply wooded sandstone gorges like the long meander around Durham's defensive peninsula. High-energy spates run quickly off these saturated uplands, and Weardale's early miners learned to harness the headwaters' erosive energy with a technique known as 'hushing': using torrents of water to expose seams and heavy nuggets of lead, which dropped out of suspension more quickly than the lighter gravels. With this history of hydraulic mining over 4-500 years, the upper river is dominated by species of plants and invertebrates which can tolerate highly mobile substrates as well as concentrations of heavy metals: a fascinating study area for the Wear Rivers Trust in a future partnership project with the North Pennines Area of Outstanding Natural Beauty.

"Apart from dissolved lead there's also the question of atmospheric lead deposits," Ivan tells me. "At Rookhope, there was a two-mile-long chimney designed to carry toxic fumes from the smelter up onto the high moors for dispersal. Some of the lead and silver in the fumes redeposited in the flue – in fact it was periodically scraped out for recycling – but we believe that the atmospheric lead would have been significant, and may still be influencing plant and invertebrate communities across the region."

Until the early twentieth century, the north Pennine lead field was one of the most important deposits in the world, and

get fish over an immovable concrete weir. Going forward, the Wear has been named as a pilot catchment for designing new forms of river basin management between the EA and organisations like ours, so we hope to be able to apply to Defra to fund many more of these projects. With training from the Riverfly Partnership, our invertebrate monitoring scheme is steadily expanding, and we've been running very successful community engagement sessions at Durham Regatta and other events. And of course local angling clubs are constantly looking out for the river: for example, Fish Legal has been acting on behalf of Chester-le-Street Angling Club in relation to large-scale run-off, erosion and sedimentation from an industrial estate via the Red House

mining this resource proved hugely profitable for the whole area. Twenty miles west of Durham, Stanhope became the richest parish in England, and acres of Weardale lead covered the roofs of Durham's cathedral and castle. Igneous deposits of fluorspar (calcium fluoride) were also exploited as a flux for steelmaking. Coal mining flourished for nearly eight centuries: by 1923, 170,000 miners were working the shafts around Durham, with no fewer than eight separate pitheads visible from the cathedral, and the river was frequently described as a coal-black sewer.

In the meantime, although County Durham produced millions of tonnes of coal before the last pit closed in 1994, the city preserved most of its narrow medieval street plan by remaining largely unindustrialised. Framwellgate Weir had been constructed for corn milling on the site of an ancient ford: north of the peninsula, Walkergate became an important local centre for weaving wool, cotton, and finally carpets on looms smuggled out of Kidderminster in the early nineteenth century. Near Prebends Bridge, a diagonal weir which served a fulling mill at one end, and a flour mill at the other, still impounds the river as far as the prehistoric earthworks at Maiden Castle, at least a mile and a half upstream.

Today, the biggest vessel on this flat stretch of water is the Prince Bishop pleasure cruiser – a recurring menace to rowers and pole-anglers from Durham City Angling Club alike – but in the eighteenth century there were far more ambitious plans to provide Weardale's mines with their own sea port. In 1720, the first round of proposals suggested making the whole middle and lower river navigable by re-routing the Wear to Gateshead via the Team: when this failed, a second option involved massive dredging from Durham to Sunderland. Both concepts ran aground because the ships of the time were already too big to make such large-scale engineering profitable. But there's still one reminder of the idea of Durham-on-sea, a seven-foot lead statue of Neptune in the city's market square. And it feels slightly sobering for a modern river restorationist to fish the Ferens Park stretch of the Wear at the tag-end of the season and imagine what could have been built here: quays, docksides, and straight-dredged navigation channels instead of pools, riffles and sandy bluffs already wrapped in a chilly dusk.

Autumn colours on the Wear

Cormorants on the Framwellgate weirs...

I shiver, reel up, wade back to the bank. Someday I'll be back again. But if I step it out now, there'll just be time for a pint of coal-dust porter in the Colpitts bar before catching my train.

... and anglers at Ferens Park

Durham: River Wear

Who's looking after the river?

The Wear Rivers Trust was launched in 2008 as an amalgamation of the Weardale Environmental Trust and the River Wear Environment Trust. The new organisation works on a catchment scale: raising awareness and funds, developing partnership projects, and making informed decisions about improving the river environment.

The Wear has been identified by the Environment Agency as a pilot catchment for river restoration in partnership with local groups to meet the standards of the Water Framework Directive, and the Angling Development Board has recently supported the formation of the Durham County Angling Action Group.

For the latest information, visit:
www.wear-rivers-trust.org.uk
www.environment-agency.gov.uk

Getting there

The Ferens Park stretch of the Wear is 10 minutes' walk downhill from Durham station.

Maps of Durham are available from the Tourist Information Centre in Millennium Place, DH1 1WA: OS Explorer 308 is also recommended.

Seasons and permits

Brown trout season runs from 22 March to 30 September; grayling season from 16 June to 14 March; sea trout season from 3 April to 31 October; salmon season from 1 February to 31 October.

Durham City Angling Club controls around five miles of the Wear, including most of the fishing around the peninsula below the cathedral and castle.

By long tradition, Durham City Council allows free fishing with a valid EA rod licence upstream from Kepier Farm to a point 50 yards below Framwellgate Bridge (a stretch known as Ferens Park or the Sands) and along the rowing course on either side of Baths Bridge: just over a mile in total. For full details of how to apply for membership, visit: **www.durhamanglers.co.uk**

Fishing tips

The Wear is a popular mixed fishery, with salmon and sea trout into double figures as well as barbel, chub, roach, dace, and trout to 5lbs in exceptional cases. Grayling numbers seem to be cyclical, but are currently recovering as a result of an EA restocking programme in the River Browney above Durham.

Ferens Park is heavily fished with all methods, so a subtle imitative approach can pay dividends, with a rod of 9 to 10ft rated for a 3 to 5 weight line. The river's most famous traditional fly is the Greenwell's Glory, reputedly invented by Canon Greenwell as an olive imitation in the 1850s, and it's still a pattern that performs well in dry, wet and spider tyings.

According to local experts like Pete McParlin and David Holland, other flies to try include Black Gnats, Partridge and Orange spiders, Waterhen Bloas and modern shrimp patterns.

Don't miss

- Durham's Norman cathedral and castle: a World Heritage Site almost encircled by the Wear's sandstone gorge. At the top of 325 steep spiral steps, the view from the 278-foot cathedral tower is spectacular
- Framwellgate, Elvet, Prebends, Kingsgate and Millennium Bridges: from ancient to modern, a full range of engineering styles
- Local museums of mining history at Durham and Killhope

Grayling season in Durham

14

FAKENHAM

River Wensum

After the street parties packed up and the bunting was furled away, the end of the Second World War brought little lasting euphoria to the people of north-west Europe. Industry and agriculture lay in ruins after years of total war: hunger stalked the continent, and resources had to be shared to save whole nations from starvation. In Britain, food rationing would last until 1953.

Stability and efficiency, declared the Agriculture Act of 1947, were the twin pillars of the government's agricultural policy, and as a bitter winter ended with devastating floods, few politicians were in a mood to argue against the need to produce cheap food at almost any cost.

During the Industrial Revolution, the natural landscapes of the midlands and north had already been transformed by old-fashioned smokestack manufacturing. Now, on this new home front, it was the turn of rivers like the Wensum, and the fields and wetlands surrounding them, to be tamed for the needs of industrial agriculture.

In fact, by the time the baton of stability and efficiency was passed to the new East Suffolk and Norfolk River Board in 1948, the Wensum had already been tinkered-with for centuries. This small chalk river falls less than 115ft over its whole 44-mile course across Norfolk's sandy, gravelly glacial fans, and more than half its gradient is robbed by mill impoundments, some so close to each other on the valley's shallow slope that the ponding between them is almost continuous. For many years, Fakenham's three corn and seed mills co-ordinated their water releases by means of smoke signals, and the channels that linked them were designed to be self-cleaning, flushing away silt with a five-foot head of water accumulated and released on alternate days.

As long as the mills remained economically viable, this careful balance successfully counteracted many of the sedimentation problems usually created by weirs and other impoundments. While the town prospered with printing works, a brewery and a cattle market, eighteenth century accounts praised the variety of the weed, the profusion of the mayfly hatches, and the quality of the fishing for trout, dace and roach.

But the river declined as the mills fell into disuse, and a local water bailiff

Fakenham Mill on the Wensum: a river devastated by dredging for agribusiness in the 1950s

recorded the destruction of the upper Wensum's delicate artificial ecosystem in the name of agricultural drainage: a testimony published in a preliminary report for the River Wensum Restoration Strategy in 2008:

"Very soon after the new River Board took control, a statement appeared in the local press announcing that they intended to carry out a major drainage programme. This would entail the use of a deep dragline over a five-mile stretch of the river from Shereford (through Fakenham) to Sennowe Park.

Sometimes size doesn't matter: proof that this stretch of the Wensum still holds a beautiful strain of wild trout

"The notice invited interested parties to make enquiries or protests to the river board's old head office... but no amount of protest was considered. We were told that whilst everything would be done to protect fisheries, and the flora and fauna, the needs of agriculture and drainage took precedence. For almost three years the dredger carried out the programme as stated, the river above Goggs' Mill (which was demolished as part of the works) suffered the worst as the laid gravel was easily removed, and as the dragline required an operational width of 15ft, all shrubs, trees and vegetation was destroyed on the south bank.

"After the work was completed in 1957, the character of the river was completely changed. It became more like a deep muddy canal. The attractive bends were mostly gone, and the fast gravel and chalk runs were replaced with mud and silt... The otters and the kingfishers have gone, and so have the roach and wild brown trout. In June there is no mayfly hatch from the muddy bottom, and with the coming of the nitrate problem, the river has been taken over by the worst types of weed and algae. The worst irony of the whole sorry mess is that the year after the work was completed, the Sculthorpe Fen was flooded, something that before was almost unheard of..."

Fast-forward fifty years, and it's fortunate that attitudes to unique chalk river habitats like the Wensum have changed significantly. Despite the scale of its problems, the entire river is designated as a Special Site of Scientific Interest and Special Area of Conservation, and a growing number of local and national organisations are deeply concerned with its health. In the late 1990s, 'very poor' fisheries surveys induced Environment Agency team leader Simon Johnson to commission the first phase of the River Wensum Rehabilitation Study: a report which finally brought the river's impoverishment and lack of diversity into full focus. Fast-forward another fifteen years, and Simon is now director of the Eden Rivers Trust, while the River Wensum Restoration Strategy is spearheaded by the EA's John Abraham in partnership with Natural England and a range of other groups.

"There are 33 river SSSIs across the country," John tells me, "and there are other schemes around, but here on the Wensum we managed to pull it all together before anyone else.

"The major drainage works of the 1950s were designed to pin the water table down to release more arable land, which as we've seen didn't work too well because it destroyed the river's hard gravel bed, and left unofficial floodbanks of spoil which also cut the river off from its floodplain, and made a lot of flooding worse."

To cover the whole Wensum, the EA team split it into nine manageable units, held six consultation events to capture information from the public, and published science-based feasibility studies and detailed plans in summer 2011. "We're taking a holistic approach to restoring the river's diversity," says John, "but what works in one area may still not be appropriate for another, and there's a whole spectrum of views to take into consideration.

"For instance, just above Fakenham Mill, a border of reeds and fishing platforms was installed in 2001 to alleviate erosion of

Above Fakenham Mill, river restoration has created a reedy riparian fringe more than 2 metres wide: perfect habitat for water voles

the bank, but we may not be able to do much more in that location because the majority of feedback told us local people rather like the ponded effect. In other areas we're using large woody debris and low-level berms to narrow over-wide stretches back to a sustainable width within the artificial channel.

91

But you don't want to force river restoration on people, dragging them kicking and screaming into it… if we run into resistance in one area, there's always somewhere else to work, and people will gradually recognise the benefits."

In this new implementation phase of the project, one of those other locations is Bintree Mill, where successful bank reprofiling over several years, combined with water quality improvements from phosphate stripping and catchment sensitive farming programmes, resulted in NE reassessing the river from 'declining' to 'recovering' status in early 2011. Officially, the Wensum is on its way back from the brink.

"When I was speaking to the River Restoration Centre the other day," says John, "they told me we're the most advanced project in the whole of Europe. We know we're trailblazing here on the Wensum, we know there's no-one else to learn from, but there'll be plenty of others who can learn from our mistakes, and now we want to keep that momentum going!"

Fakenham's market square is paved with plaques memorialising the town's printing heritage, but teasels by the river are a reminder of the wool industry too

Fakenham: River Wensum

Who's looking after the river?

In summer 2011, as part of the River Wensum Restoration Strategy, Natural England and the Environment Agency published feasibility studies and detailed plans for restoring the habitat diversity of the Wensum. These are available to anyone wishing to consider partnership projects: local groups in the Fakenham area may already be involved.

As part of the Riverfly Partnership's *Anglers' Monitoring Initiative*, a network of at least 8 invertebrate sampling sites was launched in 2011. Volunteers monitor the river above and below Fakenham with standard 3-minute kick samples (aligned with the EA's own methodologies), and aim to research the effects of contrasting river management techniques on invertebrate populations.

For the latest information, visit:
www.environment-agency.gov.uk
www.riverflies.org

Getting there

Both of Fakenham's stations closed by the 1960s, but a new rail link may be planned. In the meantime, there's plenty of car parking in and around this practical little market town.

Maps of Fakenham are available from the Tourist Information Centre on Oak Street, NR21 9DY: OS Explorer 251 is also recommended.

Seasons and permits

Brown trout season runs from 1 April to 29 October. Grayling seem to have disappeared from the Fakenham area of the river in the 1990s.

Fakenham Town Council allows free fishing with a valid EA rod licence along the Causeway to the first bridge above Fakenham Mill, and downstream from the mill along the footpath for about a mile and a half to the old railway bridge. Fakenham Angling Club controls an additional mile and a half upstream of the Causeway. For full details, visit: www.fakenhamanglingclub.co.uk

Fishing tips

In its lower reaches, the Wensum is a well-known barbel river, but wild trout, roach and dace dominate the headwaters around Fakenham. Most trout fall within the 4- to 6-inch range, growing up to 2lbs or even larger where habitat pockets allow; roach can reach 2lbs. Otters are now seen regularly downstream at Pensthorpe nature reserve, a sure sign that the fishery's biomass is recovering.

For stalking trout in shallow, narrow water, a rod of 6 to 7ft is ideal, rated for a 1 to 4 weight line, although a longer rod of similar weight will help when fishing nymphs down high banks and over reed beds. Weed growth can be prolific from July onwards, so local fly-fishers recommend switching from nymphs to dry flies as the season progresses. Black gnats, sedges, small pale olive imitations and mayflies can all work well.

Don't miss

● Fakenham Museum of Gas and Local History: mothballed in 1965, the only surviving town gas coking works in England and Wales. Their effect on the Wensum is unknown, but similar coal gas production helped to destroy the Irwell and many more industrialised rivers

● Fakenham Market Square: cast-iron panels commemorating the town's printing heritage

● Burnham Thorpe: 10 miles from Fakenham, the birthplace of Horatio Nelson

15

GRANTHAM

River Witham

Fifteen minutes out of Peterborough on the main east coast railway line, the flat arable landscape starts rolling up into hillier country.

Watching carefully from the windows of the high-speed train, you begin to notice that more of the older farmhouses are built from golden stone than dark red brick, and the railway cuttings get deeper and more frequent between walls of pale, fissured rock. If you've ever sat thinking about the architecture of trout rivers, something might click in your head at this point, and you won't surprised to hear what Grantham Angling Association's habitat improvement officer tells you about the Witham's geology when he meets you at the station.

"Yes, it's oolitic limestone," confirms Colin Hides. "Look at a geological map of Britain, and you'll see a ridge of this rock running all the way from the Cotswolds to the Humber. The limestone in the local Ancaster beds is a bit finer and lighter than the stuff in Northamptonshire, so the medieval masons favoured it for cathedrals: in fact they're still quarrying it for building work and repairs at Blenheim Palace and the Tower of London."

Between Grantham and Leadenham, ten miles to the north, the Lincolnshire Edge is formed from a double scarp of 200-million-year-old Jurassic ironstone overlaid by younger limestone: a geological succession that defined Grantham's industrial history as surely as the springs seeping from the folds of the Kesteven Uplands give rise to the headwaters of the River Witham.

Until the railway arrived, the town's economy was based on fulling, tanning and servicing the stagecoach stop-over between London and Lincoln, but from 1850 Grantham started exploiting its mineral deposits to become a centre for heavy engineering. Quarries at Honington sent limestone as far afield as the huge ironworks at Stanton on the Erewash: in Grantham itself, steam locomotives and traction engines were only the start of the output from Hornsby's foundries. Caterpillar tracks were devised by the company's chief engineer before the concept was sold to an American competitor due to lack of interest from the War Office, and the factory began making heavy oil engines in 1891, a full eight years before the better-known Rudolf Diesel started commercial production.

Tanks were built in Grantham during both World Wars, as well as Bren guns and 20mm Hispano-Suiza cannons for Spitfire and Hurricane fighters. Between 1915

Repeating history: Colin Hides drifts a dry fly past the undercut where he caught his first Witham trout in 1975

and 1918 the town had already hosted the British army's biggest depot and training camp, stretching for two miles across the grounds of Belton House: a quarter of a million men were billeted on a town of less than ten thousand, and the local authorities were forced to appoint the first-ever

Swords into ploughshares: Grantham's heavy engineering plants are gradually being replaced by smart new apartments

policewoman to handle the prostitutes who flocked to the area. Less than forty miles from the east coast, Grantham's concentra-

tion of heavy industry, armaments factories and key intersections of the road and rail network later proved an irresistible target for the Luftwaffe, so the town was more heavily bombed per head of population than any other in Britain.

"Grantham probably reached its industrial height in the last war," says Colin, "but in the 1960s the Ruston and Hornsby site still stretched from the station to the river, with three foundries, a heat treatment works, and 6,000 employees. I started my own career up the road as an apprentice machinist at Aveling and Barford, making diggers, graders and road rollers. It was all heavy machinery then, and a lot of water was abstracted from the river for the foundries and heat treatments. Of course water quality is a lot better now than it was, but it's still an anomaly: we've read all the books, we know what habitat trout need, and the Witham doesn't offer much of it. There are a hell of a lot of problems with the river in town, but there are also a hell of a lot of trout!"

Sight-fishing up the river through Grantham's parks at mayfly time, it's impossible not to agree. Although most of the riverside's industrial landmarks are disappearing under new housing developments, the Witham is still defined by its past: slowed and ponded by the almost-continuous effect of six weirs and one impassable mill, with a profusion of silt and ribbon weed, and few obvious opportunities for spawning.

But maybe there's more to this fragmented, canalised ecosystem than meets the eye. Rising out of the flatter lands on either side, the Lincolnshire Edge and Kesteven Uplands produce their own weather system, and the region is well-known for sudden heavy thunderstorms which can raise river levels dramatically. When the urban Witham's bed was dropped by 8ft for flood defence in the 1970s, engineers capped the pile-driven sidings with an overhanging ledge of concrete: today, if these corrugated revetments haven't been buried in decades of silt, they offer tempting undercuts adjacent to deep pools. And the trout are down there: a healthy population pyramid sliding in and out of cover, chasing chublets back into the weed, grazing on shrimp, olives and caddis, and leaving the early hatch of mayflies to the robins and sparrows.

I've already banked one specimen this afternoon – a big-shouldered wild trout that took a Deer Hair Emerger on its third drift past a tangle of twigs and floating debris – so I wave Colin forward to catch another where he landed his first Witham trout on Cup Final day in 1975. Blissfully ignoring his back-cast, an elderly local rumbles over the footbridge on her mobility scooter. "There's all sorts ends up in there!" she assures us. "Shopping trolleys, traffic cones… my wheelchair got thrown in last week, but I was happy about that because I got two grand for this new one!"

Compared to many urban rivers, the Witham is startlingly litter-free, and there's a very good reason why. Around 2004, John Knowles started investigating the strange legal loophole that keeps rubbish in rivers uncleared by local councils on

Hook-jawed and leopard-spotted, the author's big Witham trout

health and safety grounds, and ignored by the Environment Agency unless it creates a flood risk, a problem with water quality, or a danger to public health.

Now vice chairman of Grantham Civic Society, he recalls how he developed his own branch of the RiverCare movement. "Once I'd established that the river was never going to be cleaned up by anything short of volunteer slave labour, I called our first meeting in my living room, and we went on from there to adopt this stretch of the Witham.

"Every couple of months we load our refuse bags, gloves, litter pickers, grappling hooks, nets and first aid kit into a wheelbarrow, go out there, and clean up. Fifteen or twenty of our thirty supporters appear each time, which is about right because it's hard to supervise otherwise. There's an extraordinary cross-section of society – young and old, eight years old to eighty – including a retired barrister who insists on wearing a suit and always gets absolutely filthy! South Kesteven District Council's contracts unit kindly relieves us of the rubbish: we've got an excellent relationship with them, and the people in the EA are also very appreciative of what we're doing."

Since instigating these clean-ups, John has also maintained a relentless pressure on the supermarkets whose trolleys end up in the river. "On one occasion, I gave them an unofficial ultimatum, telling the managers when we'd be clearing out their trolleys, and asking them to come and collect them. But no-one showed from the supermarkets, and you can imagine how the *Grantham Journal* loved that story! We still have to pull out trolleys, but a lot less than

in the past. The amount of other rubbish is slowly reducing too, so I think people are becoming more protective of the river and its wildlife, and we're helping Colin and the fishing club with habitat work to benefit the swans, otters, kingfishers, water voles, trout and white-clawed crayfish.

"You can feel the sense of ownership increasing. And it's mostly due to the clean-ups, which are really such a simple thing to organise."

One that got away: trolleys and other rubbish are regularly removed by Grantham Civic Society's RiverCare group

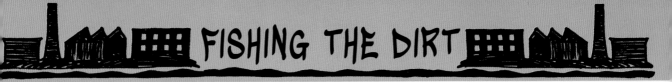

Grantham: River Witham

Who's looking after the river?

Grantham Angling Association was formed in 1872 and fought its first anti-pollution case in 1968 as a founder member of the Anglers' Conservation Association (now the Angling Trust). In recognition of its habitat work, including the restoration of pools and riffles in dredged areas below Grantham, the club was awarded the Wild Trout Trust's Conservation Award in 2002, and the Lincolnshire Community Environmental Award in 2008.

In 2004, as one of more than 30 River-Care groups supported by Anglian Water, Grantham Civic Society adopted the urban stretches of the Witham. River clean-ups every couple of months are dedicated to the practical aspects of cleaning out rubbish from the river, enhancing the landscape for wildlife and people. Within Grantham, the Environment Agency has also installed willow spiling to reduce erosion.

For the latest information, visit:
www.granthamaa.co.uk
www.granthamcivicsociety.co.uk
www.environment-agency.gov.uk

Grantham Angling Association controls much of the Witham above and below Grantham. South Kesteven District Council allows free fishing with a valid EA rod licence wherever access is possible from the riverside footpath through the town: about 2 miles of fishing in total.

Fishing tips

The Witham's limestone geology and good water quality conspire to create a fishery famous for trout up to 3lbs as well as grayling to 2lbs, dace to 1lb, and chub from 2 to 7lbs. Fly-life is abundant, with March browns, large dark olives, mayflies, pale watery olives, sedges and terrestrials of all kinds.

For sight-fishing on Grantham's heavily-canalised town water, two lengths of rod are possible: 6 to 7ft for wading, or 9 to 10ft for casting from the bank, rated in either case for a 3 to 5 weight line. For locals like Colin Hides, favourite patterns include the traditional Greenwells Glory, Kite's Imperial, Grey Duster and Grey Wulff. Large foam beetles, cast to land with an audible plop, have also proved their value for many anglers.

Getting there

The Witham is 10 minutes' walk from Grantham station.

Maps of Grantham are available from the Tourist Information Centre on Saint Peter's Hill, NG31 62AB: OS Explorer 247 is also recommended.

Seasons and permits

Brown trout season runs from 1 April to 29 October; grayling season from 16 June to 14 March.

Don't miss

● The National Trust's Belton House: reputedly the quintessential English country house and estate

● 2-6 North Parade: birthplace of Margaret Thatcher, Britain's first woman Prime Minister whose policies inadvertently led to the recovery of many urban rivers

16

KIDDERMINSTER

River Stour

On the high embankment above the flood flume at Puxton Marsh, the grey steel railings are lined with urgent warning signs. *Danger! Vertical drop! Strong currents, confined space! Keep out, no swimming, children must be supervised at all times!*

"This river's a fierce one when it floods," nods the only other angler I've seen all day, who's fishing the pool from his seat-box at the downstream end of the culvert. He eyes my ultralight rig for a moment, clearly decides I'm offering no competition to his own quest, and suddenly becomes quite chatty.

"Mind you, the town's had no trouble since they put all them waterworks in, so maybe you could say they've helped. There's a 15lb pike down there, and I want to get him out... deadbait'll do it. You seen the big barbel down by Tesco's, and the chub? Trout, you say? A friend of mine fly-fishes for them and does quite well, but you won't get them now, the banks are too overgrown and nobody's cutting the bushes back. Sometimes I get rainbow trout that come up from a fish farm on the Severn, and you hear of decent grayling in the winter. Used to be horribly polluted, this river... I remember catching gudgeon that were stained with red and yellow on their bellies with the dyes from the carpet factories, but it's a lot better now..."

Spend a day exploring the streets of Kidderminster and fishing the urban Stour, and you may end up absorbing all you'll ever need to know about Britain's rise and fall as a manufacturing power, as well as flood defence, the growth of consumer society, and the rebirth of a river against all reasonable odds.

Before the Industrial Revolution swept across the Black Country, the Stour was well known as a trout stream: rising on the north-eastern edge of the red sandstone Clent Hills, meandering slowly across a sandy, gravelly plateau, finally finding the Severn at Stourport. For a river whose mainstem measures only 25 miles long, its catchment is extensive, laced with more than a hundred miles of brooks and other tributaries, and this network of feeder streams and refuge areas has probably helped its swift recovery and repopulation with fish and invertebrates after a long industrial history.

Unlike many other wool towns, Kidderminster's textile trade survived its downturn at the end of the seventeenth century by diversifying: firstly into 'Kitterminster stuff', made with a linen warp and

Trout, chub or barbel? A perfect pool for a nymph rig in central Kidderminster

a worsted woollen weft, then into bomba-zine, a woven mixture of silk and wool which was widely adopted for mourning clothes. The first double-sided Kidder-minster carpet was woven by entrepreneur John Pearsall in 1735, and the new industry expanded rapidly. Domestic weaving and loom-shops were overtaken by steam engines, power looms and purpose-built mills, and a major building programme at the end of the nineteenth century saw a dozen carpet factories constructed in less than two decades.

Thanks to continuous innovation and investment, Kidderminster's woven carpets dominated the world market for at least two hundred years, employing 12,000

Industrial drain: how this whole stretch of the Kidderminster Stour once looked

Some urban culverts invite exploration …others don't

people at the height of the 1950s' economic explosion. Post-war housing required wall-to-wall carpets: a newly affluent population had the money to pay for them, and it was said that the factories could hardly keep up with demand. Throughout these boom times, the old town suffered almost as badly as the river. While sheep dip from raw wool, chemicals from dyeing and pesticides from moth-proofing all poured into the Stour to mix with discharges from nail mills at Kinver and galvanised steel hollowware factories at Lye, Kidderminster's medieval streetscape of ancient inns and weavers' terraces was methodically trashed to make way for a futuristic new ring-road. Many historic buildings continued to be lost when the carpet industry finally crashed in the late 1970s, and controversy still surrounds the demolition of Brintons' wool hall in 2001 during the early stages of the Weavers' Wharf redevelopment.

These days, the mills that were built to fuel a consumer boom have been supplanted by its most successful retailers, and this 18-acre site is anchored by a slew of familiar brands: Marks and Spencer, McDonalds, Next, Pizza Hut, Sports Direct and TK Maxx. But urban planning is finally catching up with the needs of the river.

In the early 1990s, one of the first tasks of the newly-formed Severn Trent Water company had been to produce an urban pollution model for the whole Stour catchment. Millions of pounds were spent on improving sewers and sewage treatment works, which can sometimes supply two thirds of the river's flow: ammonia levels dropped dramatically, and fish populations began to increase, even in the brutalist sheet-steel culverts of Kidderminster's town centre. When the declining carpet industry left large tracts of brownfield land for regeneration, Wyre Forest District Council approached the Environment Agency for advice on making the Stour a focal point of the new developments, and the results can now be seen alongside Tesco's supermarket car park.

Taking care not to disturb centuries-old contaminated ground, contractors filled in part of the existing artificial channel and carved a whole new course for the river, complete with riffles, boulders and vegetated banks that slope naturally into gravelly margins. Total floodwater capacity has actually been increased, and while there's often a crusted mass of shopping trolleys under the footbridge, the shallows are teeming with small fish. This reconstructed reach makes a startling contrast with the unrestored section just upstream: even during the building works, local people reported seeing otters moving through the site, and the project seems have been a real success in reconnecting Kidderminster's residents with their river.

Inspired by Tesco's success, Morrison's new flagship store on the site of Stour Vale Mill was built to be 'Britain's greenest supermarket', breaking records and winning awards for eco-friendly features including a rainwater harvesting system

Recovering river: just downstream, a totally new channel has been constructed, with increased flood capacity and far greater habitat diversity

which recycles more than 60,000 gallons every year. Vertical brick walls, ornamental bridges between sections of car park, and wide swathes of Himalayan balsam out-competing planted purple loosestrife still seem designed to keep you as far from the river as possible, but the pools and riffles are down there, and I'm sure I spot a little trout darting away behind a traffic cone.

But what has really made all these enhancement works possible is a new approach to flood risk management. Rather than moving as much water downstream as fast as possible, today's practitioners prefer to increase its hangtime in storage areas like Puxton Marsh: since 2003, the Kidderminster Flood Alleviation Scheme has used that well-signed concrete flume to bottleneck up to 700,000 cubic metres of excess floodwater into the marsh, gradually releasing it back into the main channel when levels drop again. Although part of the wetland was lost to the earth embankment, the remaining area's Special Site of Scientific Interest status has been enhanced by higher water levels, and Kidderminster has escaped several floods.

And fish stocks are improving too. "Salmon were back in the river by 2004," confirms EA fisheries technical specialist Chris Bainger, "and a couple of years ago we did an electrofishing demonstration near the roundabouts in the centre of Kidderminster. Put it this way: if we'd found ourselves catching trout like that from the Test or Itchen, we'd have been laughing."

The Stour's water quality has improved dramatically, but access can still be difficult!

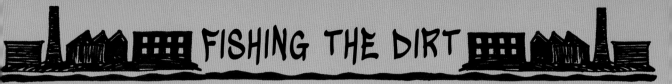

Kidderminster: River Stour

Who's looking after the river?

Since the early 1990s, the Environment Agency has been working with Severn Trent Water and Wyre Forest District Council to improve water quality and reduce pollution and flood risk. Urban regeneration projects have included ambitious river restoration projects in central Kidderminster, and flood risk management at Puxton Marsh.

The Stour is part of the larger Severn catchment, so future water quality and habitat projects may also be driven by the Severn Rivers Trust.

For the latest information, visit:
www.environment-agency.gov.uk
www.severnriverstrust.com

Getting there

The Stour at Stour Vale Mill is less than 10 minutes' walk downhill from Kidderminster station.

Maps of Kidderminster are available to download from: www.wyreforestdc.gov.uk
OS Explorer 219 is also recommended.

Seasons and permits

Brown trout season runs from 18 March to 7 October; grayling season from 16 June to 14 March.

Wyre Forest District Council allows free fishing on all stretches of the Stour through Kidderminster with a valid EA rod licence, except on Puxton Marsh: around 3 miles of fishing on the former milling channels.

Fishing tips

By all accounts the Stour's wild trout population is increasing steadily, with specimens up to a couple of pounds in weight. The river is now recognised as a healthy mixed fishery, with trophy barbel, chub, dace and roach nourished by large numbers of freshwater shrimp, and several species of cased and caseless caddis. Grayling, perch and pike are also present.

For most areas, a rod of 8 to 10ft is ideal, rated for a 3 to 5 weight line. The urban Stour is still largely unexplored as a fly-fishery, so carry a range of shrimp, caddis and midge imitations, and be prepared to match the hatch.

Don't miss

● The Kidderminster Carpet Trust's Carpet Museum in the nineteenth century Stour Vale Mill.

17

LEICESTER

Rivers Soar and Biam

Environment Agency fisheries officer Matt Buck frowns thoughtfully as he contemplates a reedy stretch of the upper Soar in Narborough. "For some reason this fishery's not prospering as it should," he tells me.

"Water quality has been improving for the past 25 years, but the trout population seems to be declining, and the cyprinid biomass is going down in spite of regular stocking, for reasons that aren't completely clear. Sure, there are all the usual problems of farmers upstream not wanting to fence their cattle out of the river, so the edges get poached and the gravels get covered in clay. But the best solution is probably significant restoration, including fish refuges and tree cover where the banks of the upper river have been resectioned in the past.

"Without those improvements we're in danger of seeing the Soar downgraded from 'moderate' to 'poor' or even 'bad' status for the Water Framework Directive, since part of that assessment is based on abundance of fish species. The irony is that the fishery actually improves downstream of Loughborough towards the confluence with the Trent, although you still get the occasional big summer fish kill when the canal locks hold up deoxygenated low quality water, and the ammonia goes up…"

As we drive around the upper catchment, I'm reminded of the value of looking at a river with an EA officer who really loves his patch. In Matt's case, this stretches all the way up to the Lathkill in Derbyshire: he's also a member of a barbel-fishing syndicate on the Welsh Wye, but it's clear that the Soar and its problems have the tightest possible hold on his imagination.

Born in Durham, Matt learned to fish on the free stretches of the River Wear before taking part in a habitat restoration project on the lower Itchen during fisheries management training at Sparsholt College. "I was so inspired by what a flow deflector could do, scouring out a hole from waist to chest deep in just one day. I thought, this is it, this is the work I want to be involved in," he says. "So now I look at the Soar, and I can see so much potential."

By this time we're walking along the canalised river beside Aylestone Meadows, well within Leicester's southern conurbation, and his spirits have lifted noticeably. Small silver fish, mainly roach and dace, are circling slowly in surprisingly clear water, and we're scanning the mixed shoals for grayling, which Matt reckons are drifting in and out of the canal from an undredged section just downstream.

Hardly classic habitat for salmonids… yet trout and even grayling are sometimes caught along the canalised River Soar

The famous Leicester Straights

Like so many other urban rivers, the course of the Soar through Leicester is complex and braided: the product of commerce and industry over many hundreds of years. Near the castle mound in the city centre, a watermill was working from the fourteenth century, and in 1557 residents agreed on a fine of sixpence for anyone throwing sewage or animal entrails into the river *'where any water for brewing is taken up'*. The Soar remained too small and shallow for barges until the late 1700s, but in 1794 the Leicester canal made almost forty miles fully navigable, straightening and raising the banks in some areas, severing the river's natural meanders in others. Leicester was one of the last major trading towns to be linked to the canal system, opening the way for importing cheap coal and exporting yarn to Europe via the Trent and Humber. By 1851 the hosiery industry alone employed ten per cent of Leicester's population, and the river reputedly ran an unusual pink colour on account of the discharges from the textile mills.

At the start of the twenty-first century, Leicester's uneasy post-industrial identity is symbolised by the debate about building Leicester City's new football training academy on part of Aylestone Meadows: an area now valued as a green lung for the city, but originally created as the cap of an early landfill site. During the 1950s, older residents remember, most of the farmland between the canal embankment and the original course of the Soar was buried by uncontrolled tipping of household and general rubbish to a depth of more than 20ft, topped with a thick skim of ash from the coal-fired power station at Raw Dykes Road.

Today, the power station too is gone, replaced by the gleaming glass and steel of Leicester City's stadium, but local fishermen like Burnie Maurins fondly recall the quality of the coarse fishing once created by the warm-water outflow below the basin where the coal barges turned. Leicester Straights in the late 1980s were renowned as the home of matchman Ivan Marks, and "people used to stand on the Walnut Street bridge throwing chips into the river, which we'd use as bait, or Red Leicester cheese. We'd cast across into the culvert to catch carp: a five-pounder was a big one. When the power station closed, the water was barely fished, and anglers moved off to the Fens and the Trent…"

Cast with care: keeping a low profile on the Biam

Regeneration is creeping south along the towpaths, but there's still something almost Soviet in the starkness of the Raw Dykes area. Pylons march across the sky in all directions from a monumental transformer farm, and there's a telltale buzzing in the handrail of a bridge where Matt and I start talking to another angler about the trout, bream and perch he's just caught. "Keep your rod tip down," Matt advises me, "you don't want to find out how many volts are going past up there!"

Still, the trout suggests we've almost reached our destination, and we follow the pylons upstream again into the valley of the secretive little River Biam. From its source in edgy Braunstone Town, most locals still regard it as just another channel of the endlessly-engineered Soar, but to the EA it's something else: a stream in its own right, briefly linked to the Soar and slightly straightened for flood conveyance, but still retaining the gravels which the main river lost long ago to dredging.

The clean riffles around a small brick pipe-bridge give the area the local name of 'Pebble Beach', and in the rough paddocks along the cress-edged stream you can make out a pattern of right-angled ridges suggesting a past life as a watermeadow system. With shifting populations of dace, roach, chub, grayling and trout feeding on healthy invertebrates, the Biam is productive enough to have attracted subsistence anglers' attention: a deep corner pool is littered with disposable barbeques and Eastern European-brand beer cans, but Matt smiles realistically as he outlines his plans for his favourite corner of the Midlands.

"We've got a lot of diverse ethnic groups in this area, all applying their own traditions to the rivers, and in the end the only solution is education," he says. "Education… and restoration to make the system resilient enough that the loss of a few fish doesn't matter. What I'd like to see here is a project to re-meander the straightened stretches with flow deflectors, perhaps using section 106 mitigation funding if the new football academy goes ahead, involving local kids with a *Get Hooked on Fishing* programme, maybe *Trout in the Classroom* too.

"I know I keep saying this, but the Biam is a real gem. Of all the places on my

Urban art: graffiti beside the Soar

patch I keep coming back to, this is my favourite. It could be the jewel in the crown of Leicester's rivers, and all it needs is a bit more time and looking after!"

Ultra-light tackle for the Soar and Biam

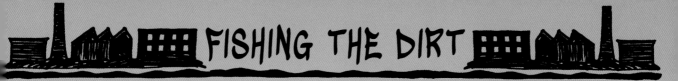
FISHING THE DIRT

Leicester: Rivers Soar and Biam

Who's looking after the rivers?

The Environment Agency took over the roles and responsibilities of the National Rivers Authority in 1996, regulating pollution, reducing flood risk and improving the environment where possible.

On rivers like the Soar and Biam, EA officers are keen to encourage partnership projects involving local communities in fishing, river restoration and environmental education.

For the latest information, visit: www.environment-agency.gov.uk

Getting there

From Leicester railway station it's about 15 minutes' walk to the Walnut Street bridge, the western side of which is arguably the best starting point for exploring the canalised Soar and Biam.

Maps of Leicester are available from the Tourist Information Centre on Town Hall Square, LE1 6AG: OS Explorer 233 is also recommended.

Seasons and permits

Brown trout season runs from 18 March to 7 October; grayling season from 16 June to 14 March.

Most of the Soar in the Aylestone and Leicester Straights area is controlled by Wigston Angling Society. On the Biam, Leicester City Council permits free fishing with a valid EA rod licence. Blaby District Council also allows free fishing in Jubilee Park at Whetstone.

For details, visit: www.wigstonanglingsociety.co.uk

Fishing tips

Right into Leicester city centre, the Soar and Biam hold sparse populations of trout and grayling mixed with dace, chub, roach, rudd, perch, carp, pike and bream. Thanks to oxygenation from boat traffic through the locks, trout and grayling are able to survive even in the canalised sections.

Average sizes aren't large, so progressive local fly-fishers favour rods of 7 to 8ft rated for 1 weight lines to maximise stealth and sport. With its natural gravels, the Biam probably has healthier invertebrate populations than most of the Soar, with olives, caddis, caenis and midges showing up in EA samples. Small dark imitative dry flies and lightly-weighted midge patterns on long, fine tippets are recommended for slow currents, while tadpole-style streamers can sometimes pull larger fish out of deep cover.

Don't miss

● Aylestone Meadows' 8-arched packhorse bridge and causeway, thought to date from the fifteenth century at least

● Leicester Straights: home water of legendary matchman Ivan Marks

● The National Space Centre and planetarium: complete with the only Soyuz spacecraft in western Europe, plus Blue Streak and Thor ballistic missiles

18

LEOMINSTER

Rivers Lugg and Kenwater

From the echoing Georgian rooms of a former hotel in the back streets of Leominster, the Angling Trust wages an endless war on behalf of healthy rivers everywhere in the United Kingdom.

Founded in 1948 by angler-barrister John Eastwood, the Anglers' Co-operative Association had just one mission: to pursue polluters of all kinds through the civil courts in an age when the needs of post-war industry still trumped concerns about environmental health. Since then the ACA and its successor the Angling Trust have lost just four out of more than 2,000 cases, developing a fearsome reputation through famous victories such as compensation for sewage pollution on the Trent and Derwent, sheep-dip damage in Beresford Dale on the Dove, and aluminium sulphate pollution that destroyed six years of painstaking habitat improvement work on the Taf Fechan.

When rivers are polluted and the Environment Agency brings criminal prosecutions against the perpetrators, any fines imposed by the courts are absorbed by the Treasury rather than going back to restore the rivers concerned. As a result, private civil suits for damages, brought by the Angling Trust on behalf of affected fishing clubs and riparian owners, can sometimes be the only hope for the future of entire fisheries, because all court awards can then go to the fishing clubs or organisations. And in some cases, record out-of-court settlements have helped local volunteers to establish sustainable Rivers Trusts, such as on the Wandle and Eden.

In 2009, the ACA merged with six other angling organisations to form the Angling Trust: a single governing body to represent the widest possible spectrum of game, coarse and sea fishing interests. Today, the Trust's team of in-house lawyers pursues around eighty court cases at any given time, which complement its local and national campaigns on fisheries and environmental issues including marine conservation, invasive non-native species, the impact of salmon farming on wild fish populations, and effective delivery of the Water Framework Directive.

In their rare moments of downtime from fighting for waters everywhere, the Angling Trust's lawyers and campaigners are also guarding the river on their own doorstep. A total of 14 staff were trained as riverfly monitors by Dai Roberts in 2010, on a busman's holiday from his beloved Rhymney, and they're keen to increase the

Endless fascination: everyone loves to lean over a bridge and catch a glimpse of a trout

coverage of the *Anglers' Monitoring Initiative* amongst coarse as well as game anglers. "Chub and barbel don't just eat ground bait," observes Angling Trust membership manager Will Smith, "and it's one of the best possible ways to get to know your river. That's why I think it's important to monitor the Lugg in the middle of Leominster – it's good PR for us, and it's more interesting too!"

A wild trout from the Kenwater

Rising at Pool Hill in upland Powys, the river runs through a rural landscape for almost all its 63-mile length down to the Wye below Hereford, and the Lugg's short urban reaches contrast completely with the rest of the catchment.

Leominster was probably founded on a defensive island site surrounded by marshes: wetland channels provided inspiration for early industrialists, and the eleventh century monks of Leominster Priory dug an extra leat known as the Kenwater to flush away waste

and drive at least one monastic mill.

Like many other towns at the time, Leominster grew so rich on the wool trade that Elizabethan poet Michael Drayton eulogised 'Lemster Ore' as the best fleece in Europe. Although the *Gazetteer of Herefordshire* grumbled in 1876 that *'there are no manufactures of any consequence, which is to be regretted, owing to the facility of water-power'*, contemporary sources show that Leominster's various river channels were powering at least nine mills, with guilds controlling industries that ranged from weaving and wool-stapling to malting, tanning and glove-making. There were also agricultural ironworks, oil and corn mills, brickfields and an ink mill which later converted to grinding coal for foundry blacking.

But perhaps a mysterious fire in 1754 had already sealed the town's fate as a backwater of the Industrial Revolution. In 1748, Lancashire cotton magnate Daniel Bourn had invested heavily in upgrading Pinsley Mill as one of only four early cotton spinning complexes, complete with his own patented carding engine. Six years later, the building burned to the ground under suspicious circumstances, and Leominster never recovered its early lead in the textiles industry. Croward's Mill was still used for pumping water until 1974, but most of the mills had gone by the time of the Second World War, and one of the last surviving sites is now a sports centre on Bridge Street.

This far upstream, the river breaks out from hard revetments into beautiful suburban pool-riffle sequences around the playing fields, punctuated with discarded shopping trolleys and the sort of steady glides that grayling love. Back in the town centre, local anglers Callum and Dex guide me onto nymphing fish that only they can see below the elegant wrought-iron footbridge. "You should've been here last week, before the pikeys came through and had all the big trout on spinners and bread!" they tell me ruefully, but thick mats of flowering ranunculus are waving in the slow currents, and I'm hypnotised by the sudden sight of leviathan grayling ghosting out of the shadows to gorge on shrimp, caddis, olives and tiny yellow stonefly nymphs.

For all its concrete, sheet-steel pilings and caged riprap revetments, the Kenwater is now the Lugg's mainstem through Leominster, and in most ways that matter it feels like a limestone stream. In fact, the relative richness of the upper catchment's Silurian silt- and mudstones is amplified by outcrops of limestone at Aymestry Gorge, and the whole-river Special Site of Scientific Interest is closely connected with its geology.

At the end of the last Ice Age, the retreating ice sheet dumped terminal moraines of boulder clay, sand and gravel about ten miles north-west of Leominster, while outflow from the melting glaciers covered the rest of the Herefordshire plain with deep, fertile deposits of fine silt and alluvium.

Especially below the town, intensive modern agribusiness on these soils is now causing severe problems for the Lugg. Phosphate and nitrate fertilisers leach into the river, while strawberry, potato and maize fields are often ploughed at right angles to the contour, allowing rain to carry topsoil straight into the channel. Some pulses of pesticide are apparently 100 times over the legal limits of the European Drinking Water Directive, and according to Natural England, the Lugg is losing soil eleven times faster than the natural rate. Every year, an estimated 700,000 tonnes are being washed down into the middle and lower Wye, where salmon recruitment on the gravel fords has all but disappeared.

"When they redid the calculations for the proposed Severn barrage," says Simon Evans of the Wye and Usk Foundation, "the scientists discovered that the annual rate of soil loss from these upstream catchments had tripled from under ten to around thirty million tonnes in just three decades. It's all down to intensification of agriculture: farmers now have to lease huge, costly

Even flood walls offer habitat niches

machines from contractors at times that may not be optimum for their soil. To plough silty clay soils, for instance, there's often only a four-week window in autumn, and if you miss that because the machines are booked elsewhere, you stand a very good chance of destroying your soil's structure, and making it vulnerable to erosion.

"All this expensive extra horsepower has taken the timeliness out of farming, some farmers still don't realise there's even a problem, and we urgently need to work out how to deal with the consequences."

But his infectious grin is guaranteed to return whenever he thinks about the Kenwater. "Trapezoidal concrete channel and all, I still reckon it's some of the best fishing in the catchment!"

Urban beauty: a Kenwater grayling, sight-fished with a tiny nymph between flowering rafts of ranunculus

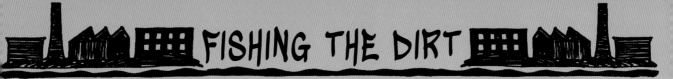

Leominster: Rivers Lugg and Kenwater

Who's looking after the rivers?

The Angling Trust was formed in 2009 to build on the work of the Anglers' Co-operative Association over 6 preceding decades to make polluters pay for damaging fisheries and the freshwater environment. It has only lost 4 civil court cases in its entire history, and is now the governing body for game, coarse and sea-fishing interests in England.

On the Lugg, Angling Trust staff are trained to monitor fly-life as part of the Riverfly Partnership's national *Anglers' Monitoring Initiative*. They also carry out rolling whole-catchment litter clean-ups in partnership with the Lugg and Arrow Fisheries Association and the Wye and Usk Foundation, which are leading additional projects to tackle the river's invasive species and water quality issues.

For the latest information, visit:
www.anglingtrust.net
www.wyeuskfoundation.org

Getting there

From Leominster station, it's about 15 minutes' walk to the Kenwater, which forms the Lugg's main channel through town. The Lugg itself can be found behind the petrol station on the A49 roundabout at the end of Mill Street.

Maps of Leominster are available from the Tourist Information Centre on Corn Square, HR6 8LR: OS Explorer 202 and 203 are also recommended.

Seasons and permits

Brown trout season runs from 3 March to 30 September; grayling season from 16 June to 14 March.

Leominster Town Council allows free fishing with a valid EA rod licence on the Lugg and Kenwater through Leominster: over half a mile of fishing.

Fishing tips

Thanks to nutrient-rich geology, the Lugg and Kenwater are capable of producing trout and grayling up to a couple of pounds.

A rod of 7 to 8ft, rated for a 1 to 4 weight line, is ideal for delicate presentation in clear water. Since the 1930s a significant local fly-tying tradition has been based on the idea of reverse-hackled dry flies: patterns tied back to front with a simple collar hackle in the gape of the hook to mimic the natural posture of olives and sedges on the surface of the water. Barrett's Bane and Barrett's Professor are the classics of this genre. Modern Deer Hair Emergers and similar imitations are also effective.

Don't miss

● Grange Court: Leominster's spectacular half-timbered market hall, dismantled and moved to Grange Park in 1853

● Leominster Priory's ducking stool: last used by order of Leominster's magistrates to duck a scold in the Kenwater in 1890, the final recorded usage of a ducking stool in England

19

LONG EATON

· ·

River Erewash

Urban fishing takes you to some strange places, but this is one of the weirdest, I think, as the police sergeant strolls deliberately back towards me round the end of Long Eaton's Kwik Fit garage. There's more than a hint of swagger as he hooks his thumbs into his stab vest and leans confidentially across my personal space. "Now, sir, I wanted to check that you haven't been paying this chap for his taxi services? Because if you have, well, we were informed that he was driving suspiciously, and, err…"

I suppress both indignation and the urge to take a step backwards. "No, sergeant. I haven't. Mick is a pal of mine who's showing me round the voluntary restoration work he's been doing on the River Erewash. And he's certainly not charging me for the time he's taking off from his day job of driving deaf kids around for Erewash Council's social services!"

Half an hour later we've finally escaped Derbyshire Constabulary's finest – having been stung for the price of a new offside front tyre as well as three licence points and a fixed penalty for its predecessor's slightly bald patch – and Mick Martin, Derbyshire blogger and leader of the River Erewash Foundation's *Trout in the Town* chapter, can finally show me the rest of his

patch. We've already walked the Erewash at Toton Fields, where the river's original, tightly-meandering course has been sliced into two separate channels for flood defence purposes, leaving twin stretches of relatively natural river topped or tailed with straight-sided canals, and a playing field on the island between them. And now we're on our way up-catchment to regain our trail above Toton Sidings.

The Erewash is a post-industrial paradox. On one hand it flows down a green corridor that sometimes feels almost totally rural: on the other, this corridor is never more than two or three hundred yards wide, and you're scarcely further than that from housing estates, railway yards, the Erewash canal, or the M1 motorway which crosses the river twice. Add the remains of the valley's silk and metalworking mills, either recently demolished or freshly renovated into luxury apartments, and you're looking at the whole history of Britain's transport and industrial infrastructure, condensed into one river valley halfway between Nottingham and Derby.

Ironworking began in this area in Roman times, exploiting small quantities of black band iron ore alongside Carboniferous-era coal measures, but large-scale

Looking north up the Erewash river corridor, a distinctive Stanton-style chimney dominates the skyline

119

Mick Martin surveys his river from one of the valley's characteristic iron bridges

the German high command wanted to capture it intact. In peacetime, Stanton's forges and foundries turned their output to heavy-duty civil engineering: iron and concrete pipes, street furniture including lamp posts and manhole covers, and even tunnel castings for the London Underground and Mersey tunnels. Carbonisation works produced coking gas and bitumen, while slag provided the final component for national road building programmes.

Wandle Trust volunteer Henry Wood lived in the Erewash valley at the height of the ironworks' production after the Second World War. "The Erewash ran cobalt blue," he recollects, "and it was said to be the second-worst polluted river in Europe.

"You wouldn't notice the steelworks so much in the daytime – they were all hidden behind clouds of steam and smoke – but at night the glare from the blast furnaces would light up the whole sky. I remember doing a night hike through the works with the scouts... we walked for about twelve miles without leaving the site. In the middle of the night we came upon a street of derelict houses, with just one house in the middle knocked down, and a massive pipe running through the gap. And the whole scene was lit up in the glow of the ironworks like something out of Hieronymous Bosch!"

The blast furnaces cooled in 1974, but Stanton's production only finally ceased in 2007, when much of the remaining factory complex was dismantled and shipped to Turkey as recycled building materials. As Mick and I peer through the gates, the site stands huge and empty, awaiting redevelopment with 3,000 new homes whose

production only reached the Erewash catchment in the nineteenth century. Chesterfield entrepreneurs Josiah and Benjamin Smith constructed three furnaces at Stanton, six miles above the confluence of the Erewash and the Trent: massive expansion followed as a result of the Franco-Prussian War of 1870, and vast numbers of shells were cast for the week-long bombardments on the Western Front between 1914 and 1918. During the Second World War, the Stanton Gate foundry produced air-raid shelters and almost a million bomb casings, as well as experimental concrete torpedoes, and it's said that the Luftwaffe held back from targeting this strategic works because

sewage will need proper treatment before it's discharged into the Erewash. "I did ask the question at the earliest planning stages," says Mick, "because there are already seven sewage works on the river, without much spare capacity in any of them. As far as I know they're still thinking about that one…"

Mick's vision for the Erewash also began taking shape in 2007, the year when one of his friends came back from a day's fishing with news of a 3lb trout. "Half a dozen of us decided to take a walk along the river for a closer look," he tells me, "and it all grew from there with clean-ups and then ideas for river restoration. To get future support from local people, your first priority is improving the river visually, then maintaining it.

"The Wild Trout Trust did two separate surveys for us, and we discovered that there are probably populations of wild trout in tributaries like the Nut Brook, even though at least a quarter of a mile is culverted through the ironworks! Over the years, long stretches of the Erewash above Toton Sidings have been straightened, and the spates have basically flattened the gravels, so a lot of the habitat consists of long, shallow uniform glides.

"Even without the sewage works, the river is naturally eutrophic: it's overwide

In summer 2011, the Wild Trout Trust's Tim Jacklin taught River Erewash Foundation volunteers how to clean spawning gravels with a leaf-blower

and there's not much shade, so the water heats up very easily. The obvious answer is to add more roughness, depth and general refuge from predators with lots of big bankside structures like tree kickers and what I call spawning logs, which is exactly what we're doing as part of our *Trout in the Town* project.

"There's many a summer evening we've spent raking and stirring the gravels about, and it's good to see our effect: one of the coarse fishermen caught several little wild trout from one of these areas, and our aim is to get patches of clean spawning gravel all the way up the river, enough for the trout to use if they're there, as well as removing barriers at the mouth of the Nut Brook to provide an accessible spawning stream. We're also venturing into the power tools method of de-silting gravels with huge backpack leaf blowers, which Tim Jacklin came to teach us in summer 2011.

"Since our very first river clean-up we've also had lots of encouragement from Warren Slaney, who started the whole *Going Wild* project at Haddon Hall on the Derbyshire Wye. He's provided us with grayling fishing days for fundraising in the winter, and huge moral and practical support. We've still got a long way to go, with six tributaries and twenty miles of main Erewash to work on. But as Warren is so fond of saying about habitat improvements: build it and they will come! Even the water voles have made it down through the concrete channels at the sidings... this is a really good little river, and we can see it getting better every year."

By the 1950s, Toton Sidings was the largest marshalling yard in Europe, shunting more than a million wagons of coal every year to fuel the local steelworks

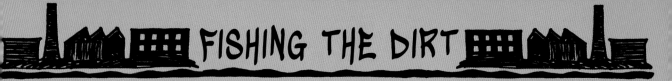

Long Eaton: River Erewash

Who's looking after the river?

The River Erewash Foundation was formed in 2007 to restore and conserve the biodiversity of the Erewash and its tributaries through regular monitoring and restoration work, and inspire local members to take responsibility for their own areas of the river, including rubbish clearance and eradication of invasive non-native plants. In conjunction with the Riverfly Partnership, invertebrate monitoring sites have been established below each of the river's 7 sewage treatment works.

In 2010 the Foundation won the Mayor's Award (Erewash) for its services to the local community, based on flexible, successful engagement with Erewash and Broxtowe Borough Councils, local landowners, wildlife groups and residents. As one of the Wild Trout Trust's *Trout in the Town* chapters, the Foundation is now working in partnership with the Environment Agency to clean gravels, install large woody debris, and improve spawning and other habitat on 3 miles of the river above Toton Sidings.

For the latest information, visit:
www.rivererewashfoundation.co.uk
http://derbyshireonthefly.blogspot.com

Getting there

The Erewash is about 20 minutes' walk from Long Eaton station. Riverside access along the Erewash Valley Trail is blocked by Toton Sidings, so head either for Toton Fields local nature reserve in Toton, or for the stretch of river above the railway lines towards Dockholme Lock and Sandiacre.

Maps of the Erewash Valley Trail are available to download from www.broxtowe.gov.uk OS Explorer 260 is also recommended.

Seasons and permits

Brown trout season runs from 18 March to 7 October; grayling season from 16 June to 14 March.

Broxtowe Borough Council allows free fishing with a valid EA rod licence on both channels of the river through Manor Farm recreation ground and Toton Fields local nature reserve. The River Erewash Foundation has negotiated a similar arrangement with Erewash Borough Council and the EA on their project stretch above Toton Sidings.

For full details, visit
www.rivererewashfoundation.co.uk

Fishing tips

The Erewash is rapidly recovering as a mixed fishery, with isolated trout to 3lbs as well as 10lb barbel, 5lb chub, 1lb roach, dace to 8oz, and even occasional sea trout. More than 2,000 grayling have recently been stocked by the EA: a tribute to the river's improving water quality.

In the tight confines of the flood relief channels at Toton Fields, you may prefer a rod of 6 to 7ft, but in general a length of about 9ft is ideal, rated for a 3 weight line. Local fly-fishers like Mick Martin recommend Balloon Caddis attractor patterns backed up with F-flies: trailing a New Zealand style nymph below a larger floating fly is also successful.

Don't miss

● The Erewash valley's classic mill chimneys: a characteristic hexagonal red brick design that's always visible somewhere on the horizon

● Attenborough Nature Reserve: 360 acres of wetlands created in gravel pits around the confluence of the Erewash and Trent

20

LUDLOW

River Teme

As you work your way down the slopes of Whitcliffe Common, cross the triple arches of Ludford Bridge and start the long climb up to Ludlow's southern gatehouse, it's impossible to ignore the Normans' ability to dominate a landscape.

For world-travellers at the start of the twenty-first century, the idea of a walled hill town evokes images of Tuscany, Andalucia or the Pyrenees, but Ludlow's castle and fortifications are every bit the twelfth-century English equal of San Gimignano, Ronda or Luz. Poised on a rocky outcrop above a roaring loop of the River Teme, this was a military, economic and political power-base from which ambitious marcher lords could project their influence across both sides of a contested border.

With military power came long-term stability and prosperity: more than half a millennium later, Ludlow's gridiron street pattern and tall town houses still conceal elongated gardens, each burgage plot calculated to feed a medieval family, and the smaller cottages on Broadgate crowd the semi-defended area between the bridge and the old town walls. According to modern urban archaeologists, Ludlow occupies one of the best hydropower locations for its size anywhere in Britain, and the town's wealth grew steadily despite the baronial conflicts of the Middle Ages.

Although the most actively-eroding area of the Teme catchment lies above Leintwardine, Ludlow's stretch of the river was steep enough to accommodate four major weirs: a variety of massive structures designed to tame the torrent that once put the *'lud'* (loud) into the town's name. The Mill Street impoundment was probably the earliest, but the unusual horseshoe-shaped weir below Ludford Bridge was also operating by 1241, powering the Old Street mill on the north bank as well as two mills on the opposite side of the river. Thirty years later, Case Mill Weir was constructed, and the Castle Mills at Dinham were last to come online in the early fourteenth century. Corn milling was quickly overtaken by more profitable fulling and cloth-making, a booming business until around 1600, when Ludlow's mills began diversifying into paper, silk-weaving, and glove-making.

Perhaps because Ludlow was the only significant town in the catchment, the Teme appears to have resisted any real ecological damage during this extended industrial age. Salmon continued to run the weirs in high water, and Sir Humphrey Davy located *Salmonia*'s grayling-fishing

Sandstone slabs form braided runs and islands in the Teme above Ludford Bridge

tutorial at Leintwardine, enthusing that *'there is no stream in England more productive of grayling'*. In the early 1900s, the area around Dinham Mill was famous for the quality of its fishing, with record-breaking bags of grayling, trout and pike. (WJ Perry, the landlord of a nearby inn, was one of those successful anglers, but he apparently proved less talented as a swimmer when he drowned in a barrel of his own beer).

In 1746, less than a century after Thomas Barker had written about Shrews-bury's winged palmers, Richard and Charles Bowlker followed his lead by publishing Ludlow's own first contribution to the literature of the sport. With a list of 29 fly patterns including the first published reference to a Red Spinner, some of the most advanced entomology yet, and a note that *'the largest greyling ever caught in England was taken in Ludlow; it measured half-a-yard in length, and weighed four pounds and a half'*, their all-new *Art of Angling* was reprinted in more than twelve editions and became the

According to Teme fishermen Richard and Charles Bowlker in 1746, 'the principal months to angle for Greyling are September, October and November'

....

definitive fishing text for over a hundred years. As a result, the Teme's traditions of tackle and fly-tying were instantly immortalised as part of the standard national approach, but successful local flies like the Red Tag, created by Thomas Flynn around 1850, continued to be absorbed so rapidly into the mainstream that the region's own undercurrent of tying characteristics has only just begun to re-emerge.

Today, thanks to modern researchers like Michael Leighton, Christopher Knowles and Roger Smith, a tradition as distinctive as chalkstream dries or north country spiders is coming back into focus, and it's possible to identify the unique look and feel of Borders flies: suggestive, impressionistic, tied from freely-obtainable furs and feathers, sometimes reverse-hackled, and almost always bushy for bouncing off vegetation and floating on rough water.

By the time of the Industrial Revolution, two wheels at Dinham were powering corn and saw mills, as well as an iron and brass foundry, but production declined at most of Ludlow's milling sites from 1850 onwards, and the weirs began to disintegrate due to lack of maintenance and the raw power of the river.

In the mid-1990s, a groundswell of interest in the town's industrial archaeology saw the formation of the Teme Weirs Trust, and Horseshoe, Mill Street and Case Mill Weirs were restored between 2002 and 2005 at a combined cost of more than £1 million, with contributions from the Heritage Lottery Fund, Biffaward, Ludlow Town and Parish Councils, the local Rotary Club and many private donations. An additional £100,000 was also raised by the

A salmon parr from the Teme

Friends of Whitcliffe Common to stabilise the historic Breadwalk and install concrete slips as access for anglers.

With fish passage a priority for the Teme as a Special Site of Scientific Interest the designs were closely scrutinised by the Environment Agency's fish passage group: Case Mill Weir now incorporates a low flow notch, and a Larinier pass was installed on Horseshoe Weir. Up to fifty salmon an hour have since been seen leaping Dinham Weir in winter floods, and Ludlow's weirs may now be more passable for all species than at any previous point in the last 800 years: a factor contributing to the overall 'recovering' SSSI status of this near-natural sand- and mudstone river, although the catchment as a whole is still suffering from agricultural abstraction and diffuse pollution as a result of increasingly intensive cattle farming on the its tributaries.

The historic structures still result in extensive upstream ponding, but the Teme has a natural tendency to narrow itself into deep slots in Ludlow's bedrock, so the weirs' extra wetted width and diversity of habitat niches is generally regarded as a benefit in this area. Olives, yellow stoneflies, small dark shrimp, and cased and caseless caddis live among the tumbled, eroded plates of sandstone in the short torrential stretches between the impoundments, while the slow-water sections favour populations of mayflies, banded demoiselles and large red damselflies, and new masonry cavities and nest-boxes in the renovated sluices offer nesting sites for kingfishers, dippers and grey wagtails. The river is a refuge for the nationally-threatened white-clawed crayfish, and otter spraints are frequently found on the weirs.

The deep water clearly provides cover for fish of impressive size: whilst this book's publisher Merlin Unwin and I are rigging up for a couple of hours' fishing amongst the clear runs and rock-ribbed islands below the Breadwalk, a local lad scrambles up the ledges with a pound-plus grayling which he's just taken on a gold spinner. Bigger still, a trout of about six pounds was recently caught near Horseshoe Weir.

"We've got a little bit of almost every kind of geology on the Teme," says Merlin, "and I think that can lead to very good fly-life and fishing. Twenty years ago, when we first moved our publishing business to Ludlow, I was stunned: there was a shower of rain, and all of a sudden a great fall of mayfly spinners covered the wet pavement outside our office. I knew at that moment we'd moved to the right place!"

Above: A half-pound grayling below the Mill Street weir

Below: Ludlow boasts almost 500 listed buildings, including many from the Tudor, Elizabethan and Georgian periods

Ludlow: River Teme

Who's looking after the river?

The Teme Weirs Trust was formed in 1997 to restore and maintain Ludlow's weirs, protect the ecology of the river established over the course of 800 years, and enhance the cultural, historic, scenic and recreational aspects of the river for local residents and visitors.

Major reinstatement works took place between 2002 and 2005, involving many partners including the Environment Agency, Natural England, the Friends of Whitcliffe Common, Shropshire Wildlife Trust and the British Canoe Union.

For the latest information, visit: www.temeweirstrust.org.uk

Getting there

The lower end of the Breadwalk at Ludford Bridge is just over 10 minutes' walk from Ludlow station.

Maps of Ludlow are available from the Visitor Information Centre on Castle Square, SY8 1AS: OS Explorer 203 is also recommended.

Seasons and permits

Brown trout season runs from 18 March to 7 October; grayling season from 16 June to 14 March.

By long tradition, Plymouth Settled Estates, Shropshire Wildlife Trust and the Friends of Whitcliffe Common allow free fishing with a valid EA rod licence along the Breadwalk between Ludford and Dinham bridges: about half a mile.

There are also short free fishing stretches along Temeside and above Dinham Weir.

Fishing tips

The Teme boasts a long history of excellent trout and grayling fishing in its upper reaches, and Ludlow is usually regarded as the crossover point between the river's game and coarse fisheries. The weirs at Ludlow provide habitat for large trout and grayling: trout up to 6lbs and grayling to 2lbs, although most of the largest specimens are caught by coarse anglers.

A rod of 9 to 10ft is ideal, rated for a 3 to 5 weight line. Richard Bowlker recommended imitative Blue Duns and Willow Flies for the best of the grayling fishing in early autumn, but the river has also developed a strong tradition of fancy attractor patterns such as the Red Tag, Brookes' Fancy, Grant's Murderer and Sanders' Special.

Don't miss

- Ludlow's Michelin-starred restaurants and nearly 500 listed buildings
- AE Housman's grave: marked with a cherry tree in St Laurence's churchyard
- Ludford Corner: the geological type site for the Ludlow Bone Bed, a layer of primitive garfish and bichir teeth, bones and scales laid down between 416 and 418 million years ago

21

SHREWSBURY

Rea Brook

"In low water conditions you wouldn't think that little river could pack so much punch," says Environment Agency ecological appraisal officer Martin Fenn. "But the Rea Brook has always had a reputation for high-energy flooding, so we really needed to move quickly when that culvert under the Kingfisher embankment started to crack.

"A lot of Shrewsbury was flooded by the Severn and Rea Brook during the previous summer, and the Council found the cracks at the end of January 2008. The Brook's whole channel ran through one small culvert in the embankment, with sewage pipes and a gas main above, and we couldn't risk another quick spate taking it all down."

For a small stream in the rolling Shropshire hills, the Rea Brook enjoys a lot of local respect for the power of its water. Compared to the Severn, which has always been known for its fluctuating water levels and frequent floods, the Brook rises and falls quickly, with mean flows from its source at Marton Pool reliable enough to drive numerous mills by the time of the Norman Conquest. In 1086, Domesday Book implied that the Shrewsbury mills were some of the most profitable anywhere

in England, providing an enormous income for Shrewsbury Abbey based on water drawn off the Rea Brook via a high-level contour leat. This had been abandoned by the late nineteenth century, but as you look at the old railway embankment and contrast the leat's grand arch with the diminutive culvert designed for what was left of the river, it's evident where most of the flow went while the mills were still operational.

By 2008, with the leat redundant and the culvert collapsing, it was time to give the Brook's full force all the space it needed again. "Working with contractors," says Martin, "we took about three weeks to excavate two or three hundred yards of new channel, much of it along the southern end of the old mill race, under the higher-capacity arch in the embankment. We were able to create excellent riffles as we went along, simply by exposing gravels previously deposited in the floodplain. And because we didn't just want to make a featureless canal, we studded the sandy banks with lots of large boulders, which will also help to increase oxygenation and control erosion at critical points."

Spoil from the excavations was used to backfill the upper end of the old riverbed, but much of the channel was retained as valuable backwater and wetland habitat. The resident fish needed to be relocated too, so Martin and his team waded in with electrofishing equipment, much to the delight of the local press.

Today, the redesigned channel and backwater form a neat little case study in environmental engineering, not just protecting infrastructure but also adding diversity of habitat. In reality, the Rea Brook is that rare occurrence in the world of river restoration: an urban stream that hasn't lost its natural topography despite centuries of industrial activity. Superstores,

A selection of contemporary palmer patterns for the Rea Brook, none larger than a size 18

petrol stations and out-of-town eateries now crowd both ends of the Rea Brook Valley Country Park, and 1980s housing estates sprawl along the rim of the valley, but the stream's volatile flow regime kept all except the most determined medieval millers at bay, and it still provides a green corridor from the Shropshire hills to the centre of Shrewsbury.

From early medieval corn milling, some sites diversified into snuff, hemp and bleach-making, and the large commercial Salop Sanitary Steam Laundry complex took over the Burnt Mills site in 1888. Throughout the eighteenth and nineteenth centuries, Shrewsbury's suburb of Sutton boasted a popular spa whose salt- and iron-rich waters were said to rival Cheltenham's, and Sutton Lower Mill also took advantage of local geology by grinding barytes ore for use as a paint pigment. After grinding, processing 'off-colour' barium sulphate could require heating and bleaching with sulphuric acid, which was then washed away with large volumes of water, so the ecology of both the lower Brook and its leat probably suffered severely at this time.

Almost all the mills had been demolished by the 1960s, and the Rea Brook now has good connectivity throughout almost its entire length. Mayflies, olives, midges and caddis are evident from a few moments' observation and stone-turning, and general water quality seems good, though algae-covered rocks suggest nutrient enrichment from the large golf course at the top of the fishery, as well as storm runoff from the surrounding housing estates.

Due to frequent flooding and the softness of the rich alluvial soil, most of the Brook's deep natural meanders were never dredged out for intensive agriculture. As a result, Shropshire Council now manages a miraculously preserved landscape: a flood-plain patchwork of streamside meadows, hedges and copses long vanished from many less developed areas. Some of the most successful management approaches have proved to be the most traditional: cattle grazing and small-scale haymaking to promote wildflower biodiversity, and hedge-laying and coppicing for woodland management. But more modern methods have also been shown to work, such as encouraging local volunteers to create new meadows and wetlands in areas of low wildlife interest, engaging the probation service in controlling invasive Himalayan balsam, and West Mercia Police's annual *Get*

Hooked on Fishing event and stream clean-up for kids from the surrounding estates.

Sometimes, exploring such a strangely *rus in urbe* landscape with a fly-rod can almost feel too good to be true: the slightly prickling sensation of being observed, when it's not unpleasant to shut down the sightlines by sliding down steeply-incised banks to fish unwatched with the lightest of lines and the subtlest of movements. All through this August afternoon, I work my way up the deep bends below Meole Brace,

In 2008 the Environment Agency cut a new channel for the Rea Brook, diverting it through an old embankment arch which once carried a leat to Shrewsbury's mills

floating close-copy palmered imitations in cathedral-like quiet over midge- and aphid-focused grayling, trout and chub. But it's only when I start breaking down my rod for the long walk back into Shrewsbury that I realise: someone really was here before me.

Thomas Barker published his *Art of Angling* in 1651, including the first image of a fly reel, the first description of the Hawthorn fly, and the first complete, detailed fly-tying instructions ever printed. By this time he was working as a chef in a Cromwellian household near the Thames in Westminster, but he was born and educated in Bracemeole: the name of Meole Brace until the twentieth century.

With Izaak Walton and Robert Venables, Barker laid the foundations of the English fly-fishing and writing tradition, and his craft was finely tuned to clear, low-running streams like this: '*your rod must be light and tender… and if you can attain to angle with one haire, you shall have the more rises*'. As an expert fly tyer, he also insisted that that after learning the basics of tying '*a man's own judgement with some experience must guide him*'. Best of all, his signature pattern was the winged palmer: the tying template handed down the generations which I'd adapted for myself and subconsciously selected to fish his own home water that quiet summer afternoon:

'*First, a black Palmer ribbed with silver. Secondly, a black Palmer ribbed with an orenge-tawny body. Thirdly, a black Palmer made all of black. Fourthly, a red Palmer ribbed with gold. Fifthly, a red Palmer mixed with an orenge tawny body of cruell. All these flyes must be made with hackles, and they will serve all the year long morning and evening, windy or cloudy. Without*

Fishing town: Shrewsbury has a long history as an angling destination

these flyes you cannot make a dayes angling good…'

There have been many more famous rivers in fly-fishing history, but maybe the Rea Brook made its mark before all of them.

Palmered-hackle flies still catch Rea Brook grayling

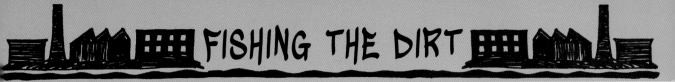

Shrewsbury: Rea Brook

Who's looking after the river?

In consultation with as many stakeholders as possible, the Environment Agency, Shropshire Council, Shropshire Wildlife Trust and Shropshire Anglers' Federation are developing a management plan for the Rea Brook Valley Country Park local nature reserve, with the Rea Brook as its central feature.

The Anglers' Federation is actively seeking grants from the Heritage Lottery Fund and other sources to improve and manage the fishery and its surroundings.

For the latest information, visit:
www.environment-agency.gov.uk
www.shropshire.gov.uk
www.shropshirewildlifetrust.org.uk
www.shropshireanglersfederation.in

Getting there

The lower end of the Rea Brook is about 15 minutes' walk from Shrewsbury station. Most of this lower section is heavily canalised, but a further 15 minutes will bring you to wilder water.

Maps of Shrewsbury are available from the Visitor Information Centre on Barker Street, SY1 1QH: OS Explorer 241 is also recommended.

Seasons and permits

Brown trout season runs from 18 March to 7 October; grayling season from 16 June to 14 March.

Shropshire Anglers' Federation controls more than 3 miles of fishing on the Rea Brook from its confluence with the Severn upstream to the Meole Brace roundabout. For full details and a list of day ticket outlets, visit:
www.shropshireanglersfederation.in

Fishing tips

The Rea Brook holds such a diverse range of species that it's often electrofished by the EA to stock display tanks for country shows. Salmon, pike, perch, roach, dace, chub and barbel are all present, with trout to 1lb and grayling to 1½lbs.

Unchanged in many essentials since the early seventeenth century, this stream responds very well to an ultralight approach with a rod of 6 to 8ft rated for a 1 to 4 weight line. In homage to Thomas Barker and the Rea Brook's unsung contribution to fly-fishing history, it's well worth fishing lightly-dressed palmered patterns on fine tippets, which can still produce outstanding sport in conditions of clear water and selective fish.

Don't miss

● Lord Hill's Column: dominating the skyline at the north end of the Rea Brook valley, the 133-foot tallest free-standing Doric column in the world

● Shrewsbury Abbey: used as the location for filming the *Brother Cadfael* television series

● Ditherington flax mill: derelict but due for renovation, the world's first iron-framed building, reputedly 'grandfather of the skyscraper'

22

STROUD

River Frome and Nailsworth Stream

Underneath a railway arch and the Uptown/Downtown nightclub, the tiny Slad Brook trickles out of one culvert, into another, and re-emerges below a framer's shop with the unmistakeable tang of a sewer misconnection.

But as soon as you double back round the car-breaker's yard and follow the main river upstream into its deepening green gorge, the modern world fades as fast as that whiff of raw sewage. The roar of rush hour on the bypass dulls to a murmur behind the trees. Arching above the Frome, the hazels and alders are coming into full leaf, while the celandines and wild garlic are over, but the stream bubbles clear and shallow in its bed of Jurassic limestone cobbles, and you start searching for signs of fly-life on the water and the flick of red-finned trout rising freely to intercept them.

Geology placed the old wool-trading town of Stroud at the steeply-dropping junction of five tumbling streams which cut deep clefts in the Cotswolds' high limestone plateau, converging from Caudle Green, Nailsworth, Painswick, and the Slad and Toadsmoor valleys. So geology also concentrated Gloucestershire's first large-scale industry on these streams, where the surrounding upper layers of limestone are

separated by an easily-mined volcanic bed of clay and gypsum known as fuller's earth. Until the later twelfth century, the vital first process of degreasing sheep's wool was laboriously carried out by trampling the fleeces in vats of stale urine, or mixtures of fuller's earth and water. Around 1170, Cistercian monks introduced the idea of water-powered fulling, with water wheels lifting and dropping large wooden mallets or stocks: firstly to scour grease out of the woollen fabric by driving fuller's earth through the wool, then to shrink and pound the open weave together into felt, which had the added benefit of not needing to be hemmed.

With its combination of water power and unlimited supplies of local wool and fuller's earth, Stroud was perfectly placed to exploit the monks' labour-saving new technology. Between the sixteenth and eighteenth centuries, the number of fulling mills and dyeworks in the area grew from 14 to 35. The steepest part of the main river, from the Golden Valley down to Stroud, falls 28ft per mile for more than five miles, and the ecological connectivity of this stretch alone was fractured by the weirs of more than thirty mill sites, with another twenty on the shallower slope

A river runs under it. In Stroud's industrial estates: one picture tells the Frome's whole story

137

Above the Bath Road bridge in Stroud

With architecture that's more reminiscent of a chateau than a factory, Milliken's Lodgemore Mill is still producing snooker baize and tennis balls, but from the 1830s, Stroud's cloth industry suffered a long decline caused by overproduction, changing fashions and competition from other regions. In particular, South Yorkshire out-competed the south-west by weaving cheaper worsteds and woollens for lower-priced emerging markets, and many of Stroud's mills closed in the 1840s, with a second downturn thirty years later.

But depression in the cloth industry provided a golden opportunity for different sectors. Holloway Brothers of Stroud boasted of being the first to use steam-powered sewing machines for clothing production, building a business that survived until 1975 by supplying uniforms to Harrods, the armed forces, and even the cast of the original *St Trinian's* film. In 1840, William Dangerfield began making umbrella and parasol sticks, later diversifying into buttons and steel pen handles, and employing another thousand local people.

Heavy engineering businesses also moved into Stroud's redundant woollen mills. The Phoenix Ironworks invented lawnmowers and adjustable spanners: other foundries made valves, engines, park benches, and the original two-man chainsaws which were later airdropped into Malaya to clear the jungle for the War Office. During the First World War, the Erinoid works at Lightpill on the Nailsworth stream became the international centre for producing plastic: a revolutionary new material which was odourless, non-flammable, non-conductive and could

from Stroud to the Severn. Eventually there were more than 150 mills on the whole Frome system, and milling records show how severely the river's flow regime was affected by these impoundments: in 1834, Ebley Mill provided employment for nearly 1,000 workers, but until the owners built their own reservoir, work often couldn't start before noon because so much water had been held back upstream by other mills.

At the height of Stroud's prosperity, the town and its satellite villages merged to form a single industrial corridor that drove the mechanisation of the Cotswolds woollen industry.

Heavily-felted broadcloth was dyed in strong colours like 'Stroud Scarlet' and 'Uley Blue' before being exported all over the world by the East India, Levant, Hudson Bay and Royal African trading companies: customers ranged from the court of King George III to indigenous North Americans who loved the densely-woven scarlet fabric and its decorative selvedge so much that some even named their wives after the faraway town where it was made.

be sawed, drilled, glued and turned like wood.

Predictably, the demands of these industries went far beyond the Frome's capacity to power them, and many mills installed auxiliary steam engines which needed constant supplies of coal from the pits of Staffordshire, Shropshire and the Forest of Dean. As early as 1728, engineers had been floating the idea of making the whole river navigable, an idea fortunately sunk by the sheer number of mills and their continuing need for water power. Several contentious Acts of Parliament later, a plan was finally approved to link Stroud's western edge to the Severn through a completely separate channel, and the Stroudwater Canal was opened in 1779. In the long term, the Frome's base flows proved more consistent than the Churnet's, which supplied the eastern Thames and Severn Canal, and the Stroudwater's commercial traffic lasted until the 1940s.

On the Nailsworth Stream and other tributaries, several milling sites like the former woollen, hosiery and stickmaking Dunkirk Mills have already been converted into apartments, while others have been occupied by supermarkets and car parks. The scruffy surroundings of Stroud's canals are now the focus of major regeneration schemes, and the river and its tributaries will inevitably be affected: at the time of writing, several new hydropower schemes

Look at the fins on that! Limestone streams can make unforgettable trout

The Frome still feels like a working river

are under consideration, all of which would pose problems for fish migration. But for now the new turbines and ancient clattering fulling stocks are silent, the heavy engineering and plastics works have long since stopped discharging their noxious brews of cooling oil and vinyl compounds, and the quiet gorges of these reclusive little streams are ready for rediscovery by light-footed urban fly-fishers.

"It's quite phenomenal down there," sighs Chris Bainger, the Environment Agency's local fisheries technical specialist. "Over the next few years we'll need to put a lot of effort into addressing all the weirs and constraints that will otherwise fail the Frome against its Water Framework Directive targets, and we want to get more local people involved in looking after the river too. But when I jumped in to do a kick-

sample behind the supermarket a few weeks ago, there were caddis, heptagenids, even signs of otters, right through the middle of Stroud. It's very productive, almost a chalk-stream… just a fantastic little trout river."

Keep out: there's plenty of other water to fish

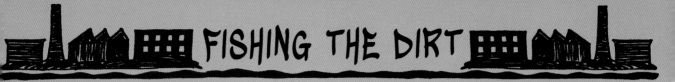

Stroud: Rivers Frome and Nailsworth

Who's looking after the rivers?

The Environment Agency took over the roles and responsibilities of the National Rivers Authority in 1996, regulating pollution, reducing flood risk, and improving the environment where possible. Over the next few years, local EA officers will be looking at ways of solving the Frome's historic connectivity problems to meet the requirements of the Water Framework Directive, and encouraging local people to take more ownership of the river.

The *Stroud Valleys Project* organises occasional litter clearances and habitat projects around the Frome and its tributaries, while Stroud and District Angling Club is gradually restoring sections of the Thames and Severn Canal as a stillwater coarse fishery.

For the latest information, visit:
www.environment-agency.gov.uk
www.stroudvalleysproject.org.uk

Getting there

The Frome is about 5 minutes' walk from Stroud station, while the Nailsworth Stream enters the main river about 20 minutes further down the valley.

Maps of Stroud are available from the Tourist Information Centre on George Street, GL5 1AE: OS Explorer 168 is also recommended.

Seasons and permits

Brown trout season runs from 18 March to 7 October.

Where footpaths permit public access to the Frome and Nailsworth Stream, Stroud District Council allows free fishing with a valid EA rod licence. However, many stretches are still inaccessible due to security fences around industrial and post-industrial premises.

Fishing tips

With their heavily-industrialised past and legacy of habitat fragmentation, the Frome and Nailsworth Stream are still recovering urban rivers. Wild trout are often warily selective: most run from 6 to 8 inches, but the potential is there for a larger trophy shot.

A rod of 7 to 8ft, rated for a 1 to 4 weight line, will help you infiltrate the more inaccessible areas and make the most of small, wild fish. The area's limestone geology encourages fly-life including caddis, olives, heptagenids and shrimp, but there are few traditional patterns on rivers industrialised from the sixteenth century onwards, and progressive fly-fishers can safely take an experimental approach.

Don't miss

- The Slad Valley: Laurie Lee's setting for *Cider with Rosie*
- Dunkirk Mill in Nailsworth: complete with milling displays and Gloucestershire's largest surviving working water wheel

23

COLNE

••

Colne Water

To understand what went wrong for so many of Britain's rivers during the Industrial Revolution, there's no better place to start than a vintage map. And the 1910 Ordnance Survey map of central Colne comes as a revelation.

From east to west along the banks of this first-order tributary in the upper reaches of the Ribble catchment, the impact of the cotton industry can clearly be seen. A chain of mills imprisons the river: most are cotton mills, but there's also a foundry, a dyeworks, a gaslight and coking company, and at least two tanneries. Almost every square yard of space is occupied, and the mills are hemmed into the valley bottom by steep streets of terraced houses running down the hills on either side.

As one of nearly 300 factory towns in this region of Lancashire, Yorkshire and Cheshire, Colne was almost perfectly suited to processing cotton. By helping the cotton fibres to stretch and cling together, the damp west Pennine air reduced the strain placed on them by machinery, so production costs were at least ten per cent less than in drier areas. Lancashire's coalfields provided the mills with supplementary power, while the canal system carried raw materials into the area, and finished goods back to the docksides at Liverpool. Between 1891 and 1911, Colne's population doubled to 26,000: at the industry's peak, local cotton magnates boasted that their looms had met the demands of the home market by breakfast time, and the rest of the day's production could be dedicated to export.

Even into the 1970s, Colne Water ran indigo blue from dyeing denim. But peering over Primet Bridge in the centre of town today, there's a strong sensation of historical vertigo as you contemplate an industry that grew so fast and only entered its final catastrophic decline within the memory of the anglers now looking after the river. Beside and behind you, a chimney and a railway viaduct still soar into the sky: in front, more than six storeys high, a canyon of semi-derelict mill buildings curves steadily away to its vanishing point, hundreds of yards downstream. Below a bricked-up doorway, part of the riverbed is paved with worn-out millstones, and the wreckage of a small platform shows where boilermen once shovelled hot ash straight into the river.

Bob Pearce and Graham Counsell, both committee members of Colne Water Angling Club, remember those days clearly, pointing out the remains of pumps,

Dark satanic mills: a few of Colne's factories still tower several storeys over the river

condenser pipes, and all the other nuances of industrial archaeology as we walk the river.

Over the course of a long career including years as an army driver and council water bailiff, Bob also spent time as a specialist loom mechanic in the mills where his father had worked as a fire-fighter before him. "The fine cotton 'dawn' would build up under the looms so quickly that it needed to be cleared every week at least," he says, "and of course many mills didn't. But being full of natural oils, it was quite capable of self-combusting: the flames would flash over between the looms, filling the whole weaving floor almost instantly with choking black smoke: terrifying and a real problem if you were caught in it!"

Today, even as we watch, many of Colne's historic mills are facing demolition, their brownfield sites being cleared for housing, car parks and dealerships, gyms and big box retail spaces, and occasional community parkland. At the heart of this shape-shifting landscape, still constrained by blockstone weirs and 20ft walls, the river is slowly rebuilding some of its own natural riffle sequences and gravel shoals, but it's easy to imagine how fast the spates must run off the new era's extensive hard surfaces, exaggerating the natural flashiness of this upper catchment, and threatening the survival of all but the hardiest fish and invertebrate populations.

In classic form, the diversity and abundance of most indicator species decline as you follow Colne Water down its urban reaches, and Graham and Bob are quietly determined to track those insidious water

Bob Pearce fishes beside the M65

quality problems back to their source.

In fact, this isn't the first time that volunteers from Colne Water Angling Club have shouldered responsibility for addressing the river's challenges. In 1966 an article in *The Field* recorded how an earlier generation reclaimed Colne Water as a trout fishery with a comprehensive programme of diplomacy focused on water quality improvement, restocking and education.

The mayor and corporation rewarded their persuasiveness by building a new sewage treatment works, and at least one tannery installed an expensive effluent purification plant. Under the leadership of local businessman Derrick Pickup, serious poaching problems were reduced by tactful education, while *'working parties removed the bedsteads and bicycle wheels... and the club introduced not only trout but water plants and crustaceans (which) has resulted in trout up to 3lb being taken... By hard work, by sound planning, by harnessing civic pride and industrial common sense and generosity, the club has brought a river back to life, turned an eyesore into something of beauty, and has made miles of fishing available to local people.'*

Half a century later, with more and more of the area's industrial infrastructure falling into disrepair, the club's talent for diplomacy is still in evidence. In 2008, Pendle Council signed a fifty-year peppercorn lease on condition that the club invested the full rental value in improving the river, on the basis of a habitat survey conducted by the Wild Trout Trust. The Environment Agency agreed to match-fund this commitment with £10,000 of their own, and a new *Trout in the Town* chapter was born.

After removing several tonnes of scrap metal with successful river clean-ups, Graham, Bob and fellow committee member Andy Pritchard decided to start river restoration at the top of the catchment. Sediment loading from the upper reaches had already been identified as a possible block on the river's productivity, and one of the newest sources was obvious: just below the confluence of the Laneshaw and Wycoller becks, gabion basket foundations for a new footbridge had completely re-routed the river's 15ft peak flows, eroding raw earth from one bank before swinging back to undercut a magnificent line of mature trees.

In November 2009, with guidance from the Wild Trout Trust, the club began urgent work to stabilise these banks: pinning a total of a 142 logs into place with two-metre lengths of reinforcing bar from Graham's metal fabrication business, and backfilling the void with more than 14 wagonloads of Christmas trees and brashings from Natural England's forestry management programme around Stocks reservoir. "We reckoned we'd invented a new alpine sport that winter," smiles Graham, "bouncing Christmas trees down the hill from the road, and seeing who could catch them before they hit the river!"

Less than two years after the works were completed, the soft revetments are filling with natural sediment and coarse woody debris, and fly-life in the area is already improving.

So what's next? At the time of writing, with the threat of a recommissioned weir successfully deflected, the club's next habitat enhancement project lies just downstream alongside the old tannery

Bob Pearce, Graham Counsell... and 142 pinned logs

145

lodges of Ball Grove Park, where they plan to install a sequence of upstream-pointing wooden Vs to increase diversity and create pockets of adult trout habitat in a straight, featureless milling channel.

"There's a lot needs doing to this river," concludes Bob. "Everything we've managed so far, it's been a concerted effort by a small number of people. But with more hands on, and more support, we could do so much more!"

Fully reinforced: at Spring Gardens the whole riverbed is paved with blocks of stone

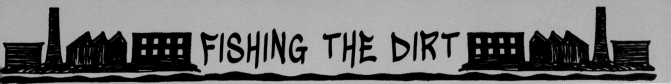

Colne: Colne Water

Who's looking after the river?

Colne Water Angling Club was founded in 1952 to restore Colne Water as an urban trout fishery. Since 2008 the club has been one of the flagship chapters of the Wild Trout Trust's *Trout in the Town* programme, working with the Environment Agency, Natural England, Pendle Borough Council and several local Friends groups to secure the future of wild trout in the river.

Numerous voluntary clean-ups have removed tonnes of rubbish, and the club has now begun a series of upper-river restoration works including soft revetments and other in-channel structures, with partnership match-funding from the Environment Agency. Angling coaches have been trained, an invertebrate monitoring network has been established, and future projects may also be planned with the Ribble Catchment Conservation Trust.

For the latest information, visit: www.colnewaterangling.club.officelive.com

Getting there

Colne Water is less than 5 minutes' walk downhill from Colne station. From here, it's at least 45 minutes on foot upstream to the Ball Grove area.

Maps are available from the Discover Pendle Centre on Vivary Way, BB8 9NW: OS Explorer OL 21 is also recommended.

Seasons and permits

Brown trout season runs from 15 March to 30 September.

Colne Water Angling Club controls the full 3-mile length of Colne Water, down to the confluence with Barrowford Water, as well as 3 local stillwaters. For full details, visit: www.colnewaterangling.club.officelive.com

Fishing tips

Colne Water has not been stocked for at least a decade, and wild trout now average between 8 and 10 inches, with very occasional specimens up to 3lbs. Although Colne Water Angling Club's rules allow members and day ticket holders to take a brace of trout per week, it's feared that the river lacks the productivity to sustain this level of harvest: in some areas, populations may have been severely damaged by poaching.

Local fly-fishers like Graham Counsell and Bob Pearce rely on rods of 9 to 10ft, rated for a 4 to 5 weight line, on all but the smallest headwaters. Favourite Colne flies include attractor caddis and CDC patterns to match the hatches which are improving noticeably on the restored stretches, with an array of marker species including heptagenids, freshwater shrimp, caddis, olives and blue-winged olives, as well as a mayfly hatch. Further downstream, the more sensitive species decline, and midges dominate the menu.

Don't miss

● Wycoller village, hall and ancient stone bridges: reputedly the setting for Charlotte Bronte's *Jane Eyre*
● Colne Cemetery: the tomb of Wallace Hartley, bandmaster on the *Titanic,* who reputedly led the orchestra in playing *Nearer My God to Thee* as the liner sank

24

HUDDERSFIELD

··

River Holme

"Shiny brass beadhead flies may work in other parts of the country," argues professional fly-tyer Jez Mallinson, "but they're not nearly as useful as copper beads when you're fishing in Yorkshire.

"Think about it: everything's down to the dominant colours of the water. When you've got peat-fed freestone rivers flowing off the moors and millstone grit of the Pennines with that coppery, peaty tinge, you want to match those tones when you're tying your flies. Insects camouflage themselves naturally against the rocks and silt of their river – it's a survival strategy – and the trout and grayling are programmed to respond to that. I've fished copper and gold bead-heads as a team of two nymphs on many occasions, switching them around to see if depth makes a difference, and I'd say that the copper usually outperforms the gold by about three to one".

Born in the village of Kirkburton in the hills above Huddersfield, Jez moved to south London and the Wandle catchment at an early age, but regular holidays kept him in touch with his roots among the Pennine becks that converge to form the little river Holme. "My uncle Eric taught me the family tradition of tickling trout in Mark's Bottom," he winks, "before giving me my first cane rod and centrepin reel, which I fly-fished with a silk line.

"Later on, when I started work as a long-distance haulier, I'd always time my journeys so as to fit in a few hours on the rivers around home – you had to obey the tachometer, and it was better than sitting in a layby somewhere! For years, driving over the Tinsley viaduct at Sheffield, I'd smell the smoke drifting over from the chimneys and think, ah, I'm home."

Even in the early 1970s, Jez remembers, Yorkshire's proud textile industry was in decline. For at least a century and a half the region had successfully out-competed the south west: first by producing woollen and worsted fabrics more cheaply through a system of artisan clothiers working out of their own homes, later by surviving the civil unrest of the Luddite movement and exploiting the energy of steeply-falling Pennine rivers to drive weaving complexes specialising in fine woollens. But the development of synthetic fabrics after the Second World War was the killing blow. "People started wearing rayon, and it was all over," says Jez sadly. "Only a city gent could afford to pay a thousand pounds for a fine wool suit, and even that didn't last long."

Today, a handful of specialist weavers

One pipe going in, this one coming out: a classic northern mill on the Holme

still supply Italian designers with their finest threads, but the old woollen economy is gone, and many of the mills around Huddersfield have been occupied by other industries: together with underperforming sewage treatment works, a very present threat to the rivers like the Holme. In 2007, Yorkshire Water was fined £10,000 and ordered to pay £754 costs after exceeding its discharge consents from treatment works at Neiley near Holmfirth on five occasions in 2005, suffocating at least four miles of river with a spike of biochemical oxygen demand (the measure of water de-oxygen-ation caused by bacteria breaking down organic material like sewage).

Later in 2007, a much worse incident occurred at the other end of the Holme. When a small company called Dr Clean (UK) went out of business, its owner arranged to have a surplus pallet of five-litre containers of washing-up liquid removed from a unit on the Queens Mill Road indus-trial estate. A large amount of this detergent was spilled whilst being loaded into a truck, and ran into the river: when the Environ-ment Agency arrived, several feet of foam were covering the channel from bank to bank, with broken-off chunks still visible two miles below the Holme's confluence with the Colne.

By the end of the investigation, at least 750 dead trout, grayling and other fish had been collected, whilst many more probably drifted downstream beyond the immediate mile and a half of ecological impact, and

Beadhead flies for the Holme, tied by Jez Mallinson, who suggests matching dressings to the river's predominant colour

Richard Baker holds a fine wild trout from central Huddersfield

the EA knew they were dealing with West Yorkshire's most serious pollution incident in 15 years. The judge at Bradford crown court agreed, emphasising that the public would be outraged if he failed to impose a suitably deterrent penalty for such a reckless breach of water resources legislation, and fining Dr Clean's owner £50,000 plus £5,000 costs.

Ironically, a fish kill on an urban river can often be the most effective fishery survey in decades, and the body count after Dr Clean's spillage showed just how far the Holme had recovered since 1894, when Tom Bradley's *Yorkshire Angler's Guide* described the whole 8½-mile river as *'unfishable on account of the pollutions'* except in the mile above Holme Bridge. Throughout the Industrial Revolution, while the green valleys filled with gritstone terraces and the dark satanic mills of William Blake's imagi-

nation, trout had survived in the Holme's upper tributaries and headwater reservoirs: when general water quality began to improve, they started drifting down again to the confluence with the Colne and the wider Calder catchment. Grayling also appeared, possibly reintroduced by anglers, though their upstream progress is hampered by several very large weirs.

By long necessity and tradition, most local angling clubs concentrated on coarse-fishing Huddersfield's canals and mill lodges, but a few fly-fishers noticed the upturn of water quality and the rivers' fortunes, and it was their tenacity that finally brought the town into the modern age of river restoration.

In 2008, Slaithwaite and District Angling Club on the Colne offered a day's guided fishing on the Holme for the Wild Trout Trust charity auction: an annual

151

selection of freely-donated gifts, promises and hard-to-access fishing permits that now raises more than £50,000 every year in unrestricted core funds for the Trust's work. The winner was Bryan Russell, a businessman from Essex who found himself forcibly struck by the contradictions of urban fly-fishing.

"Shortly before I visited the Holme," Bryan tells me, "I fished the Itchen on another Wild Trout Trust auction lot I'd won, which was a wonderful experience, full of beautiful fish. Then I came up to Huddersfield, where I caught just as many trout, all just as big and healthy, but we were catching them from a river that was literally full of rubbish. Concrete blocks, old pipes, sheets of metal, wire cable and plastic bags hanging off the trees and waving from side to side in the current like weeds. It was so disappointing… I live in Essex and I care about the river. Did anyone in Lockwood?"

As it turned out, people in Lockwood did care about the Holme: a catalyst was all that was needed. Local MP Barry Sheerman, an old friend of Bryan's, predicted that the benefits of a single clean-up would only last for a couple of months, so he used his influence to call a meeting of stakeholders and possible project partners including the EA, Kirklees Council, the Calder and Colne Rivers Trust, the Wild Trout Trust and local employer Britvic. Within months, a whole new *Trout in the Town* chapter had launched, complete with almost £100,000 of foundation funding for clean-ups, invertebrate monitoring and river-based educational programmes across Huddersfield.

"One of the first clean-ups was sponsored by McDonalds," says Bryan, "and posters went up in burger restaurants all around the city. On the day of the event, we were absolutely inundated with volunteers, who cleared away more than a hundred sacks of rubbish. The *Greenstreams* campaign has already moved far beyond trout and grayling fishing to help everyone embrace Huddersfield's rivers again. I suppose that's what you'd call a success story!"

The Holme's litter problem inspired the launch of the Greenstreams project in 2008

FISHING THE DIRT

Huddersfield: River Holme

Who's looking after the river?

The *Greenstreams* campaign was launched in 2008 to work with local people to re-establish Huddersfield's rivers and canals as community assets. Managed by environmental charity and consultancy Urban Mines Ltd, in association with the Environmental Alliance and the Cobbett Environmental Enterprise Centre, the campaign clears litter, enhances riverside habitats and runs educational programmes including *Mayfly in the Classroom*. Future plans include river restoration as part of the Wild Trout Trust's *Trout in the Town* programme.

For the latest information, visit:
www.urbanmines.org.uk
www.environmental-alliance.co.uk

Getting there

The lower Holme is about 15 minutes' walk from Huddersfield station.

Maps of Huddersfield are available from Huddersfield Visitor Information Centre and Library on Princess Alexandra Walk, HD1 2SU; OS Explorer 288 is also recommended.

Seasons and permits

Brown trout season runs from 25 March to 30 September; grayling season from 16 June to 14 March.

Kirklees Council allows free fishing on the Holme in Huddersfield with a valid EA rod licence. Above Lockwood Bridge, where bank access is restricted by Huddersfield rugby club, wading may be the only option.

Fishing tips

Despite recent pollutions, the Holme's average water quality is good, with enough invertebrates to sustain a prolific trout and grayling fishery, including many fish around the ½ lb mark. Given the right pockets of habitat, specimens of both species can reach 1½ lbs.

A rod of 7 to 8ft, rated for a 1 to 4 weight line, is ideal for presenting dry flies and nymphs under overhanging alder branches between rock riprap walls. Long-time Holme fly-fishers like Jez Mallinson recommend small Klinkhamers and similar parachute dressings to imitate caddis and olives, backed up with copper beadhead nymphs matched to the natural tannins of the river.

Don't miss

● Lockwood Viaduct: Grade II listed, carrying the railway line from Huddersfield to Sheffield over the Holme on 32 gritstone arches

'Run your nymphs through there': Adrian Grose-Hodge shows the boys a perfect pool

25

KENDAL

River Kent

Under the soles of my wading boots, the smooth shale pebbles slide and resettle themselves as I creep into the river at a half-crouch against an imperceptible current. After several weeks without rain, the Kent is as low as I've ever seen it: a skim of brown algae on the surface of the stones gives the river an illusion of colour, but this evening the water is harder and clearer than plate glass under a brassy sun.

Big red spinners are spiralling in the air, and a trout starts rising below one of the bridges, where a gravel bar and scattered boulder garden add a little diversity to Kendal's heavily-revetted flood channel. I consider my options, tie on a dry Pheasant Tail pattern and start my stalk. The trout maintains its rhythm as I sidle into range.

Still watching, I feed line out into the slow current behind me, take up the tension on the long rod and water-haul the fly forward. A lucky gust of wind whistles between the buildings and whips the tippet round in a perfect shepherd's crook, and a big head and shoulders erupt from the surface to meet it. The trout takes the fly at a flat-out run, rocketing downstream through shallow water faster than I can raise my rod tip to pick up slack. The reel starts to spin. Then, thirty yards away already, he's round the other side of the biggest boulder. For half a second, I feel the tightness of the tippet before the fly comes shooting back at me. He's gone.

This isn't the first time a strong Kent trout has beaten or even spooled me, I reflect ruefully, but this urban beat could do with a lot more rocks like that one – not least because more rocks would mean more fish. During the 1970s, as a riverside plaque reveals, the Kendal Flood Relief Scheme added the latest layer of blockstone and concrete engineering to the channel through the town, stripping it of features and leaving it hugely overwide in times of low flow.

More than many rivers, the Kent has a catchment of two halves. Above Kendal, the upper river and its tributaries converge from steep valleys of impervious metamorphic slates and grits: below the town, the Kent cuts a series of gorges through a softer limestone landscape down to Morecambe Bay. As a result of those steep, flashy headwaters, destructive flooding has been an issue for centuries. So the entire river has been heavily modified for flood defence as well as water-powered industry, leaving plenty of work for the modern South Cumbria Rivers Trust to do.

Public viewing: local schoolkids spot a salmon – and a bicycle – from a high vantage point

Rock and a hard place: the boulder where the author lost his latest Kendal trout

"The whole catchment is awash with dozens of weirs and other structures," the Trust's manager Peter Evoy tells me, "but most of those have been made passable for salmonids at one time or another. Eels have been disregarded historically, so we've started looking at their needs, and installed eel passes within Kendal during 2010. But overall, what's done most damage to the river has been the flood engineering: lots of dredging and straightening above and below Kendal, with armoured beds, gravel traps and berms all over the place.

"Long stretches of the river have been completely cut off from their floodplain, and we're approaching landowners who are seeking payments through the Higher Level Stewardship Scheme, to influence them to take the flood embankments down as part of a Cumbria-wide river restoration partnership with the Eden and Derwent Rivers Trusts."

Ironically, although the Kent has been so heavily modified that it can only qualify for 'good ecological potential' status under the Water Framework Directive, it's also one of the most important refuges for white-clawed crayfish anywhere in the UK. According to Natural England's Special Site of Scientific Interest and Special Area of Conservation notifications, this may now be the only major river system in England where native crayfish can still be found in high densities and a variety of habitats, from the lower reaches up to an altitude of 250 metres above sea level.

The catchment's flashiness keeps its substrates mobile and silt-free, and the crayfish find refuge everywhere: in small marginal areas of cobble and stones in the headwaters, under mats of ranunculus in the middle reaches, and deep in the limestone gorges below the town of Kendal. Although the Mint tributary has suffered from cypermethrin pollution, including one incident in 2004 which killed more than 5,000 crayfish, the river's usual high water quality, calcium-rich geology and salmonid populations also benefit freshwater pearl mussels, and one of the UK's only two breeding colonies co-exists with the crayfish in the Kent system.

Straddling the geological succession between the upper and lower catchment, Kendal was founded in the eighth century as the settlement of Kirkland near a ford across the Kent. Until the Industrial Revolution, local wool was the main source of income: 'Kendal green' cloth, coloured with dyer's greenweed and woad or indigo, was reputedly worn by local bowmen at the battles of Crecy and Poitiers, and certainly got a mention from Shakespeare in *Henry IV (Part I)*.

The powerful barons of Kendal laid out the town on a grid of long burgage plots, some running down to the river's wool-washing steps in parallel lines: a street pattern which survived well into the late eighteenth and early nineteenth centuries, when these narrow yards and lanes were developed for heavier industry, including an organ works.

In 1848 the fifty-acre Kentmere reservoir was constructed to regulate the river's flow for paper mills, snuff mills and gunpowder works, and Robert Miller Somervell laid the foundations of the town's footwear industry by relocating his leather-finishing business to the eastern side of Nether Bridge. This was a site where a cluster of tanneries had historically occupied the town's noxious-trades quarter: now, Somervell became Kendal's largest employer, making shoes with imported American sewing machines, and introducing the 'K' trademark in 1865. Wartime production included tents, aero-engine and wing covers, and fleece-lined flying boots with hidden compartments for compasses and German money: shoes were still made in Kendal until 2003.

Today, apart from its world-famous Kendal mint cake, much of the town's industrial flavour has vanished, but its modern residents are working hard to preserve their river's SSSI and SAC status. Across the UK, Himalayan balsam has become one of the most damaging invasive non-native species,

shading out native plants with dense stands of foliage that die back in winter, leaving bare, rootless riverbanks vulnerable to erosion, and dumping silt into spawning gravels: a national problem that the Environment Agency estimated in 2010 would take £150-300 million to solve.

Environmental experts agree that the best way to clear this aggressive invader is to take a whole-catchment approach, starting from the top – and the Kent Invasive Plants Action Group has done exactly that. "Janet Antrobus and Judith Wallen are simply

A red spinner on the Kent

brilliant!" exults Bekka Close from her perspective as Cumbria's freshwater invasive non-native species initiative co-ordinator. "As passionate local people they've been working on it for six or seven years now, organising at least fifteen voluntary work parties to pull it by hand during growing season, as well as monitoring other invasives like giant hogweed and Japanese knotweed.

"Those thirty or forty volunteers have made such an impact, delivering real improvements to an SSSI and SAC, that Natural England and the EA are now funding the group to employ contractors to spray and strim the worst infestations, which can then be revisited to pick off any late-germinating stragglers by hand. There's lots of river still to cover, but they've basically dealt with the problem right down through Kendal. And they've spread the message to so many others that you now get lots of residents pulling up odd plants when they're out walking their dogs. Real local empowerment and ownership – isn't that just what you want to achieve?"

Starting from the top of the catchment, the Kent Invasive Plants Action Group has cleared Himalayan balsam from the river banks right through Kendal

Kendal: River Kent

Who's looking after the river?

The South Cumbria Rivers Trust began to evolve in 2000 as a result of local anglers' concerns about fish stocks in the Rivers Leven and Crake, and then in Windermere and Coniston. The project area expanded to cover the Kent, Bela and Duddon, and the present organisation was formed in 2006. The Trust now hosts the *Cumbria Freshwater Invasive Non-Native Species Initiative*, with responsibility for delivering Cumbria's Biodiversity Action Plan and the *Cumbria Freshwater Biosecurity Campaign*.

The Trust also supports the Kent Invasive Plants Action Group: an active voluntary organisation part-funded by Natural England and the Environment Agency to eradicate Himalayan balsam from the full length of the river.

For the latest information, visit: www.scrt.co.uk

Getting there

Oxenholme is now the nearest mainline station, about 2 miles south-west of Kendal.

Maps of Kendal are available from Made in Cumbria on Stramongate, LA9 4BH: OS Explorer OL 7 is also recommended.

Seasons and permits

Brown trout season runs from 15 March to 30 September; sea trout and salmon season from 1 January to 31 October.

Kendal Town Council allows free fishing with a valid EA rod licence from the pool below Nether Bridge upstream to Victoria Bridge: about a mile of fishing.

Fishing tips

The Kent is south Cumbria's main game fishing river, with hard-fighting wild trout which average around ¾ lb, and a few elusive specimens from 3 to 7lbs: a thriving goosander population may be affecting recruitment of smaller fish. Most of the river's angling pressure is focused on salmon and sea trout, which run between June and October, so the banks are often deserted throughout the early season.

A rod of 9 to 10ft is ideal, rated for a 3 to 5 weight line. Local tackle shop owner Geoff Waites recommends small flies during the cooler months, getting larger as the weather warms up, with darker patterns throughout the day and lighter colours later. Different sizes of F-flies and Grey Dusters cover many situations, from large dark olives and black gnats to caddis and caenis, but Kite's Imperials, Tups Indispensables and Klinkhamers are also invaluable in summer. In rain or wind, try a daddy-long-legs under the trees.

Don't miss

● The Museum of Lakeland Life and Industry: complete with a room dedicated to fishing writer Arthur Ransome, usually featuring his rods, reels, flies and other tackle

● Kendal mint cake: created accidentally by a confectioner making glacier mints, the favourite high altitude pick-me-up for Edmund Hillary's conquest of Everest in 1953

26

MANCHESTER

River Irwell

Mike Duddy, President of Salford Friendly Anglers' Society, is a master of the deadpan. "This is the river that nobody wants in the land that time forgot," he says, waiting just long enough before raising a quizzical eyebrow to make you think he's completely serious.

Deadpan or not, it's also a very accurate description of the Irwell. In its lower reaches, the river runs through some of the UK's most disadvantaged areas of post-industrial multiple deprivation: further north, below its confluence with the Roch, the Environment Agency still gives the river almost the worst possible classifications for chemical and biological water quality. Near its headwaters at Irwell Springs, a treatment plant worth £1 million buffers the fourth worst case of minewater pollution in the UK. But then there are anglers' photos too… and some of those show trout so large you'd swear they swam in rivers in Slovenia or the Andes if it weren't for the debris banks of bollards, tyres, mattresses and shopping trolleys in the background of almost every shot.

The Irwell's original medieval fishery survived until the end of the eighteenth century. Trout were taken for granted, salmon ran the river in countless numbers,

and the niche occupied by grayling in other catchments was held by indigenous 'graining' or 'shoalers', a rare herring-sized form of dace now found only in Switzerland. Underpinning the ecosystem, fly-life was so prolific that Salford residents could stand on the bridges and knock hunting swallows and house martins out of the air with short-handled whips.

But all the way down the river's 39 miles from the moors above Bacup to its confluence with the Mersey at Irlam, the Industrial Revolution had already started to take hold, converting domestic-scale fulling and weaving into organised, empire-building mass production. In 1773, calico printing works near Summerseat brought the cotton industry to the upper river and its tributaries, and clusters of mills sprang up in the ancient settlements of Bury and Radcliffe. Ramsbottom was purpose-built as a new industrial town, with spinning mills closely followed by paper, soap, bleach and chemical factories, tin works and foundries, and glass printing five miles upstream at Rossendale. Many of the weirs first built at this time can still be seen: huge structures designed to divert water from the river for power and fabric processing. Most would have been impassable to migratory

No need to lie: Adrian Grose-Hodge looks justifiably stunned as he hefts his season's best trout for the camera

Like Slovenia.... but with more litter

salmonid populations in the early twentieth century. Until then, supply far exceeded demand for the poisonous by-products of town gas production, and the carbonisation works that lined the Irwell simply washed them away with water already used to cool the white-hot coke.

The famous Warrington salmon disappeared, and so did the graining. Around 1826 the river enjoyed a short reprieve when coal-gas production became temporarily uneconomic, but it was soon on a downward spiral again, with cotton mills, coal mines, print and bleach works, paper mills and chemical factories all using its waters as a waste dump. By the 1860s contemporary writers agreed that the Irwell was *'considerably less a river than a flood of liquid manure, in which all life dies, whether animal or vegetable'* and *'there was scarcely a blade of grass or a bunch of rushes near the river itself, and only such trees as were high enough above its banks to keep most of their roots out of its reach, and luckily so placed as not to be destroyed at the top by chemical fumes, had preserved their leaves and lives'*.

Sewage treatment improved gradually, but the apocalyptic language still continued in a Parliamentary debate of 1950, recording how the river remained polluted and lifeless for more than a century. Along fifty miles of the Irwell and Roch, over a hundred mills intercepted and polluted every drop of run-off from the hills *'so that it may be said that no natural water normally enters the river from its cradle in the moors to its grave in the Manchester Ship Canal... There are no fish, no insects, no weeds, no life of any kind except sewage fungus, nothing but chemicals and dirt which cannot be put to profitable use.*

fish even at the highest flows, but a second blow soon hit the fishery harder still.

In a process pioneered in London between 1810 and 1813, industrialists devised a method of producing flammable gas for street and domestic lighting by super-heating bituminous coal in airtight retorts. Instead of burning, the coal released its volatile constituents as a noxious brown smoke containing tar, ammonia, cyanide, carbolic acid and hydrogen sulphide. Later generations found new uses for these chemicals as insecticides, fungicides and early forms of tarmac which probably caused the black trout disease that destroyed many

MANCHESTER

Sewage effluents are hailed with delight as being the purest waters which these rivers hold…'

Worse than sewage effluent, paper mills were now using caustic soda for processing straw pulp, and industries downstream had to add water softeners before they could use re-abstracted water in their steam-boilers. At the top of the catchment, the Bacup Corporation reported that *'at eight o'clock one morning the river was a vivid orange colour, with suds rising eighteen inches high on the water, and by noon it had changed to an intense black'*.

By the 1970s, Mike still remembers it as "a miasma of colour - oranges, reds, cobalts and purples - cycling over the river to school, you'd have to hold your nose. The petrochemical industry set fire to the Ship Canal at least once, and most of the Irwell was biologically dead until the late 1980s. I won't make myself very popular with other northerners for saying this, but we were blessed with Margaret Thatcher and Michael Heseltine who kicked off the 25-year *Mersey Basin Campaign*. It's fabulous what they achieved: no salmon at all in 1999, forty in just ten days by 2006. Salmon and sea trout still can't get up the Irwell,

The Irwell near Ramsbottom

because there are at least two hydro schemes and four locks in the way, but they would if they could!"

Even if it's hard to imagine salmon spawning in the upper Irwell's high-energy gravels again, trout are certainly back. The headwaters above Bury were stocked with fingerlings in the 1980s, and the *Mersey Basin Campaign's* work continues with Salford Friendly Anglers' Society and their new pressure group Action Irwell.

Mike, Nick Carter and Tom Donnai, the club's new founding fathers, grew up on the banks of the river and watched it return from the dead whilst becoming accomplished international fishers and bloggers themselves, as much at home in Mongolia and the Pyrenees as wandering the edgelands of Salford and Manchester. Nick was the first of their acquaintance to catch a trout from the Irwell, and they resolved to protect the river's recovery by reviving the world's oldest angling club as north-west England's most powerful environmental lobbying organisation.

There are plenty of challenges ahead. In 2011 Mike identified at least 108 CSOs, 87 of them illegally unscreened in direct

Not all urban fishing is free

contravention of the Urban Waste Water Treatment Directive. Hundreds of trout were killed by two major chemical pollutions in 2010 alone, and repopulation of many stretches is restricted by the weirs which break up connectivity.

Despite a serious health advisory against humans eating trout from a river where the UK's last arsenic factory only closed in the 1970s, mink are prolific. Substrates throughout the catchment are still laced with a cocktail of lead, cadmium and other heavy metals, and the Manchester Ship Canal is so full of contaminated silt that it can probably never be dredged.

So maybe it's no coincidence that Irwell trout are often hard to hold for their Kodak moments, secreting extra slime to protect them from their post-industrial habitat. And it's all the stranger that you can sometimes fish the sandstone gorges of the upper river, surrounded by the ruins of mills crumbling back into banks of bramble and wild garlic, and genuinely feel you've been transported to the mountains of the former Yugoslavia.

In years to come, we'll probably recognise that England's very own urban Idrijca flows down through the hills north of Manchester, under the shadow of the M66 motorway. When that happens, I'll be glad that I was one of the first to rediscover it.

Tempted with an olive spider in the surface film: the author lands another spectacular Irwell trout

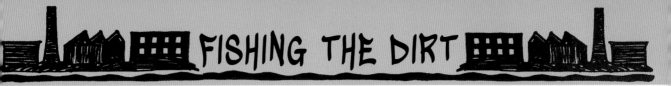

Manchester: River Irwell

Who's looking after the river?

Originally founded in 1817, Salford Friendly Anglers' Society was reconstituted in 2010 to protect the Irwell by creating north-west England's biggest environmental lobbying group.

The Society works with many local partners including councils, canoeing clubs, United Utilities and the Irwell Rivers Trust to raise the profile of the river, continue its revival, and ensure that as much as possible remains freely accessible.

In 2011 the Society joined the Wild Trout Trust's *Trout in the Town* initiative, started riverfly monitoring and launched the Action Irwell partnership.

The Irwell has also been identified by the Environment Agency as a pilot catchment for river restoration in partnership with local groups to meet the requirements of the Water Framework Directive. For more information, visit:
www.salfordfriendlyanglers.org.uk
http://actionirwell.blogspot.com plus
http://manchesterfishingfiend.blogspot.com
http://anglingforsomething.blogspot.com
http://tominargentina.blogspot.com

Getting there

Much of the Irwell is accessible from the Manchester Metrolink and the East Lancashire Railway, with stations at walking distances from the river.

Maps are available from local tourist information centres: OS Explorer 277 and 287 are also recommended.

Seasons and permits

Brown trout season runs from 15 March to 30 September.

Bury and District Angling Society controls 3 beats of the Irwell near Ramsbottom and Bury, but long stretches have fallen out of local clubs' interest as a result of the Irwell's industrial history. Salford Friendly Anglers' Society aims to secure as many outstanding fishing rights as possible before starting habitat work: fishing will then be available in perpetuity to all anglers with free Society membership and a valid EA rod licence. The Society has controlled the whole river within Manchester's inner ring road since the end of 2010, a total of 6 miles of double bank fishing. For full details, visit:
www.salfordfriendlyanglers.org.uk or search online for Bury and District Angling Society.

Fishing tips

Because larger fish can sometimes survive predation and pollution incidents better than smaller specimens, lower Irwell trout can run very large indeed: up to 10lbs in exceptional cases. Most are much smaller and a rod of 9 to 10ft, rated for a 4 to 6 weight line, is ideal.

The river's invertebrate populations were severely damaged by centuries of industry, and diversity is still limited in many areas. The upper river holds midge, olives, caddis and stoneflies, with shrimp and hoglice further down, but the best advice is to carry a wide selection of flies and be prepared to match the hatch.

Don't miss

● The Yorkshire and East Lancashire Railway: opened in 1846 as a transport link between Manchester and Rossendale, restored and reopened in 1987 as a heritage line

● The Irwell Sculpture Trail: one of the UK's largest public art schemes, a 33-mile walk following the river from Salford Quays to Rossendale

27

MANCHESTER AIRPORT

··

River Bollin

Fifteen years after the last muddy eco-warrior clambered out of the network of tunnels under the Bollin valley's ancient woodlands, the skies over Manchester are full of planes.

Charter-liveried Airbuses and Boeings thunder at full thrust into the clouds above Mobberley and Knutsford, heading out for sun, sea and sand. Coming home, the jumbos and twinprops stack for their final descent over Stockport's own 'Valley of the Kings', sardonically nicknamed for the landmark blue glass ziggurat office block that squats under the flightpath between the M60 and the infant Mersey. But coming or going, flaps down or throttles open, how many of Manchester Airport's twenty million annual passengers ever peer out of their portholes halfway down the mile and a half straight shot of Runway Two and think, *hang on, did we just go over a river?*

"Not many!" chuckles ecological consultant Pete Worral down the phone when I ask him this question. "But there's certainly a story to be told about the tunnel, the Bollin, the runway and the protests at

the time, and efforts of everyone involved to balance environmental and ecological needs with delivering a project at acceptable cost.

"Before the tunnel was even suggested, the local authority had mooted re-routing the river right round the end of the runway, and into a different catchment. At the time I thought I'd stymied our chances of working on this project by laughing outright – it wasn't just the technical issues but the whole principle of the idea. We studied the options between 1992 and 1993, and when the tunnel idea came forward in the mid-1990s, there was a lot of shock and horror. The public inquiry went through all the stages of asking whether we really could put a river into a 240 metre culvert on a sustainability ticket, so once the tunnel was definitely chosen, we had to make sure to do everything we could to minimise the ecological breach.

"For instance, Sheffield University looked at lighting the tunnel to sufficient lux levels to support the growth of plants: feasible, but the energy costs would have been astronomical, enough to run the

Most culverts offer very little casting space... but the Bollin tunnel is a notable exception

Proof of concept: a 17-inch trout from the Runway Two tunnel

whole airport. We studied angles of direct sunlight penetration too, which is one reason why the tunnel ended up being 25 metres high, and consideration was given to making part of the runway transparent to admit light. We went quite a long way with that one, but it was eventually rejected because of technical problems with giving glass a friction surface suitable for aircraft."

In the end, Pete and his colleagues were left with the challenge of reducing the impacts of a long dark tunnel. "Fortunately, tunnels aren't that unusual in nature: many rivers effectively run through tunnels of woodland, and a report by APEM concluded that fishery productivity is only reduced by canopy cover because shade restricts invertebrate populations so that some stretches become depauperate.

"We also examined issues of ichthyomechanics – coarse fish will move through tunnel systems, can salmonids do the same? – and we came up with a design involving a series of fixed boulders, each positioned in the channel according to the maximum water velocity against which trout can swim in a single burst. There are bat boxes at the apex of the tunnel, and we pushed

hard to incorporate weeping walls into the design: dry walls can be a real problem in preventing species from moving through areas like this."

To create the tunnel's parabolic arch at the mid-point of the runway, techniques were borrowed from the construction of Sydney's Olympic stadium: a system of wheeled hydraulic struts and trusses which travelled along tracks on either side of the river as each pour of concrete was completed. But the works were delayed by a significant stand-off with environmental activists. In January 2007, protestors started digging tunnels of their own in the Bollin valley, including one system dubbed 'Cakehole' which was described by breathless journalists as *'the most ambitious tunnel ever built in the path of a construction project… a fifty-foot-deep labyrinth with vertical climbs, acute angles, and hiding places protected by a series of steel-plated doors.'*

The previous year, activist Daniel 'Swampy' Hooper had been involved in direct action against the Newbury bypass: now he became a national celebrity after breaking all previous records with a week-long underground protest in the Bollin

168

valley. Other activists nailed themselves to trees and cemented their limbs inside oil drums, but Pete is scathing about their efforts: "I thought at the time it was a shame: they got lots of media attention, but when it came to the inquiry, there was no representation from the objector group at all. Had they turned up, they could have held a position of real power and influence. Instead they simply cost the project a lot of money and made themselves a danger to ancient woodland which wasn't even in the path of the runway, damaging trees and disturbing important badger setts."

Today, a strangely primaeval peace has returned to the jungles of willow that surround the middle Bollin. Nobody seems to notice a bloke with a fat black rod tube walking around the airport perimeter – and swinging a heavy Clouser Minnow under the cavernous arch suddenly connects me to one of the subterranean beasts I've come to find. With 747s bellowing like Jurassic monsters at either end of the tunnel, the big trout slogs angrily upstream through two sets of rapids, and I finally scramble down a battered ladder to wrestle him to hand on slipping sandstone-shingle banks in the neon half-light.

It's a visceral, Lost World experience, and it proves how successful this river-reconstruction project has been. As part of the Mersey system, within the economic catchment of the world's first industrial cities, the Bollin produced some of the earliest cotton, silk and woollen factory goods for export via the dockyards at Manchester and Liverpool. Even during the tunnel's planning phases, the river was heavily polluted with sewage from Macclesfield, but the £1 billion *Mersey Basin Campaign* eventually achieved major water quality improvements, and most of the catchment's natural processes were still miraculously intact.

Whereas the Bollin retained many of its natural meanders above the tunnel, the channel had already been straightened just downstream during the construction of Runway One. Adding the huge culvert would have created one continuous canalised section, so the decision was taken to return the downstream stretch to its pre-1970s state: using excavators and dumpers to re-cut three meanders, add riprap, scrapes and backwaters, and installing pre-planted coir rolls, mattresses and marginal vegetation. Along those

Cowslips have re-colonised the riprap banks at the end of Runway One

· ·

Keep clear: Manchester is the UK's third busiest airport

restored meanders, willow thickets now overhang current-sculpted sand and gravel pools, with good numbers of olives, caddis and midge, and local Environment Agency fisheries officer Andy Eaves confirms that he's seen trout up to three pounds in the tunnel area.

Since the 1990s, Pete has also worked on the Twin Rivers diversion around Heathrow Airport's Terminal 5 development, and his thoughts on ecological connectivity via rivers and woodland corri-

dors led directly to the development of the EA's big-picture *Mersey Life* programme. And he agrees that this level of river reconstruction really does work.

"What we've learned from the results of the Terminal 5 and Bollin projects is that river ecology can function even when it's confronted with almost insurmountable difficulties. Rivers and fish are adaptable: the system doesn't collapse, and the tunnel hasn't done the damage that most people had feared. On the contrary, I think it's a case study of what can be achieved even in the most adverse circumstances – a major civil engineering project delivering real environmental benefits. And I'd be quite surprised if there weren't one or two Mersey salmon running up and under the runway right now!"

Plane-spotters' paradise: a distant view of the airport's terminal buildings

Manchester Airport: River Bollin

Who's looking after the river?

Between 1985 and 2010, the 25-year *Mersey Basin Campaign* converted the Mersey from Europe's most polluted estuary to a haven for biodiversity that won the first International Riverprize in 1999. Inspired by the return of salmon to the system, the Environment Agency's *Mersey Life* programme is now addressing degraded and fragmented river habitats through a phased programme of river restoration.

More than 160 possible projects have been identified: the Bollin Valley Partnership and other local groups are involved in clearing invasive Himalayan balsam, known as 'Mersey weed' since it was introduced to the UK in 1839. Working with the Wild Trout Trust, the National Trust has also installed large woody debris in the river at Styal.

For the latest information, visit www.environment-agency.gov.uk

Getting there

The Bollin tunnel is about 45 minutes' walk from Mobberley station. Maps of the Runway Two Trail are available to download from: www.manchesterairport.co.uk OS Explorer 268 is also recommended.

Seasons and permits

Brown trout season runs from 15 March to 30 September; grayling season from 16 June to 14 March.

Manchester Airport's environment section allows free fishing with a valid EA rod licence in the Bollin tunnel area.

Fishing tips

In fly-fishing terms the middle Bollin is still largely undiscovered. Even before the installation of state-of-the-art fish passes on the lower Mersey, salmon and sea-trout were known to be running this river as well as the Goyt, Etherow and lower Tame, and they are now spawning successfully.

Trout to 3lbs have been caught in several areas, and grayling are present both upstream and downstream of Manchester Airport. The river also holds chub, dace, roach, perch and pike.

A rod of 9 to 10ft, rated for a 4 to 6 weight line, should cover most eventualities. Carry a well-stocked fly-box and be prepared to fish heavy nymphs or streamers through the dark, turbulent boulder cascades within the tunnel itself.

Don't miss

● The Bollin tunnel: 60ft high, 78ft wide and 260 yards long under Runway Two of Manchester's international airport

● Manchester Airport's Runway Visitor Park: complete with decommissioned Nimrod and Concorde aircraft

● The National Trust's Quarry Bank Mill at Styal: one of the best-preserved textile mills of the Industrial Revolution, now a working museum of the cotton industry with the largest working water wheel in Europe

28

NEW MILLS

Rivers Goyt and Sett

"Tree-kickers are just great as river restoration structures for urban rivers," enthuses Andrew Parker, leader of Disley and New Mills Angling Club's *Trout in the Town* chapter.

"The first time you get your chainsaw out and drop a tree in full leaf across the channel, it seems to fill the whole river and you think, *no, surely we'll never get away with this!* But you hinge the cut end of the trunk off the stump or another nearby tree, with bolts and 12mm braided steel cable, and the next spate simply picks the whole tree up and swings it parallel to the bank.

"Pretty quickly the leaves and twigs break off, and then you're left with this wonderful big piece of large woody debris scouring and size-sorting the gravels in the middle of the channel, and trapping sediment where the current is stilled among the larger branches. Anywhere the bank is unstable or prone to erosion, you're helping to prevent that, and the branches provide the perfect refuge for juvenile trout and grayling in high flows, or when the cormorants and goosanders are about. Frankly, for a river like the Goyt, it's hard to think of anything a tree-kicker isn't good for..."

Another sudden smile flashes across his face. "Well, that's not quite true... we did get one or two canoeists in the early days who thought we were trying to kill them. But we weren't, they lived to tell the tale, and we've managed to make some history by proving that tree-kickers can work just as well in this country as in the USA."

With only four years' work, Andrew and his small team have made a big impact on the Goyt, a classic Pennine spate river that rises on Axe Edge with the Rivers Dane, Dove, Manifold and Wye before flowing 24 miles north, across more than ten post-industrial weirs, to meet the Tame and form the Mersey at Stockport.

Where the Goyt joins the Sett between Disley and New Mills, the sudden combined force of the two rivers has sliced a gorge through sandstone cliffs 70ft high: a perfect location for hydropower old and new, but a stern challenge for any form of soft revetment or other river restoration structure.

A mile and a half downstream at Strines, the Goyt's floodwaters have usually lost little of the savagery that swept away bridges and mills in 1872 and 1930, and it was here that the fishing club and the Wild Trout Trust received consent from the Environment Agency to trial the UK's first urban tree-kickers in 2008.

Valley of viaducts: Torr Vale is a striking post-industrial archaeological park

Secured with steel cable, a tree kicker gets to work in a big Goyt spate

Four large alders were duly felled and anchored into position, where they held firm through a winter of spates that carried a much larger tree downstream and left it wedged against the buttresses of Strines Bridge. The most effective structures proved to be the ones anchored in the deepest water, where they could work in the widest range of flows. Best of all, when the EA electrofished this stretch in 2009, they found evidence of trout recruitment in an area that had always been devoid of juvenile fish: little trout that appeared when the electrodes were swept directly through the tree-kickers' tangled branches. "They do say trout live in trees," Andrew reminds me gleefully, "and if it can work on the Goyt, it can work in a lot of other places too."

The success of the Goyt's tree-kickers has interesting implications for urban river restoration everywhere. The EA's own guidelines are careful to grade the relative benefits of 'enhancement' and 'restoration': whereas enhancements are concerned with connectivity and smaller-scale works, restoration demands wholesale recreation of catchment-scale physical and biological processes, including *'significant increase in diversity of hydromorphological features'*: just the benefits that simple tree-kickers can start to provide.

Fresh from similar debates about flood defence on his home waters in Sheffield, the Wild Trout Trust's Paul Gaskell becomes almost lyrical when he's explaining how putting large woody debris back into urban rivers can actually help to reduce flood risk at a catchment scale. "It can sound counter-intuitive at first, but using wood in the channel to produce turbulence and greater hydrological roughness will spread the peak flood flows over a greater timespan. This does two things: it reduces the risk of a highly synchronous arrival of peak flows at a vulnerable bottleneck such as a bridge, and it reduces the maximum height of the flood peak. You still get the same area under the curve, but it's spread over a longer period, so the peak is lower."

Now, with EA permissions in place to extend the tree-kicker programme, and much more work already done with brash bundles and mid-channel cover logs, the whole Goyt catchment looks set to benefit from these learnings. And maybe not before time, because due to its location at the convergence of two capricious moorland rivers, New Mills has more reason than many small industrial towns to look askance at their flashiness and power.

After an early history of coal mining, cotton mills and print works were built in Torr Vale from 1788, with workers' cottages scrambling up the towering cliffs above them, sometimes perched one on top of another with doors at different street levels.

By 1810, there were nine spinning mills, three weaving operations, and at least three print factories, one of which invented the method of roller-based calico printing that later became the industry standard. Iron and brass foundries moved into the gorge after the flood of 1872, and the river was still plagued by pollutions until the early years of the twenty-first century.

Defying New Mills Council's efforts to clean up the river throughout the 1970s, anti-frothing agents from the bleach- and dyeworks further up the Goyt at Whaley Bridge were a persistent problem. In 2000 a spillage of sodium hypochlorite from a paper mill destroyed six miles of the river below New Mills: members of the fishing club apparently collected 90 dead fish from just one bend. Around the same time, cotton production finally ceased in Torr Vale Mill after more than 200 years, and its fire-damaged Grade II★ listed stonework now provides a poignant contrast to the gleaming Millennium Walkway which arcs almost 180 degrees around it on the other side of the river.

Bracketed by new and old, shiny and crumbling, the gorge is a good place to cast a line across the tannin-stained currents, and contemplate the parallel curves of industry and river restoration. Grayling lie in the deeper water where the mill's old tail race still cuts a channel into the bed of the river, rocketing up to snatch a fly from the meniscus so positively you'd think they were trying to make a point. And as we climb the hill back to the station, Andrew has his own philosophical moment. "You've got to take a long-term view of river restoration," he insists.

"Inevitably there's lots of excitement around a new project – in fact you've got to generate that excitement to make it happen – but that also means more publicity, more pressure on the fishery. If by chance you get a hard winter or two on top of that, it can really knock the fish stocks back, and people easily jump to the wrong conclusions. I know a couple of guides who say they used to catch three-pounders every time they fished the Goyt. Now, they complain about only catching them once a season.

"In the end, you just need to be realistic and concentrate on making the whole river system as sustainable and resilient as possible. So now I want to get more of those tree-kickers installed!"

Opposite Torr Vale Mill, the award-winning Millennium Walkway is daringly cantilevered off New Mills' Victorian railway embankment

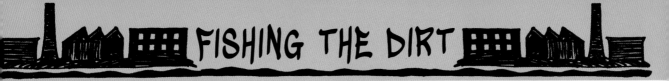

New Mills: Rivers Goyt and Sett

Who's looking after the rivers?

Since the 1970s, Disley and New Mills Angling Club has worked with New Mills Council to improve the condition of the river: hard work spearheaded by Martin Doughty who received a knighthood for his regeneration work in this area. The club joined the Wild Trout Trust's *Trout in the Town* programme in 2008, organising river clean-ups in partnership with other local groups, invertebrate monitoring, and pioneering the use of tree-kickers as river restoration structures in urban areas with partnership funding from the Environment Agency.

The river is also a key sub-catchment of the *Mersey Life* project. For the latest information, visit:
www.environment-agency.gov.uk
www.dnmac.org.uk

Getting there

The confluence of the Goyt and Sett is no more than 10 minutes' walk from either of New Mills' stations: New Mills Central and New Mills Newtown.

Maps of New Mills and Disley are available from New Mills Heritage and Information Centre, SK22 3BN: OS Explorer OL1 is also recommended.

Seasons and permits

Brown trout season runs from 15 March to 30 September; grayling season from 16 June to 14 March.

Disley and New Mills Angling Club controls long stretches of fishing on the upper Goyt and its tributary the Sett. For full details and a list of membership outlets, visit:
www.dnmac.org.uk

Fishing tips

In the 1970s Disley and New Mills Angling Club stocked the Sett with fingerling trout and grayling, which soon started trickling downstream to establish self-sustaining populations.

Both species now average around 10 inches, although exceptional trout can reach 3 to 5lbs, and grayling up to 16 inches have been recorded. The Goyt and Sett benefit from the tailwater effects of canal-supply reservoirs on their headwaters, while United Utilities' ongoing programme of moorland restoration will also reduce the catchment's flashiness, and protective structures like tree-kickers should help to prevent future loss of whole grayling year classes in peak flows.

In normal water conditions, local fly-fishers recommend using a rod of 8 to 9ft, rated for a 4 to 5 weight line. Flies with yellow and red tags are almost always useful for targeting grayling, while Andrew Parker recommends modern trout patterns like JT Olives, Deer Hair Emergers and very small CDC F-flies for imitating olives, sedges, buzzers and late-season terrestrial falls.

Don't miss

● The Torrs Millennium Walkway: opened in April 2000, partly supported on stilts sunk into the river bed, partly cantilevered off the sheer side of the railway embankment
● The One World Festival: a yearly event designed to raise awareness of environmental organisations and initiatives, including a campaign to make New Mills plastic bag free

White water: a kayaker prepares to paddle an autumn spate on the Sett

29

SADDLEWORTH

River Tame

In the steely sunlight of an early spring after-noon, heather is burning on the thousand-foot heights of the moor. Smoke curls away northward on the blustering wind: scarcely noticed by the day-trippers thronging Saddleworth's six villages on the first warm day after a long cold winter, less than the memory of the fog of manufacturing that once hung thick in the steep cloughs of the little River Tame.

Walking the photogenic streets of Denshaw, Delph, Dobcross, Diggle, Upper-mill and Greenfield today, you can read these valleys' whole industrial history in the architecture of their buildings.

Most are constructed from locally-quarried millstone grit: a greenish, coarse-grained sandstone composed of gravelly particles cemented with calcium carbonate. Gritstone is hard to carve, so Saddleworth's houses are plain and functional, lit by the long rows of south-facing mullioned windows that reveal their origins as weavers' cottages, often with date stones as their only external decoration.

In the sixteenth and seventeenth centuries, local farmers struggled to make a living from the Pennines' thin soils, and turned to cloth-making to supplement their income, weaving coarse woollen fabrics

as outwork from small-scale fulling mills. As home weaving became more profit-able, and new technologies like spinning jennies and flying shuttle looms required more space, many of Saddleworth's houses were extended vertically from two to three storeys, each with a dry, well-lit loomshop above the domestic living area. Designed to resist the rigours of the local climate, this was practical architecture as characteristic as the single-roofed chalet-barns of the Alps, and it helped Saddleworth's yeoman clothiers increase production from 8,640 pieces of cloth in 1740 to 35,639 in 1790.

At the same time, the traditional weavers' business was threatened by the economies of scale emerging in larger purpose-built mills. Powered by the Tame and its tributaries, these focused on scrib-bling (sorting threads by size) and fulling at first, but slowly took control of the whole production process. New communities grew up around the mills, particularly at Greenfield and Uppermill where the valley floor widened and the Huddersfield Narrow Canal and railway bound Saddleworth into the warp and weft of Britain's wider Indus-trial Revolution.

But the price of economic expan-sion was paid in human misery and social

Slow and sure: Adrian Grose-Hodge takes a stealthy approach on the upper Tame

179

unrest. In 1806, the area's embattled home weavers petitioned Parliament to restrict the number of looms and jennies in any one building, and food riots became common between 1795 and 1812. Packed into these

The massive Alexandra Mill in Uppermill

new urban developments, factory workers suffered too, and many marched under the radical 'Black Flag of Saddleworth' to join 60,000 other pro-democracy demonstrators at St Peter's Field in Manchester in August 1819: a protest that ended in the notorious bloodbath of the Peterloo Massacre.

And industrialisation continued. In 1839, a factory inspector reported 57 woollen and 39 cotton mills in Saddleworth employing 3,489 adults and 285 children. Ten years later, according to one travelling diarist, water and steam-driven mills were still rising *'on every hand'*, switching their powerlooms between wool and cotton according to market conditions. Bankfield Mill in Dobcross boasted a gasworks, a clock

tower and a beam engine three storeys high as well as a terrace of workers' cottages; Diggle's New Mill boasted the biggest water wheel in England with a diameter of nearly 65ft; and steam-powered Alexandra Mill can still be seen, towering over the smaller vernacular buildings of Uppermill and the riprapped channel of the Tame. Products included printed cotton calico, woven cotton conveyor belts and tyre fabric, woollen shawls and flannel, and felt for pianos, corn plasters and saddle wadding. On the Chew Brook, wool processing gave way to making cigarette papers from a mixture of flax and hemp: a French monopoly until the First World War, but a profitable UK business after that until the 1990s.

"Profitable, yes… and also hugely polluting!" reminisces Herman Wagler, president of the Saddleworth Angling Society. "Almost fifty years ago, when we formed the club to start cleaning up the river, there were still about half a dozen mills with access to water from the Tame. These days, they'd have to return the water above the point of intake, but there was none of that then: all the wool and cotton dyers would just empty their tanks and clean their chemical dye-vats straight into the river and be done with it.

"You'd always get the trout dropping down from the headwaters again, but the river took time to recover from each pollution. The six of us who formed the club lived for fishing in those days, we couldn't wait that long! So we asked the farmers who owned the fields for permission to fish – a bottle at Christmas was often all it took – which then enabled us to put pressure on the polluters for loss of amenity.

"The papermill at Greenfield on the Chew Brook was by far the worst. We collected samples and supplied evidence for the Rivers Authority prosecution, and even then the mill owners got the court hearing moved over to Huddersfield so it wouldn't appear in the Oldham press. But that frightened a lot of the other companies, especially the dyeworks at Delph which always seemed to clean its tanks into the river when people were off on holiday and wouldn't notice. After that, a lot of the industry declined by itself. Looking back, we made a lot of mistakes, but we also got a lot of things right – and it taught us there's much more to fishing than catching fish!"

Like all urban rivers, the Tame still exists under the constant threat of catastrophic pollution. Down the eastern edge of Manchester towards its confluence with the Goyt at Stockport, its lower reaches suffer from a range of diffuse and point-source pollution problems serious enough to warrant ongoing suspension from most of the Environment Agency's *Mersey Life* river restoration project. And even the upper areas of its 56-square-mile catchment aren't immune.

At Greenfield, the river is influenced by nutrients from the sewage treatment works, and in June 2009, in an incident alarmingly similar to the bleach pollution less than two years earlier on the River Wandle, a tank of sodium hypochlorite overflowed at Buckton Castle sewage plant near Mossley. Workers pumped the bleach out of a containment bund into a nearby surface water drain, believing that it was connected to the foul sewer: instead, the sodium hypochlorite ran straight into the Tame, damaging invertebrate life and killing hundreds of trout, chub, pike and minnows down a mile-long stretch of river.

United Utilities was fined £24,000 and ordered to pay £4,554 in costs, a penalty derided by local anglers as no more than an operating fee. A year later, another short-lived but unidentified pollution in a similar area also killed trout, pike and chub.

"There's a lot of very high-quality salmonid habitat in the upper reaches of the

Glowing colours from the Tame

Tame," admits the EA's *Mersey Life* project manager Katherine Causer, "but until the middle river's water quality issues are addressed in future rounds of United Utilities' asset management plans, there's not a great deal more we can do to get connectivity to the rest of the Mersey. But just wait and see…

the effects of the Water Framework Directive will have to kick in eventually!"

Stalking a trout under the stone-mullioned windows of Delph's Shore Mill

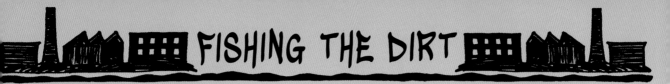

Saddleworth: River Tame

Who's looking after the river?

Saddleworth Angling Society was founded in the early 1960s by 6 local anglers determined to reduce pollution from the local textile industry and make the river sustainable as a trout fishery. The club now has around 350 members, and is working with schools in Uppermill to introduce fishing to the curriculum.

The Environment Agency monitors the river in its statutory capacity and as part of the *Mersey Life* project. For the latest information, visit:
www.environment-agency.gov.uk
www.igofilmguides.com/saddleworthangle.html

Getting there

The Tame is 5 minutes' walk from Greenfield station: from here, it's about 20 minutes into Uppermill along the main river.

Maps of Saddleworth are available from Saddleworth Museum in Uppermill, OL3 6HS; OS Explorer OL1 is also recommended.

Seasons and permits

Brown trout season runs from 15 March to 30 September.

Saddleworth Angling Society controls several miles of the upper Tame, from its confluence of the Chew Brook up to Denshaw, as well as much of the upper Huddersfield Narrow Canal and 7 mill dams and reservoirs.

For full details, visit:
www.igofilmguides.com/saddleworthangle.html

Fishing tips

The upper Tame and its tributaries are comparatively shallow headwater streams with small trout averaging 6 to 8 inches in length. Water levels in the Saddleworth area rise fast after rain, but drop and become fishable again very quickly. Some headwaters are impounded for public water supply, and compensation flows can produce tailwater effects and slightly larger trout. Unquantifiable volumes of water are also abstracted from the river by the Huddersfield Narrow Canal, and many pounds between the locks are heavily stocked with carp and roach. Grayling may also be present.

A rod of 7 to 8ft, rated for a 1 to 4 weight line, is ideal for tackling this variety of water. Invertebrate life is diverse, with reliable olive hatches throughout the year, so resident expert Richard Baker recommends imitative Griffiths Gnats and olive spiders backed up with Copper Johns and Pheasant Tail nymphs. In early season, stripping a Clouser Minnow through deep pools can pull up a few surprises.

Don't miss

- Saddleworth Museum in Uppermill: part of the former Victoria Mill, complete with salvaged looms and a replica of a local 1760s clothier's cottage
- Standedge Tunnel on the Huddersfield Narrow Canal: opened in 1811 and restored in 2001, the highest, deepest and longest canal tunnel in Britain
- Saddleworth's Whitsun weekend: internationally-famous brass band competitions and beerwalks

30

SHEFFIELD

....

River Don

"Look up there!" says Stuart Crofts as we pick our way along the roughly-eroded edge of the Don at Winn Gardens, 200 yards above the massive, aptly-named Niagara Weir. Three feet higher than his head, a continuous inch-thick seam of darker sediment runs through the sandy bank. "That's a solid layer of ash and slag," he reveals. "The Steel City gave the world some great products, but it wrecked the river at the same time. And now the river is recovering, and even the Industrial Revolution is passing into geology!"

I pick a piece of clinker out of the cliff, and ponder what Stuart has been telling me about the fall and rise of the Don. After a slow start during the late Middle Ages, Sheffield's early industrialists made up for lost time where the upper river met the Rivelin, Loxley and Sheaf on a marshy plain east of the Pennines. Making intensive use of water power, the first corn mills soon diversified into textile, paper and cutlery production: by 1770 there were 161 weirs between the growing city and the rivers' headwaters, the equivalent of a tilt forge or grinding wheel every 300 yards. The weirs and wheels cut off the salmon and sturgeon runs, while the mills also used vast quantities of river water to quench hot steel in the forges: heating, deoxygenating, and contaminating it with oil and other pollutants. By 1894, Tom Bradley wrote regretfully in his *Yorkshire Angler's Guide*, *'this once beautiful angling stream is now very highly polluted for the greater part of its course, and for a distance of forty-five miles is absolutely unfishable... about a mile below (Hazelhead) the ochre water from the Bullhouse Mines enters the river, and here the pollutions commence, and gradually increase from various sources all the way down until... the river becomes a solid, inky mass of pollution'.*

At Oughtibridge, paper mills dumped bleach and wood pulp into the channel, inflating biochemical oxygen demand even more dramatically than the sewage which poured into the river from every primitive drain and was only finally captured by the Don Valley Interceptor Sewer during the 1990s. In 1979, industrial discharges into the Don included mercury at 21 milligrammes per litre and coal solids at 100 milligrammes per litre. "You can still see fig trees growing along the Don," says Stuart, "because the mill workers would eat figs, the sewage would be piped straight down and out of the mills, and the fig seeds would root along the margins and thrive in the warm air from the forges!"

Stuart Crofts fishes upstream in the shadow of Sheffield Wednesday's Hillsborough stadium

Trout in the gutter: SPRITE's friendly angling competitions serve as useful population surveys of the Don's wild fish

From the development of crucible steel and Sheffield silver plate in the 1740s until the industry's sudden closure in the 1980s, Sheffield's heavy forges hardly missed a beat. During the First World War, the River Don Works rolled 16-inch armour plate for dreadnought battleships: in 1940 the Vickers factory was targeted by the Luftwaffe because it held the only 15-tonne drop hammer capable of forging crankshafts for the Merlin engine which powered both Spitfire and Lancaster aircraft. Even in the late 1970s and early 1980s, the arc furnaces near Rotherham were still setting new records for the quantities of steel smelted in a single day.

When Stuart took early retirement in 2009 after 33 years as a maintenance electrician in Sheffield's steel mills, he launched the *Adult Caddisfly Occurrence Scheme*, qualified as the Riverfly Partnership's northern tutor for the *Anglers' Monitoring Initiative*, and translated his 17-times experience on England's international fly-fishing team (twice as captain) into life as a full-time professional guide.

Meanwhile, shift patterns at the mills had also given him time to dedicate to restoring the Don to its former glory as a trout river. Inspired by anti-abstraction campaigner Gerald Stocks, and supported by the South Yorkshire branch of the Salmon and Trout Association, Stuart started using his civil rights to inspect the Public Water Register and force the factories to clean up their discharges by putting embarrassing information in the public domain – including an *exposé* of one mill with 28 outlets into the Don, every one of which was breaching its consents.

On the upper river above Penistone, Bullhouse mine had closed in 1957, but the abandoned workings continued overflowing into the river, coating its bed with ochre and suppressing the whole food web from diatoms up to trout. Stuart took his own campaign for remediation works onto local television, the BBC's *Countryfile* and *Today* programmes, and even arranged to have jars of the orange water displayed in the House of Lords. As a result, the Environment Agency and the Coal Board obtained part-funding from the European Commission for a £1.1 million scheme which oxygenates the minewater by passing it over cascades, encouraging the ochre it to drop out of suspension more quickly when it reaches a settling lagoon in a disused quarry. From here, the water seeps through a reedbed to trap any remaining fine particles: the final stage of a process that has restored almost four miles of the upper Don to health since 1998.

"It's miraculous how this river has been rescued in the space of two decades from problems that were just unbelievable," muses local historian Chris Firth, author of the monumental *Domesday to the Dawn of the New Millennium: 900 Years of the Don Fishery.* "But the headwaters were already clean enough in 1984 to introduce 200 grayling cropped from the Driffield West Beck by the National Rivers Authority. They spawned within months, there have been grayling in the Don ever since, and the ranunculus we brought back at the same time has now spread as far downstream as Doncaster."

With the basic ecological requirements for a thriving trout and grayling fishery in place, local people could start addressing the river's other post-indus-trial problems. To take responsibility for the stretch from Hillfoot Bridge to Winn Gardens, former Royal Marine John Blewitt formed a community interest company called SPRITE (Sheffield Partnership for Rivers in Town Environments) as part of the Wild Trout Trust's *Trout in the Town* programme. "I was fed up with the muck," he says bluntly. "The Don was the first river I fell in: I washed my face in it once and came out black! But now's the time to clean up the litter, and get the schools and youngsters involved.

"Historically the last thing riparian owners have wanted is responsibility for dealing with fly-tipping and keeping the river clean, so tracking them down for permission to remove rubbish and fish the river can be a hell of a job. And there can be up to fifty landowners per mile! But we've

Magnetic silt from the Don: largely composed of eroded slag

now achieved a general presumption that we can access the banks to improve them provided we don't try to pass the buck on the cost."

Some of the litter tells its own tales of the urban badlands, including bulk dumps of fertiliser bottles, rock wool and cannabis root balls from illicit marijuana farms. But by publicising SPRITE's clean-ups in the local press, the worst fly-tipping blackspots have already improved, and volunteers are moving onto tacking less exotic invasive plants like Himalayan balsam.

Volunteers often fish the river after clean-ups, meticulously noting their catches, and using friendly competitions as a way of recording the richness of the fishery in case of any future pollution disaster.

"Many people have said that if you cut me in half, you'd see the words River Don running right through me," Stuart told me in 2009, on the day he won the Wild Trout Trust's coveted Bernard Venables Award in recognition of his accomplishments since the 1960s.

"But that's not just me: it's also true for everyone else who's working on this river. Everything we do, we know beyond doubt that we're making a difference."

Exquisite micro dry flies for Sheffield's rivers, tied by Stuart Crofts

Paul Gaskell lands a steely grayling on his trademark beadhead duo rig

Sheffield: River Don

Who's looking after the river?

Sheffield Partnership for Rivers in Town Environments (SPRITE) was formed in 2009 as one of the Wild Trout Trust's first *Trout in the Town* chapters, working with the Upper Don Flyfishers, the Don Catchment Rivers Trust and other local groups. Seed funding was provided by sponsored fishing events organised by members of the Cressbrook and Litton Flyfishers' Club, and Yorkshire Water is investing heavily in full-catchment run-off modelling and fish refuges.

As a community interest company, SPRITE engages residents of all ages with the river, organising river clean-ups, invasive plant clearance, and invertebrate monitoring as part of the Riverfly Partnership's *Anglers' Monitoring Initiative*. SPRITE also runs a free-to-join fishing club to offer local anglers a chance to put something back into the fishing that they enjoy.

For the latest information, visit:
http://www.spanglefish.com/sprite-southyorks

Getting there

Sheffield's Supertram system provides many easy jumping-off points for the Don, via the blue and yellow lines from Sheffield station, and the Upper Don Walk also offers useful access. To reach the SPRITE-managed stretch of the river, get off the tram at Langsett or Primrose View for Hillfoot Bridge, Hillsborough for the Kraft factory area, and Middlewood Park and Ride for Niagara Weir and Winn Gardens.

Maps of Sheffield are available from Sheffield Tourist Information Centre on Norfolk Row, S1 2PA: OS Explorer 278 is also recommended.

Seasons and permits

Brown trout season runs from 25 March to 30 September; grayling season from 16 June to 14 March.

SPRITE has adopted and negotiated free fishing for its members on the River Don from Hillfoot Bridge to a point just above Niagara Weir at Winn Gardens: at least 2½ miles of fishing with a valid EA rod licence. Membership of SPRITE is free in return for contributions to the cause according to location and ability: desk-based involvement is gratefully accepted. For full details, visit:
http://www.spanglefish.com/sprite-southyorks

Fishing tips

The River Don is widely recognised as a prolific urban fishery, where trout are known to grow to more than 5lbs, and grayling to 1½lbs or more. You may also encounter barbel in deeper pools, and the lower reaches hold good populations of roach.

A rod of 9 to 10ft is ideal, rated for a 4 to 5 weight line. Due to nutrient enrichment, olives outnumber heptagenids on the main river, but the olive fishing is excellent. Stuart Crofts developed several series of dry fly patterns for the Don, including the SMC Emerging Olive, Dancer Soft-Wing Caddis, AB Midge and Greenfly. If nothing's hatching, Paul Gaskell recommends going deep with duo rigs featuring olive and other beadhead nymphs.

Don't miss

● Kelham Island Museum and Magna Science Adventure Centre near Rotherham: complete with recreated *son et lumière* steelworks

● Sheffield's famous independent breweries: including the Hillsborough Hotel which supports SPRITE with its special brew of Wobbly Wader beer

● Fish On Productions' *Urban Fly Fishing* DVD: featuring the Hillsborough Stadium stretch of the river

31

SHEFFIELD

Rivers Loxley, Sheaf and Rivelin

As you ride the intercity train into Sheffield from the south, the rails run down a broad valley with woods and terraced houses rising on either side, and you may catch tantalising glimpses of a river flowing through parklands and culverts just below the tracks. This is the Sheaf: the river that lent the city its name, and it's just one of several tributaries of the upper Don which offer urban fly-fishing as secret and intimate as the broad reaches of the main river can sometimes feel like the very public face of a still-working river.

Rising neatly parallel on the eastern slope of the Pennines, the Sheaf, Rivelin, Loxley and Porter Brook cut steep valleys into the millstone grit and iron-rich coal measures that once supplied the raw materials to launch Sheffield's development as one of the world's greatest industrial cities.

Today, those valleys are still thick with industrial archaeology and the remains of mills which once harnessed the water power generated by the rivers' torrential flows. The Sheaf falls a full 400ft to meet the Don from the point where its headwaters converge at Old Hay Brook, while the Loxley descends 280ft in six miles from Low Bradfield to Hillfoot, and the Rivelin valley

loses 260ft of altitude between Rivelin Mill Bridge and its confluence with the Loxley at Malin Bridge. As a result, each river was able to accommodate an astonishing number of mills. On the Loxley, you can easily find evidence of 24 weirs, wheels and forges, and the tree-lined gorge of the Rivelin valley still presents a patchwork of 21 dams designed to provide consistent off-line water supplies for the river's twenty mills. The Sheaf drove 24 mills along a five-mile length, plus another twenty sites on the brooks and dikes of its headwaters, and 21 on the Porter Brook which now meets the Sheaf in a culvert under Sheffield station.

Each river also developed its own industrial character. Medieval corn mills on the Loxley were converted to run cutlers' grinding wheels and forges, while the Rivelin's mills specialised in tool-making and grinding from an early date: Walkley Bank Tilt Mill used water-powered hammers to forge farming implements, Mousehole Forge became world-famous for its anvils, and the Nether Cut Wheel was still grinding scythes in 1939. A few miles further south, the Sheaf's millers diversified into paper-milling, saw-making and using water-powered bellows to smelt lead

Shaun Leonard and Paul Gaskell spot trout for Stuart Crofts on the Rivelin

from Derbyshire in specially-designed ore hearths. Some areas of the Rivelin's banks and bed are still composed of solid iron slag, and local fly-fishers like John Blewitt advise you not to disturb the sediments in the lower Sheaf's culverted stretches. "Offal was once dumped in the river where it ran past the city's slaughterhouses, and if you break through the overlying crust of newer silt and gravel you can still smell it!"

Throughout the industrial years, trout survived in the comparatively unpolluted headwaters, and even thrived in the Rivelin Valley and Damflask reservoirs, constructed between 1845 and 1896 to collect valuable rainfall for milling power and public water supply. According to angling historian Conrad Voss Bark, these impoundments became the cradle of modern stillwater fly-fishing in the 1880s, and Paul Gaskell, the Wild Trout Trust's *Trout in the Town* programme manager, can't resist a chuckle as he explains how the area's parsimonious industrialists inadvertently helped to secure the rivers' recovery when Sheffield's factories finally closed.

"The old mill-owners bulldozed legislation through Parliament to make sure

Safely released: a Sheaf trout goes back

they always had enough water and power for their mills, so we still get very significant compensation flows in the Loxley and Rivelin. That's important when you remember that the Don and Sheaf actually ran dry through the centre of Sheffield during the 1976 drought! I do wonder how much the reservoirs dampen the rivers' natural disturbance regimes, which can sometimes help diversity, but the flows are still very volatile, and the steep bedslopes mean that that most of the historic pollution has long since been swept away."

By design as well as by accident, Sheffield now claims to be one of the UK's greenest cities, and the Don and its tributaries have been the key to this modern urban landscape. Perhaps inspired by Sir Horace Walpole's description of *'one of the foulest towns in England, set in the most charming situation'*, 1920s urban planner Sir Patrick Abercrombie pitched the ambitious idea of surrounding Sheffield with a network of radial parks: riverside parkways along the Don, Rivelin, Loxley and Sheaf, modelled on *'the finest example in this country'* set by the tiny Porter Brook.

"There's definitely a local culture of public access hardwired into Sheffielders' consciousness," Paul tells me. "The 1932 mass trespass on Kinder Scout took place not far away, and the city fathers were very concerned to provide mill workers with exercise and access to green spaces, all the way out to the countryside, to offset the high levels of urban pollution and poverty. Those green corridors still provide us with plenty of access to the rivers, and now they're also letting wildlife back into the city: 74 species of birds, 21 of butterflies,

The reel deal: mayfly in the Steel City

and 367 of plants at the last count."

Since 2003, no-one has worked harder to enhance these river corridors than Environment Agency fisheries project manager Neil Trudgill, who has championed radical restoration works on the heavily-culverted Sheaf since 2003. The following year, Yorkshire Water took action on CSO pollution by installing a ten million litre stormwater retention tank under Millhouses Park beside the Sheaf, and in 2010 Neil finally got his chance to convert a nearby series of health-risk paddling pools into a long rock-ramp fish pass. It's a complex naturalised design incorporating pools, undercuts and resting spots to bypass two immovable weirs — and many species stand to gain from the long-term *River Sheaf*

Restoration Project, including trout, salmon, bullhead, lamprey, otters and even white-clawed crayfish, for which the river may become an important ark site.

Still, urban river restoration isn't always so straightforward, and you only need to travel a few miles across town to Malin Bridge to understand some of the tension between progressive fisheries conservationists and the old-school flood risk management section of the EA.

Where the minewater-ochreous waters of the Loxley meet the clearer, darker Rivelin between two long bridges, major flood defence works in 2009 removed over 20,000 tonnes of gravel, reinstated the head loss of long-buried weirs, and winched whole trees out of the river banks — destroying a shaded, naturalised channel, and replacing it with a shallow, featureless flat. Under pressure from the Wild Trout Trust, the Angling Trust and the Salmon and Trout Association, even senior EA figures were forced to concede that the river had been damaged, and the confluence has now been studded with boulders to improve the habitat until the area's gravels can be replenished by natural processes. But the incident still rankles. "There's simply no point in trying to make the plughole of any urban river bigger by dredging it," argues Paul, who brought the full firepower of his freshwater ecology PhD to bear on the debate from his home just around the corner.

"There are so many bridges and pinch points that you'll only make flooding worse if you speed the transit of water into these bottlenecks... instead, we need to find ways of turning down the taps and slowing down the water. Let's do what the residents did near the River Quaggy in South London: win a campaign for naturalised river channels rather than smooth, treeless concrete chutes under the slogan *'Flood the parks, not the properties'*. Reduced flood risk, better spawning habitat… result!"

Stuart Crofts fishes the Sheaf in Millhouses Park

Urban war zone: the junction of the Rivelin and Loxley before mitigation works to repair habitat destroyed by over-zealous flood risk management

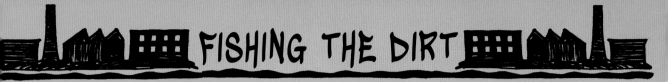

Sheffield: Rivers Loxley, Sheaf and Rivelin

Who's looking after the rivers?

Since 2003, the Environment Agency has focused on improving fish access and connectivity on the River Sheaf in conjunction with local groups including the Friends of Millhouses Park.

On the Rivelin, Sheffield Partnership for Rivers in Town Environments (SPRITE) is working with the Rivelin Valley Conservation Group to raise awareness of fisheries and invasive species issues, with joint Himalayan balsam pulling in summer 2011. The Angling Trust, Wild Trout Trust and Salmon and Trout Association have also been involved in negotiating mitigation for over-zealous flood risk management works at the confluence of the Rivelin and Loxley.

For the latest information, visit:
www.spanglefish.com/sprite-southyorks
www.rivelinvalley.org.uk
www.wildtrout.org
www.anglingtrust.net
www.salmon-trout.org
www.environment-agency.gov.uk

Getting there

The Sheaf at Millhouses Park is 2 minutes' walk from the Abbeydale Park and Ride terminus, with regular buses from central Sheffield. For the junction of the Rivelin and Loxley, head for the Supertram terminus at Malin Bridge.

Maps of Sheffield are available from Sheffield Tourist Information Centre on Norfolk Row, S1 2PA: OS Explorer 278 is also recommended.

Seasons and permits

Brown trout season runs from 25 March to 30 September. No grayling are present in the Don's tributaries.

Sheffield City Council allows free fishing on the urban, publicly-accessible stretches of the Sheaf and Rivelin with a valid EA rod licence. On the Loxley, SPRITE have negotiated two-thirds of a mile of free fishing alongside the Loxley Park mill redevelopment, up to the red and white sign denoting the start of private land. (If you park your car at Loxley Park, please leave your details at the reception desk).

Fishing tips

Apart from being significant spawning and nursery areas for the main river, the Don's tributaries hold good populations of wild trout in their own right. At around 9 inches, average size in the Sheaf is slightly larger than either the Rivelin or Loxley, but you stand a strong chance of encountering trout up to 1½ lbs almost anywhere in these torrential, feature-packed little rivers.

For most situations, a rod of 7 to 8ft is ideal, rated for a 1 to 4 weight line. If you fish a nymph, be prepared to get wrapped up in snags of subsurface industrial archaeology, especially on the Loxley. Unusually, the Don tributaries feature prolific mayfly hatches in early June: Paul Gaskell also suggests patterns to imitate olives, hydropsyche caddis and black gnats on the Sheaf, plus brook duns and heptagenids for cobbly riffles on the Loxley and Rivelin.

Don't miss

● Abbeydale Industrial Hamlet: a working museum on the River Sheaf, based on a nineteenth century steelworks

32

SLAITHWAITE

River Colne

"I simply cannot stress how good the fishing was on the Colne," declares Richard Baker. "It was better than any other river you and I have ever fished, anywhere.

"I was living in London at the time, before our work on the Wandle had really kicked off, and I hadn't yet discovered the full potential of the Tame, when I picked up a call from one of my oldest fishing pals. Andy was working as a teacher, and he was very keen and conscientious, but he told me he'd found this amazing fishing spot in Milnsbridge, and told me to drop every-thing, take a sickie if I had to, and meet him on the river right away.

"So I drove across to the Colne, and he was right. It was amazing… shallow pool after shallow pool, all stuffed with trout and grayling… you'd catch ten or fifteen fish from one pool, often with double hook-ups on a two-nymph rig. But Andy would be saying *come on, keep moving, there's plenty more water upstream that you haven't seen yet!* We ended up fishing the river for years, and it was never less than sensational."

Although Richard and Andy didn't know it at the time, the circumstances that created those hundred-fish days on the Colne were far from accidental. In the mid-1970s, as Yorkshire's textile trade contracted, and the mills and all their attendant gasworks and foundries fell silent, members of Slaithwaite and District Angling Club began to think about reviving the river as a viable fishery.

None of the river's indigenous trout had survived the Industrial Revolution, but thousands of fry were stocked over many years to kick-start a new population in the headwaters around Marsden, and the Environment Agency introduced 25 pairs of grayling to the Linthwaite area in the late 1980s. Both experiments worked: trout and grayling began breeding successfully, and club members like current chairman Ray Collier came to regard the Colne as one of the best wild salmonid fisheries in Yorkshire.

But trouble was on its way. Although the valley's industrial past had revolved around processing wool, silk and cotton, the chemical businesses that now took over many of the redundant milling sites threat-ened even worse consequences for water quality. Richard sums up the problem succinctly: "The trouble with all these old northern mills is that there's always one pipe going into the site, and one coming out. So if anything gets spilled inside the mill, it runs straight out of one of those pipes into the river. And God help the river if the spillage is poisonous!"

Hoping for a trophy, Richard Baker lets rip with his heavy-duty streamer set-up in central Slaithwaite

Forgotten wilderness: Slaithwaite's mills have mostly turned their backs on the river

Seen from this angle, the succession of pollutions that devastated the Colne between 2007 and 2010 assumes a hideous sense of inevitability. Barely two months after a deadly detergent spill on the Holme swept down into the Colne in December 2007, local EA officers were out on the river again, investigating a slower-acting pollutant that killed several hundred trout, grayling and stone loach in the four-mile stretch between Slaithwaite and the Aspley canal basin: a mysterious episode that remains unresolved.

Thirteen months later, another point-source pollution proved far more obvious. A trail of over 400 distressed and dying fish led the EA all the way from central Huddersfield to Slaithwaite's Spa Fields industrial estate, where a pipe was discharging a milky white mixture of permethrin and deltamethrin: chemicals used for making nit shampoo and other pesticides, in concentrations thirteen and four times the maximum permitted level.

In the criminal prosecution that followed this category one offence, Sub Micron Industries admitted cleaning protective overalls in a washing machine that had been inadvertently plumbed to surface water drains rather than the sewage system, and the court decided on a penalty of £4,500 plus £3,580 costs.

Yet the Colne's catastrophes still hadn't reached their crescendo when Huddersfield magistrates imposed the Sub Micron fine on Monday 17 May 2010. In the early hours of the very next Monday morning, several fierce explosions ripped through the Grosvenor Chemical works on the banks of the river between Slaithwaite and Milnsbridge, igniting a firestorm in a warehouse that took 150 fire-fighters four days to bring under control.

As a cloud of smoke and chemicals drifted down the valley, the EA scrambled quick-reaction teams from its newly-formed air quality cell for the first time since the

Buncefield blast at Hemel Hempstead, and warned local people to stay indoors and keep their livestock away from the Colne and the canal. Yorkshire Water did everything possible to contain contaminated water used to put out the fire, but toxic chemicals flooded into the river under a froth of fire-suppressant foam: a cocktail of constituents for glue, weed-killers and creosote products. British Waterways closed its lock gates all the way to the Calder, while Ray and his colleagues could only watch the unfolding disaster in disbelief.

"We didn't see as many dead fish this time," he says mournfully, "but that's because the river was still very sparsely populated after the last pollution. After the Sub Micron incident, you looked into the water and there were little gold ingots and diamonds everywhere: trout, grayling, stone loach and minnows, all dead, all littering the bed of the river. We've been talking to the Angling Trust about compensation, but we really don't know how we'd spend the money. And the risk of pollution will be with us for as long as there are chemical works in the valley."

As I write this, Grosvenor Chemicals' case has yet to come to trial, but the river is slowly recovering. Although the Milnsbridge stretch is heavily engineered and constrained by large weirs at either end, and countless numbers of invertebrates as well as trout and grayling were killed, the EA has now been able to restock more than seven thousand grayling – and there are other local initiatives that may also help to boost the river's future fly-life. As a result of the *Greenstreams* project, which covers the full 13 miles of the Colne as well as the urban centre of Huddersfield, 24 invertebrate monitors have been trained by the Riverfly Partnership to detect point source and other pollutions. And on the flipside of the Calder and Colne Rivers Trust's practical plans for reintroducing invertebrates across the catchment, the Wild Trout Trust's programme manager Paul Gaskell has already rolled out his *Mayfly in the Classroom* educational project to several schools in the city.

"Soon after the inception of *Trout in the Town*," he says, "it became clear that a cheap, simple educational tool would be a really valuable means of generating public interest and a sense of custodianship in local communities for their urban corridors. *Trout* and *Salmon in the Classroom* have been brilliantly successful where funding and support resources are available, but

Northern gold: a wild trout from the Colne

I wanted to find an alternative, cheaper means of communicating the delicacy and importance of our stream foodwebs and their indicator species.

"The cost of a whole *Mayfly in the Classroom* set-up is less than £20: you could probably even reduce that by salvaging the two-litre fizzy drink bottle from your local river when you take the kids to collect the mayfly larvae! Then you use a simple aeration system and a very low-tech cooling apparatus such as freezer packs in a water bath to keep the nymphs alive for approximately two weeks, transferring them into a perforated box in a refrigerator when they hatch. The kids maintain all the correct temperatures for the nymphs and adults, observe the mayflies until they undergo their unique second moult from duns into full imagos, and then release them as adult flies at the streamside. It's a great way of using the iconic life-cycle and literary status of the mayfly, to say nothing of all those Shakespearean sex-and-death overtones, to make a really profound impression and get people thinking about their local river!"

Between Slaithwaite and Linthwaite, a bank of invasive Japanese knotweed buffers the river from a vast covered wood-yard

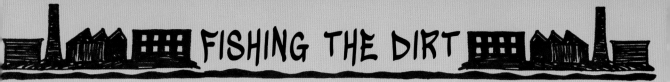

Slaithwaite: River Colne

Who's looking after the river?

Slaithwaite Angling Club and the Environment Agency have been working to improve fish populations in the Colne since the 1970s, and are now partners in the *Greenstreams* campaign, which was launched in 2008 to re-establish Huddersfield's rivers and canals as community assets.

Future river restoration work will be guided by the Wild Trout Trust's *Trout in the Town* programme, which has also provided formal 'train the trainer' sessions to roll out the successful *Mayfly in the Classroom* community engagement project across the Kirklees Education Authority area.

For the latest information, visit:
www.slaithwaitedistrictanglingclub.org
www.calderandcolneriverstrust.org
www.mayflyintheclassroom.org
www.urbanmines.org.uk

Getting there

The Colne is 5 minutes' walk from Slaithwaite station.

A map of the town water beats is available in Slaithwaite and District Angling Society's guide to fisheries: OS Explorer 288 and OL 21 are also recommended.

Seasons and permits

Brown trout season runs from 25 March to 30 September; grayling season from 16 June to 14 March.

In addition to numerous stillwaters and sections of local canals, Slaithwaite and District Angling Club controls the Colne in Slaithwaite below Linthwaite Steps and above the footbridge in the town centre: up to a mile of fishing. Kirklees Council allows free fishing with a valid EA rod licence where ownership of fishing rights is unclear. For full details and a list of membership outlets, visit: www.slaithwaitedistrictanglingclub.org

Fishing tips

Before recent catastrophic pollutions, the Colne produced a trout of 12¾ lbs in the Milnsbridge area, and populations are now recovering thanks to natural recruitment and grayling restocked by the EA. In the thin water above Slaithwaite, plenty of juvenile trout are present in the 4 to 6 inch class: further down, you may find the odd larger specimen of 9 to 12 inches that's educated enough to escape water quality problems by running up side streams, but very few smaller fish.

A rod of 8 to 9ft is ideal, rated for a 3 to 5 weight line. Even where the water is impounded by weirs, fish are active to the surface, and midge imitations work well in this chironomid-rich environment. For winter grayling fishing in deeper, faster stretches, Richard Baker proposes multi-fly rigs with tungsten bead-heads and shrimp patterns to help you cut quickly through the water column and locate tight shoals of fish.

Don't miss

● Huddersfield Narrow Canal: completely re-excavated and restored along Slaithwaite's high street

33

SOWERBY BRIDGE

River Calder

Across the spine of the Pennines at Calder Head, rainfall seeps through the stalks of heather and cotton-grass to form two rivers. To the west of the watershed, the Lancashire Calder cuts a tiny thalweg downwards to Burnley, Padiham and the Ribble at Mitton. And the Yorkshire Calder trickles east, its darkly tannic waters skirting a landfill site and the rubble of opencast mining, searching out the Aire at Castleford, the Ouse at Airmyn, and finally the North Sea at Hull.

In the steep valleys of its upper catchment, the Yorkshire Calder and its tributaries are already constrained: prevented from wandering naturally across their landscape by laboriously-constructed riprap walls planted with alders whose root systems knit the gritstone slabs in place. But the full-catchment straitjacket becomes even more formalised in the old mill towns of Hebden Bridge, Todmorden and Sowerby Bridge, with dressed-stone and concrete walls, and massive weirs impounding up to half a mile of river each.

"Apart from CSOs and the risk of accidents in chemical factories, the 400 weirs in the catchment are undoubtedly the Calder's biggest problem," says Ian Oates, director of the Calder and Colne Rivers Trust. "Once upon a time, these structures might have had the benefit of buffering interruptions to the river's flow, even providing refuges when the mills were filling their offline reservoirs and whole sections of the channel would often run dry – which often used to happen here, as well as on the Sheffield Don and many other rivers – but that's not a worry any more.

"Most of them are totally impassable obstructions that stop fish from following their migratory instincts, give them nowhere to hide in case of pollution, and force them to complete their whole life-cycle in just one area of habitat. For instance, we frequently find good-sized trout dropping down into the weirs from the upper tributaries when flows are lower in summer, and not being able to get back up again on their natural spawning run. There's just enough gravel for them to spawn in some of the weir sections, so they breed there and turn carnivorous, eating their own fry.

"Fortunately for everyone, and thanks to a fish pass that's recently been installed at Castleford, we know that salmon are now making their way up the lower Calder as far as Brighouse – and of course salmon are a priority under the Water Framework Directive! So we're collaborating with the

Urban warriors: Duncan Soar, Adrian Grose-Hodge and Richard Baker gear up for sub-arctic grayling in Sowerby Bridge

A Calder grayling for Paul Gaskell

Environment Agency and British Water-ways, taking an opportunistic approach to demolishing or mitigating their weirs one by one, working our way up from the very bottom of the river. What's passable for salmon should also be passable for eels and many other species: we've already got confirmed otter sprainting sites throughout the catchment, dippers and kingfishers are increasing in numbers as water quality continues to improve, and even Daubenton's bats are finding usable habitat once more."

As we weave back and forth across the Calder's narrow bridges in Ian's battered four-by-four, it's impossible to miss the vast ponded areas behind each weir, the acres of invasive Himalayan balsam and Japanese knotweed spreading along the banks, and the towering walls of the old woollen and cotton mills falling sheer to the water's edge. In this crowded, claustro-phobic valley, there hardly seems enough room for the roads, the railway, the mills and the river. Almost every square foot of land is occupied, and many of the older buildings are already being converted into apartments for Manchester's affluent new commuter belt. It's a re-imagining of the post-industrial landscape that often retains the picturesque shells of the multi-storey spinning mills, but sweeps away the single-storey weaving sheds with their saw-tooth roofline of north-facing skylights: too hard to convert from industrial to chic, and a waste of valuable real estate.

Having spent the last 27 years restoring his own rural tributary to a state

204

of near perfection, Ian is rolling out everything he's learned to these urban corridors of the Calder and Colne. By taking down the weirs, he explains, flood risk for the residential developments will be reduced, and the river will be able to start re-cutting its own pool and riffle sequence: maybe with results not too different from the new canoe slalom course in the middle of Sowerby Bridge, where carefully-positioned boulders create a highly-fishable sequence of pinch-points, pools and runs in the over-wide channel. "But we've also got to think about water quality," he emphasises.

"Because today's road and urban drainage systems are so efficient, the whole of the upper catchment suffers pervasive point-source pollution from overloaded sewers that cause CSOs to discharge before the rivers are running high enough to dilute them, especially because many of the headwaters are buffered by reservoirs. Then there are the misconnections, which are next-to-impossible to trace. When old farm buildings are converted for residen-

tial use, the sewers are often plumbed into the nearest big pipe, with no real knowledge of where the pipe actually goes, even if it's straight into the nearest river. It's well known that trout don't mind a bit of organic enrichment, but a constant stream of raw sewage is no good for the fish or the invertebrates."

Although the upper Calder powered plenty of medieval corn and fulling mills, and Yorkshire's first fully integrated woollen mill complex was established at Sowerby Bridge between 1778 and 1792, the river's original fishery seems to have been resilient enough to resist the effects of industrial intensification and population growth until 1850. Fish were a major source of nutrition for the valley's residents, and commercial netsmen operated throughout the catchment: five different types of salmon were said to run the river, and the vicar of Knottingley described 'Graylings, Chubs, Barbules and Smelts' as his favourite catches.

Under the arches: upstream nymphing

When the ecosystem did collapse, it failed so spectacularly in just two years that the government sent inspectors to investigate, but their findings made no difference. By 1894, the river could only be described by Tom Bradley in his *Yorkshire Angler's Guide* as *'an inky cesspool'*, a condition it retained until sewage treatment improved in the 1950s.

Since then, serious coarse angling has already migrated downstream by ten or fifteen miles, many local clubs have developed game fishing sections, and I can't help recalling something I heard from photographer Rod Calbrade in 2003 after he'd shot an urban fishing story a few miles below Sowerby Bridge. "As the river became cleaner, trout started taking over from roach and bream in the canalised stretches, and the coarse fishermen were saying to the EA: give us our pollution back again!"

It's a tale that rings true on many urban rivers, and it's entirely typical that Ian also plans to go one better. "In recent years we've had a couple of sewage and diesel pollutions in this area," he says, "but now we're achieving a baseline of decent water quality, I want to get the fly-life back too. I know how to do it, because I did it on my home river: collecting spinners from other waters over the course of several evenings, keeping them on ice in a cool-box, then releasing them to lay their eggs in an area where I'd already got the habitat absolutely right. That's why I'm now seeing some of the best hatches in Yorkshire: blue-winged olives, mayflies, turkey browns, iron blues, you name it."

He winks at me. "I get things done!"

Fishing the canoe course in Sowerby Bridge

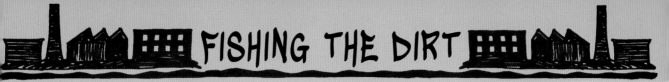
Sowerby Bridge: River Calder

Who's looking after the river?

The Calder and Colne Rivers Trust was formed in 2008, and became a charitable trust in 2010. Inspired by steady improvements to the catchment's water quality, the Trust now intends to tackle connectivity problems, point-source pollution and other legacies of the Industrial Revolution, and ensure that the health and biodiversity of the Calder and its tributaries continue to improve.

Other initiatives include catchment-wide riverfly monitoring, educational schemes with riverside visits linked to the national curriculum, and coaching teenagers in fly-fishing as a life skill.

For the latest information, visit:
www.calderandcolneriverstrust.org

Getting there

The Calder is less than 5 minutes' walk from Sowerby Bridge station.

A map of the town water beats is available in Ryburn and Halifax Angling Society's membership booket; OS Explorer OL 21 is also recommended.

Seasons and permits

Brown trout season runs from 25 March to 30 September; grayling season from 16 June to 14 March.

Ryburn and Halifax Angling Society controls long stretches of the Calder above and below the centre of Sowerby Bridge, as well as 2 miles of the Calder and Hebble Canal. Calderdale Council allows free fishing with a valid EA rod licence from the bridge below the canoe slalom course upstream to the cricket pavilion: about 400 yards of free fishing.

For full details and contacts for membership enquiries, visit: www.ryburnandhalifax.com

Fishing tips

Compared to smaller tributaries like the Colne, the Calder is a challenging river to fish, with a reputation for being the place where local guides spend their days off. As such, its large impoundments have been known to hold trout up to 8lbs and grayling over 3lbs, but productive areas can be very localised as well as heavily dependent on the river's recent pollution history.

A rod of 9 to 10ft, rated for a 4 to 6 weight line, is ideal for the Calder's wide water and specimen fish.

Ian Oates strongly recommends sedge and large dark olive patterns for your dry fly box: small Pheasant Tail nymphs and Yorkshire spiders are sufficient for subsurface work in low water, but tungsten-loaded Czech-style shrimp, olive and heptagenid patterns may be needed in winter.

Don't miss

● Wainhouse Tower: reputedly the world's tallest folly at 275ft, originally designed as a chimney for John Wainhouse's dyeworks in the 1870s, but completed as an ornate tower with 403 internal stairs to a viewing platform

34

BARGOED

Rhymney River

"It's complicated!" Dai Roberts lowers his pint, wipes his beard thoughtfully, and gazes out of the window of the Bedwellty Church Inn, down into the valley where the Rhymney flows invisibly through its deep screen of trees.

"Not long ago, someone from the Environment Agency told me that this is a very unlucky river, and I think she was right. You know the way all rivers aggregate the problems in their catchments? Well, all those other rivers' problems are represented on the Rhymney, so a lot of people can learn valuable lessons from what we've achieved. But that still doesn't help us very much right now…"

As secretary of Aberbargoed Anglers, Dai couldn't have been in a better position to notice when the full complexity of the Rhymney's modern problems began to emerge in 2002. "During our start of season competition that year, not a single member caught or even saw a fish. We began turning over the rocks, and found the river almost devoid of insect life. When we contacted the Agency, their appraisal team came to the same conclusion, and offered to help us investigate."

From his previous career as a biochemist, Dai knew that freshwater shrimp could be used like the traditional miners' canaries as a proxy test for chemical water quality, and he designed a cage that would allow him to suspend a number of shrimps in the river's water column and check for mortalities on a daily basis.

It was labour-intensive work, but with every successive spate he was able to trace the source of the shrimp-killing pollution further upstream through the river and its tributaries, finally narrowing the search to a single culvert entering the tiny headwater Nant Melyn.

At that point, the EA stepped in with more technical equipment: semi-permeable monitoring devices that use a layer of fat on a thin membrane to absorb minute traces of chemical pollution, each of which cost £300 to analyse.

"Pyrethroid insecticides occur naturally in chrysanthemums," Dai explains, "but they're not very stable, so the laboratories developed a range of much more stable and toxic synthetic pyrethroids. These were used for cypermethrin sheep dip and spraying newly-planted trees in forestry operations: in this instance we discovered that there was a factory making wooden buildings on an industrial estate near Tredegar that was treating its timber

Industrial archaeology on the Rhymney

with permethrin and then storing it uncovered in the yard.

"Whenever it rained, polluted water was running off the wood and sawdust, down a surface water drain, straight into the Nant Melyn and then the Rhymney. After the collieries and steelworks closed in this area, the Welsh Development Agency built enormous numbers of factories to attract new industry and investment, but there was never much scrutiny of what those factories might actually be making or discharging

into the local environment. And this was a case in point."

Indeed it was. For the very first time, sharing data and establishing trust between the angling community and statutory bodies like the EA led to an outstandingly successful criminal prosecution in 2009, when Abertillery Magistrates' Court fined Kingspan Off-Site almost £7,000 under the Water Resources Act 1991. By this time the business had already relocated its activities to Milton Keynes, and Dai could turn his attention to the Rhymney's remaining problems.

Meanwhile, others had also been worrying about rapidly declining fly-life in Britain's rivers. From 2001, when the Natural History Museum started working with English Nature, the Riverfly Recording Schemes and the John Spedan Lewis Trust to train fly-fishers to gather and identify standardised samples of aquatic invertebrates and use the results to assess water quality, this backwater of citizen science became steadily more mainstream.

After the first Riverfly Conference in 2004, the Riverfly Partnership was created, supported by a steadily-growing network of observers under the banner of the national *Anglers' Monitoring Initiative*. Based on Dai's learnings and the EA's Biological Monitoring Working Party protocols, trained *AMI* volunteers make regular visits to key locations on their rivers: for instance, where a tributary joins the main river, or just above and below a suspected source of pollution. At each site, a standardised three-minute kick-sample is taken, and the abundance and diversity of eight key groups of invertebrates are counted and translated into a simple algorithm to indicate the river's ongoing water quality.

The most pollution-sensitive species such as stoneflies and mayflies score highest, while a river containing only leeches and hoglice is clearly suffering from problems: as seen on the Rhymney, shrimp can't endure chemical pollution, but can often thrive on organic enrichment from sewage and phosphate fertilisers. If invertebrate levels drop dramatically between one monitoring visit and the next, this suggests that pollution has occurred, and each *AMI*'s co-ordinator has a hotline to the EA to trigger an official investigation.

Because the EA's own monitoring programme has been steadily eroded from regular twice-yearly visits to little more than reactivity to suspected problems, such constant surveillance by enlightened fishers

Dai Roberts' gammarus cage: each cell holds a shrimp to detect chemical pollution

can add a layer of real science to the usual eyes and ears on the riverbank. "Since the Kingspan case, other local industries know we're watching," Dai smiles with satisfaction, "and I'm pretty sure the numbers of pollution incidents have dropped as a result."

Even so, the Rhymney continues to be haunted by its industrial heritage. In the early 1900s, while every stream in the area ran Bible-black with coal dust, Bargoed colliery set at least two world records for the weight of coal produced in single shifts. When the pit finally closed in the 1970s, its legacy was Europe's largest colliery slag heap, burning internally and towering 400ft over the river.

Most of the colliery site is now occupied by Bargoed Woodland Park, but only because the land proved too contaminated to redevelop for housing and a new electronics factory, and Dai fears that PCBs, PAHs and other insidious pollutants are still leaching into the Rhymney. Iron-rich water also overflows into the river from abandoned mine-workings, coating rocks in orange ochre and reducing the amount of algae and diatoms for invertebrates to feed on: another stress on the system. And the sandstone valley is so steep that the area's main trunk sewer follows the Rhymney all the way, studded with CSOs that overflow every time it rains, and advertise their presence with a constant tang in the air and debris on surrounding trees.

"When the Rhymney Valley Trunk Sewer was built in 1926," Dai concludes, "Bargoed's population was smaller, and people used less water. Now most of the sewers are surcharged even at low summer levels, and there's a lot of consented industrial effluent. At the same time, maintenance of the infrastructure has gone downhill: whereas the old water companies used to send teams round once a month to deal with blockages, Welsh Water's current approach is 'repair and maintain', so it took them six weeks to repair one 20ft section of pipe, and six years to dig out another collapsed pipe that was causing a CSO to overflow almost continuously.

"The Nant Bargoed branch is now being replaced, but the whole trunk sewer really needs relaying. And how soon can you see that happening, here or in any of the other valleys? This is one of the best maintained and keepered stretches of river in the whole of south Wales – but until the CSO problem is solved, there may really be a limit to what we can do for the Rhymney."

One picture, many problems: CSOs, fly-tipping, Himalayan balsam and Japanese knotweed

FISHING THE DIRT

Bargoed: Rhymney River

Who's looking after the river?

Since 2004, thanks to Aberbargoed Anglers, the Rhymney has been the most intensively monitored catchment in Britain, with 18 invertebrate sampling sites on 26 miles of river.

As the Riverfly Partnership's pilot for the national *Anglers' Monitoring Initiative*, the club's volunteers have supplied key evidence for the Environment Agency to successfully prosecute an industrial polluter on the upper river, as well as on the neighbouring Sirhowy. Other projects include clearing invasive plants, reducing overshading, installing soft bank revetments, and close collaboration with the Rhymney River Federation of Angling Clubs and Rhymney River Task Group (Caerphilly County Borough Council, EA, Welsh Water and the Coal Authority).

The Riverfly Partnership is a national organisation which aims to further the understanding and conservation of riverflies and protect the quality of Britain's rivers, by bringing together anglers, conservationists, entomologists, scientists, water course managers and statutory authorities to increase understanding of riverfly populations.

For the latest information, visit: www.riverflies.org

Getting there

The Rhymney River is 5 minutes' walk downhill from Bargoed station. OS Explorer 166 is recommended.

Seasons and permits

Brown trout season runs from 3 March to 30 September.

Aberbargoed Anglers control a mile and a half of fishing on the west bank of the upper Rhymney, above the bridge over the river at Bargoed. Caerphilly County Borough Council also allows free fishing for about 3 miles downstream through Bargoed Woodland Park.

For full details, search online for Aberbargoed Anglers, or contact the Riverfly Partnership: www.riverflies.org

Fishing tips

The lower Rhymney around Caerphilly holds good numbers of trout and grayling, but the upper river at Bargoed has suffered severely from the effects of permethrin and mining-related pollution. Nevertheless, salmon are returning, spawning is good, and trout now average between 6 and 8 inches in this area.

For small wild fish, a rod of 7 to 8ft, rated for a 1 to 4 weight line, should be more than sufficient. Dai Roberts does most of his fishing with dry flies, mainly olive imitations, although standard beadhead Pheasant Tail nymphs can also work well. In this upper river gorge, trout are most likely to rise in areas where the trees have been coppiced and skylighted to allow more light to penetrate, but it's also worth trying terrestrial patterns in the darker tunnel stretches.

Don't miss

● The Winding House at New Tredegar: showcasing one of the winding engines used to raise and lower mine shaft cages, transporting men and coal between the surface and the depths of the pits

35

BRIDGEND

River Ogmore

When Bridgend County Borough Council secured around £2.5 million in funding from the European Union and Welsh Assembly to build a sinuous modern walkway along the top of the town centre's brutalist 1980s flood defences, fishing rights and access were almost certainly the least of their concerns. But the councillors soon discovered how much those rights meant to the members of the Ogmore Angling Association.

"We're a little club," says vice president Ian Finylas, "but we've been fishing this river since 1891, and we didn't want to be steamrollered. It was a matter of principle: the walkway was designed as part of a larger regeneration programme without any consultation or concern for angling, which created this health and safety problem of anglers casting and endangering passers-by. Under those circumstances, do you bow out and stop fishing, or do you uphold your fishing rights? We wanted to draw a line in the sand and make sure others will consult us and take us seriously in the future. And now they will!"

Under the terms of the eventual out-of-court settlement, the total compensation paid to the Ogmore Angling Association can't be revealed, but this wasn't the first time the club has staunchly upheld the interests of its members.

In 2002, Ian led a determined campaign to deal with the problem of shopping trolleys being dumped in the river alongside the Tesco superstore, and a hard core of dedicated committee members still runs monthly clean-ups through these town centre pools that once regularly yielded four or five trolleys each.

Bridgend's inhabitants weren't always so concerned about the welfare of the river, or even their fellow humans. "This was always supposed to be a cobblers' town," winks Ian, "but I'm not sure how much cobbling ever went on. There were all sorts of smuggling antics, and the communities out on the coast near Kenfig had a reputation as wreckers, tying lanterns onto their sheep and cattle to convince sailors that they were heading for a safe harbour."

With one notorious local wrecker known for his prosthetic hook as 'Mat of the Iron Hand', it's little wonder that George Agar Hansard found a cast of similar characters still at work on the Ogmore and its tributary the Ewenny in the course of researching his comprehensive *Trout and Salmon Fishing in Wales* during the early 1830s:

Evolved to grow through solidified lava, only Japanese knotweed is tough enough to penetrate Bridgend's brutal flood defences

Gnat attack: very small flies are recommended for targeting resident Ogmore trout

'Notwithstanding every destructive engine that ingenuity can invent is made use of for their capture by the idle and dissolute population of Bridgend, the supply of salmon and sewin appears to suffer no diminution... From the commencement of the spawning season, at the latter end of September, until January, parties are engaged every moonless night in spearing salmon by torchlight...the quantity thus destroyed in one season is immense, every farm and mill being supplied with its stock of dried salmon. One Thomas of the Leychard, about two miles from Bridgend, is the most skilful and determined poacher of this description in Glamorganshire. Thomas Johns of Bryn-y-minyin is another worthy of the same stamp. There are some excellent anglers and fly-tiers who haunt and poach [the Ewenny].

A shoemaker and a deaf and dumb man of the village near its mouth; Stradling of Bridgend, and Jenkins, a one-armed man, of the same place, are also capital fishermen; yet to employ or encourage them in any way serves only to confirm them in their malpractices...'

In the end, only the mining industry was able to kill the Ogmore's runs of migratory fish, but even these began to return in the 1980s. The river now enjoys the best runs of salmon and sewin of all the catchments covered by the South East Wales Rivers Trust – perhaps because its steep course, from the confluence of three former mining valleys at Dimbath Special Site of Scientific Interest to the sea at Merthyr Mawr, offers few serious obstructions to migration.

In 2008, an advisory visit by the Wild Trout Trust's conservation officer Andy Thomas rated its spawning potential as excellent. Good quantities of large woody debris in the headwaters are credited with stopping too much of the river's shale substrate being washed out of these critical areas, and there's also the EA's intriguing idea of recycling shale, removed from the lower river for flood defence, to supplement the natural supply of spawning gravel in the upper reaches.

Even in the dredged, sheer-sided canyons of Bridgend town centre where much of the loose shale gets deposited by the Ogmore's high-energy spates, boulder weirs provide oxygenation and a hint of habitat diversity, and long paving slabs overhang the edges as platforms for anglers or cover for fish. "It's obviously some of the most productive angling water on the river," declares Andy, "so I'd love to see those defended margins softened with some scrubby natural cover and shade. With the right permissions, it shouldn't be too difficult to bolt or weld a few reverse pockets onto the steel piling and plant them with sallow or goat willow as low marginal vegetation, which would certainly enhance the pools for the main fishing focus on the migratory trout."

While we're watching the water under a concrete-grey sky that threatens rain, a white-nosed salmon sidles out from the ancient hump-backed bridge, and a pod of little brownies starts competing with the wagtails for a hatch of needle flies and pale watery duns.

"As soon as I joined the club committee in 2006," says Ian, "I started arguing scientifically for reducing the stocking policy. The river might need a bit of supplementary stocking to keep the members happy, but nowhere near thirty or forty fish per pool at three or four pounds each. Currently we're trickle-stocking about 1500 trout a year, all around ten or eleven inches: that's much more sustainable for the river, and less of a target for organised poachers too."

In his capacity as the club's habitat improvement officer, Ian has also led the way on riverfly monitoring as a means of measuring the Ogmore's health. With funding from the EA, around twenty monitors were trained by the Riverfly Partnership in May 2010, and the results have already demonstrated how shrimp populations can boom unnaturally just downstream from tributaries affected by organic enrichment via sewer misconnections and CSOs. Although cypermethrin sheep dip has been withdrawn from sale since 2010, there's still the danger of residual stockpiles being used by hard-pressed farmers, so catchment-wide invertebrate monitoring will help to deter

In central Bridgend, concrete ramps provide access for anglers and heavy shale-removing machinery

and detect any future problems.

"All in all," says Ian, "the Ogmore is only fifteen miles from source to sea, and that makes for quite a manageable catchment. If we can get it back to where it was in Hansard's day, when he could go out and catch seven big trout without moving more than twenty yards, I'll be a very happy man."

Right: Under Bridgend's ornamental walkway, a rusty shopping trolley lies buried in a sandbank

Below: Since 2002, local anglers have worked with supermarkets to reduce the number of trolleys in the river

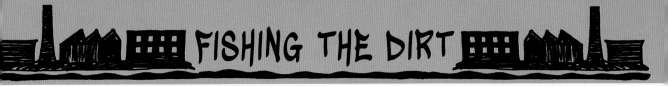

Bridgend: River Ogmore

Who's looking after the river?

The Ogmore Angling Association was founded in 1891, and is now working with Environment Agency Wales, the South East Wales Rivers Trust, the Wild Trout Trust and other partners to improve the fishing on the Ogmore.

When anglers' access to the river in Bridgend was threatened by a new waterside walkway, the club successfully defended its members' fishing rights and gained recognition as a consultee for future riparian developments. Monthly clean-ups remove bikes, scooters, shopping trolleys and other rubbish, and 20 invertebrate monitors were trained by the Riverfly Partnership in 2010, with funding secured from the EA through the South East Wales Rivers Trust.

For the latest information, visit:
www.ogmoreanglingassociation.com
www.southeastwalesriverstrust.org.uk

Getting there

The Ogmore is 10 minutes' walk from Bridgend station.

Maps are available from the Bridgend Tourist Information Centre in the Bridgend Designer Outlet, CF32 9SU: OS Explorer 151 is also recommended.

Seasons and permits

Brown trout season runs from 3 March to 30 September; sewin (sea trout) and salmon season from 1 April to 17 October.

Ogmore Angling Association controls almost all the fishing on the Ogmore and Ewenny. In the walkway area of Bridgend, the club encourages only experienced fly-casters to fish and wade, with appropriate care for

the safety of passers-by: the club will not become involved if any incidents occur.

For full details and a list of day and season ticket outlets, visit:
www.ogmoreanglingassociation.com

Fishing tips

The Ogmore is better known for its migratory salmonids than for its resident trout. The river's salmon run mainly as grilse, but its 3-year cycle of Tay-strain sewin average 2½ lbs, with notable fish reaching 4 to 5 or even 15 to 16lbs. Resident trout are smaller, with a 9-incher regarded as a good specimen from the river's headwaters, and a supplementary stocking of 11 to 12 inch trout in the Bridgend area each year. Grayling are only present in the limestone-influenced Ewenny.

Targeting larger sewin with snake-fly variants will demand heavier tackle, but a rod of 9 to 10ft, rated for a 4 to 5 weight line, should be perfect for normal daylight fishing on the town water. Experienced local anglers like Ian Finylas fish imitatively for resident trout, matching freshwater shrimp, pale watery olives, iron blue duns, stoneflies and midges, and getting up at dawn for prolific hatches of caenis. Traditional flies include Coch-y-bonddhu and Blue Dun patterns: Griffiths Gnats are almost always a reliable modern standby.

Don't miss

● Bridgend's Old Bridge: surviving in the midst of modern flood defence works, the steep, narrow bridge which reputedly gave the town its name
● Ogmore Castle: a romantic Norman ruin guarding a strategic tidal ford near the confluence of the Ogmore and Ewenny
● Bridgend's traditional tradesmen's signs: painted on many older buildings' walls

Danger
Deep water

36

CWMBRAN

Afon Lwyd

There's a wolfish grin on Tom Richards' face as he clambers out of the driver's seat and pulls his spraying kit out of the blue Wye and Usk Foundation van.

"I hate giant hogweed," he announces, "but I love going after it. If I find a patch on this river, there's no mercy, no escape… one good drink of glyphosate and that's that. We're very proactive, here at the Wye and Usk Foundation, and as deputy operations director I'd much rather just jump in and deal with a problem myself than record it and wait for someone else.

"Then there's Japanese knotweed. In the last three years or so we've really started to understand the benefits of spraying it in late summer, so each plant takes the poison down into the rhizomes as it's dying back naturally. Let it grow, hit it hard at the end of the season, whack it out!"

Halfway down the Afon Lwyd's 12 mile course from the high moors around Blaenavon to the tidal Usk at Caerleon, Tom is assembling his kit in front of Croesy-ceiliog school at letting-out time, and the kids crowd around, shrieking "Who ya gonna call? Ghostbusters!" at his white overalls and yellow electronic backpack.

"Did you ever hear the Genesis song about *The Return of the Giant Hogweed*?"

he asks them. "You haven't? Well, look it up on the internet, you'll find out how dangerous it is. So if you spot any more here in the school grounds, don't touch it: tell a teacher and I'll come and kill it for you!" Then, as good as his word, he's off to spray the spiky, stinging leaves in the school's riverside wetland, and strike another blow for restoring the Afon Lwyd and the Usk catchment in general.

The Wye and Usk Foundation became a fully-fledged charity in 2000, but this forward-thinking Rivers Trust had already started to build a respected name in river-mending circles. Driven by the collapse of the Wye's iconic salmon run in the 1980s, the first walk-over surveys of the upper river showed that hundreds of miles of prime spawning habitat were barred to ascending trout and salmon by man-made weirs and naturally-occurring debris dams, some up to 12ft high.

From 1996, with millions of pounds of funding from Europe and other sources, the Foundation's teams moved methodically down-catchment, clearing over 500 obstructions from the Lugg, Arrow and Monnow as well as the Wye, and installing fish passes at a time when no-one other than the statutory authorities had ever tackled

Into battle: Tom Riches sprays a patch of giant hogweed on the banks of the Afon Lwyd

CWMBRAN

....

such tasks. By 2010, when this ambitious programme of river reconnection finally reached the Afon Lwyd, the Foundation's focus had expanded to include angling access and clearing invasive non-native plants, and its experts were well versed in the balance of paperwork and practicality required for removing huge obstacles like the 12ft ironworking weir at Tynantddhu.

"We went through all the right heritage channels," Tom assures me, "including getting an archaeologist to advise us on leaving enough of the old structure for studies in the future. The weir was made of solid oak baulks, set on a sill of sandstone bedrock and held together with hand-forged iron pins. The old oak was as hard as iron, and we had to use special tungsten-tipped chainsaw blades to cut it! But the local residents didn't mind – in fact they were delighted to see the height of the weir reduced because the noise of the water kept them awake at night."

By the end of 2010, work had also been completed on a second impassable

Re-opened for fish passage: all that's left of the Tynantddhu weir

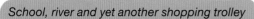
School, river and yet another shopping trolley

weir at Cwmavon, as well as emergency revetments where the river was kicking sideways across a shallow riffle to erode the football pitches in the centre of Cwmbran. Together with the Environment Agency's own £250,000 Larinier pass at Pontymoile, which overcame another 12ft barrier and eliminated a major poaching hotspot, these improvements now allow migratory fish to run and spawn all the way from the mouth of the Usk up to the World Heritage Site at Blaenavon: a full 17 acres of newly-accessible spawning gravels to add to the Wye and Usk Foundation's reopened 450 miles of tributaries.

The Afon Lwyd's modern name means *'Grey River'*, but its notoriously violent spates earned the original name of *'Torvaen'* (stone breaker) and the river's power was harnessed by ironworks at Pontypool as early as 1425. In the seventeenth century, the Hanbury dynasty of ironmasters pioneered the tinplate industry by inventing the rolling mill, the first mechanised method of flattening wrought iron bars into sheets. Nearby Pontymoel also became famous for japanning: a cheap, durable way of decorating tinplate trays, snuffboxes and other homewares with lacquer, and at least one visitor apparently prophesied that the area would become a second Birmingham on the strength of these industries alone.

Above Pontypool, the upper third of the river survived relatively unscathed until the end of the eighteenth century, but everything changed when a group of entrepreneurs from Staffordshire and Worcestershire invested £40,000 in constructing an ironworks on the bleak, peaty plateau near Garn-yr-erw.

Within ten years, Blaenavon's output of pig iron was second only to the massive Cyfarthfa forges at Merthyr Tydfil, producing over 10,000 tonnes every year as the Napoleonic Wars created constant demand for cannon balls and heavy artillery. No-one appears to have recorded the effect on the Afon Lwyd, maybe because it was so habitually polluted from such an early date: but it's all too easy to extrapolate from the fate and effect of a similarly industrialised Usk tributary a few miles to the north, and the way its effluent destroyed the trout and salmon fishing in the Usk's lower catchment. *'The angler is recommended not to commence operations until he reaches the immediate neighbourhood of Crickhowell,'* wrote George Agar Hansard in the 1830s, *'as between that town and Abergavenny the Clydach flows into the Uske, and poisons its waters by the refuse of the iron works which it carries down with it.'*

Even worse than the metalworking effluents was the problem of large-scale sewage disposal. In 1929 a typical report declared that *'the nuisance created in the vicinity of some of the sewer outfalls, during the drier periods of the year when the flow of water in the river is not sufficient to carry off the whole of the sewerage is repulsive and a probable menace to health... Anyone in the vicinity of the Afon Lwyd on a summer's morning may see colonies of all kinds of flies feeding upon the decomposing sewage matter from whence many of them gain access to the larders and food stores generally...'*

In the event, local politics and two World Wars blocked every effort to replicate

Sand-martin boxes on the newly-revetted bank in Cwmbran

the trunk sewers being installed across the rest of south Wales – until the principality's first new town at Cwmbran finally solved the Afon Lwyd's problems with sewers connected to modern treatment works. But you can't help wondering what might have happened if generations of county medical officers had won their argument earlier. Had trunk sewerage reached this valley as planned in the 1920s, would the river now be suffering the same chronic problems of collapsing pipes, overflowing CSOs and underinvestment still so evident on the Rhymney?

And so it turns out that on another summer's day, with the latest patch of giant hogweed safely sprayed, Tom and I decide we've got time to sample the fishing on the world's first official urban angling passport beat. Winding through rocky revetments in Cwmbran's well-tended parklands, the river is low and quiet, but above the boating lake there's a promising corner pool, and a maze of underwater boulders where a shockingly large, pale shape suddenly swims into focus. An upstream breeze brings the suggestion of Jammie Dodgers and Wagon Wheels from the Burton's biscuit factory: the trout snubs an olive spider pattern, then hammers a hair-winged emerger and thrashes around in the rocks, thrilling the group of kids on the bank who point, squeal, and can't quite seem to believe what they're seeing.

In last century's open sewer, this must be post-industrial urban fly-fishing at its best. As we walk back down to the van, our laughter says it all.

Twice shy? The author first caught and released this trout in May 2011: 4 months later, by the time of this second photo, the fish had gained at least an inch in length and half a pound in weight

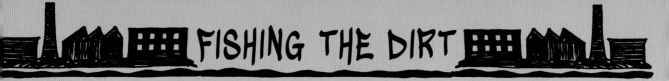

Cwmbran: Afon Lwyd

Who's looking after the river?

Since 1995 the Wye and Usk Foundation has been dedicated to addressing catchment-wide habitat problems affecting the Wye and Usk fisheries. In 2010, with 2 years' funding from Wild Fishing Wales, the *Friends of the Afon Lwyd (FOAL)* project was launched to focus on litter, fish passage, water quality and invasive species issues in partnership with Torfaen Council, local angling clubs, Keep Wales Tidy and Environment Agency Wales.

As this book went to press, at least 2 impassable weirs have been lowered: future plans include tree coppicing, eradicating Japanese knotweed, access for partially disabled anglers, and installing upstream V-weirs to retain spawning gravels in the upper river.

For the latest information, visit: www.wyeuskfoundation.org

Getting there

The Afon Lwyd is less than 10 minutes' walk from Cwmbran station.

A map of the lower beat is available in the Wye and Usk Foundation's passport booklet: OS Explorer 152 is also recommended.

Seasons and permits

Brown trout season runs from 3 March to 30 September.

Cwmbran Angling Association controls about 2 miles of the Afon Lwyd, from the bridge by the A4042 roundabout up to the Monmouth-shire and Brecon canal at Pontymoile. This is now accessible as the first urban fishery in the Wye and Usk Foundation's passport scheme: there are no riverside voucher boxes, however, and vouchers must be exchanged for tickets before fishing.

For full details and a list of day ticket outlets, visit: www.wyeuskfoundation.org

Fishing tips

Despite its diminutive size and industrial history, the Afon Lwyd has now been recolonised by wild trout up to 2 or even 3lbs. Sewin and salmon also run the river in summer and winter respectively, and popula-tions of olives, shrimp, caddis, iron blue duns and mayflies are improving.

To cope with the possibility of large trout in tight spaces, a rod of 6 to 7ft is ideal, rated for a 2 to 4 weight line. Although water quality is excellent, the river always runs with a pale grey tinge: a tone to match with Klinkhamers, Adams and similar dry parachute or hair-winged emerger patterns. If in doubt, Tom Richards suggests going down to a size 18 or 20, with part of the dressing below the surface as a trigger for rising fish.

Don't miss

● Blaenavon World Heritage Site: historic ironworks and Big Pit National Coal Museum
● Pontymoile aqueduct and fish pass: complete with hairpin bend to allow migra-tory salmonids to ascend a 12ft weir

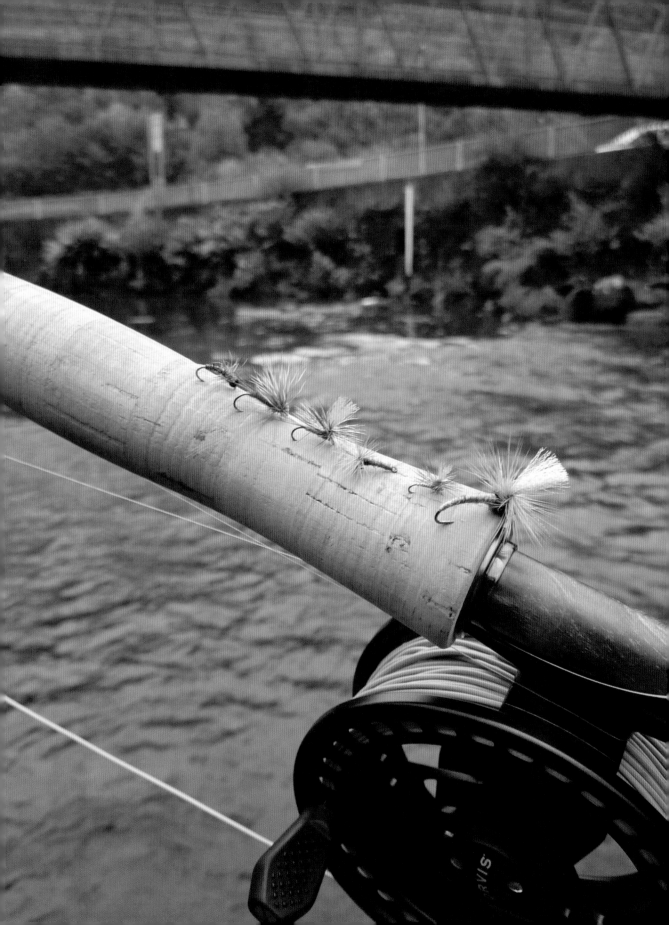

37

MERTHYR VALE

River Taff

On a late September morning in south Wales, the spars and rigging of Cardiff's Millennium Stadium emerge from low mist into a crisp blue sky.

Steam and the smell of hops drift upriver from the Brains brewery, and the Taff flows low and silent, punctuated by one huge rise mid-river, ripples spreading sideways to the walkways along either bank. At Cardiff station, bilingual announcements give this journey a strangely foreign feel, and you keep getting tantalising glimpses of the river before the train finally judders into the shiny new station at Merthyr Vale. Two minutes down the hill, and there's the Taff again, spanned by a battered blue footbridge, with trout rising delicately under a curving blockwork wall and the blackened mouth of the Vale's old colliery culvert.

Here at the top of the Taff, Merthyr Tydfil was probably the world's first and largest iron town. On the southern edge of the Brecon Beacons, Carboniferous geology offered rich deposits of coal and iron ore for smelting, limestone to act as the flux in the furnaces, and power from the river's rapid headwaters. Ironmasters from the Sussex Weald had already reconnoitred the Valleys in the sixteenth century when their local coal reserves started to fail: around 1750

they returned in earnest, and by 1801 this little mountain village had become the most extensive industrial conurbation in Wales.

New technology soon enabled coal to be converted into hotter-burning coke, and the town sprawled out around a network of multi-furnace ironworks. By the 1840s, the forges at Dowlais alone boasted 18 furnaces, 100 steam engines and 10,000 of Merthyr's 18,000 employees. In earlier times, it was said that a squirrel could make its way from Cardiff to Brecon without touching the ground: now the ancient sessile oakwoods were clear-felled for pit props, leaving the barren, fast-draining hilltops familiar to modern eyes.

Looking down from these heights in 1844, when Merthyr's annual production of iron equalled a quarter of the whole of the United States', the king of Saxony described the valley's underworld glare with a mixture of awe and horror as *'the fiery city of Pluto'*: a vision of hell for the booming population of radicalised workers who staged regular riots against the garrison posted here to keep the peace, and also for the ecology of the river. Around the same time George Agar Hansard recorded that *'the vicinity of Merthyr Tyd-vil has greatly contributed to render certain portions of the Taff unworthy the angler's* attention. *The poisonous matter discharged into it from the iron-works, and the lawless practices of the forge-men, continually diminish the stock of fish. In dry seasons these depredators assemble in bands, and wading into the streams armed with sledge hammers, contrive by violently striking the stones under which the trout are concealed, to destroy an incredible quantity of fish of all sizes.'*

Even when the seams of iron ore were worked out, pollution and pressure on the fishery only got worse. As Cardiff grew rich on Merthyr's productivity, and then on the output of the whole south Wales coalfield, many ironworks upgraded to steel-milling using imported ore. Temperatures in the blast passages under the Cyfarthfa furnaces reached 1,500 degrees, and the river was the obvious conduit for superheated water contaminated with quenching oil and other pollutants.

Today, Merthyr Tydfil Angling Association's webmaster is Gareth Lewis: one of a new generation of semi-professional fly-fishers who works hard all day in the IT sector, then comes home to tie exquisite flies, guide clients on small streams and rivers as a GAIC-qualified instructor, and blog fluently about his experiences.

Naturally, he also has an acute appreciation of the Welsh Valleys' history, and the way it once threatened the rivers he loves. "In 1872," says Gareth, "a report on the Taff stated that it was uninhabitable for fish, mainly because of tipping hot cinders into the river, and scouring the river bed by washing down cinder dumps. After the ironworks declined, the worst pollution probably occurred below the collieries at Merthyr Vale, Trelewis Drift, Taf Bargoed and Trelewis. In 1970 there were 97 parts per million of suspended solids recorded in the Taff near Mount Pleasant, and 99 parts per million near Quakers Yard. There was also raw sewage being discharged directly

A chunky little wild Taff trout falls for Gareth Lewis' Roy Christie-style reversed parachute emerger

Times change: the author casts hopefully into the culvert pool where Merthyr Vale colliery discharged its pollution until 1989

into the river, not to mention chemicals from the factories on Morlais Brook!"

But as the 1980s decimated Britain's heavy industries, the Taff's salvation was at hand. British Steel shut its last foundry in Merthyr Tydfil in 1987: despite complete renovation at a cost of £2 million in the 1960s, Merthyr Vale colliery never recovered from the miners' strikes of 1984 and 1985, and finally closed in 1989. The Morlais Brook was cleaned up, and new treatment works at Cilfynydd finally solved most of the upper river's sewage problems, although there's still the feeling amongst anglers that many industries simply see the cycle of pollution and fines as one of the costs of doing business in this area.

From 2001, Tony Rees, John Coombs and other members of Merthyr Tydfil Angling Association began large-scale restoration work on the Taf Fechan headwaters above Merthyr Tydfil, installing bank revetments and flow deflectors to create pools and riffles, and importing more than a hundred tonnes of gravel to enhance the catchment's spawning and nursery zone.

In just three years, the project made more than enough progress to win the runner-up category in the Wild Trout Trust's annual Conservation Awards. But disaster struck in August 2006, when the supposedly leak-proof water works below Ponsticill reservoir accidentally flushed three tonnes of liquid aluminium sulphate into the river, killing over 23,000 fish.

Tony and John recalled their memories of that appalling day for an Angling Trust interview in 2011. "The river turned white, and there were dead fish for more than three miles downstream of the water works... I saw one fish which leapt from the river and landed on a rock as if trying to save itself, and when some of the fish were examined afterwards, their gill filaments seemed to disintegrate. I remember thinking, this was a horrible way for fish to die."

In the criminal prosecutions that followed, fines of £16,500 plus costs were imposed on Welsh Water and United Utilities, and Welsh Water paid £22,000 to the club to cover the costs of restocking. Eventually a civil case led by the Anglers'

Conservation Association (now the Angling Trust and Fish Legal) secured an additional £25,000 compensation, in recognition of their wasted efforts and the destruction of a valuable wild trout fishery. Merthyr Tydfil Angling Association's working relationship with the water companies is now closer than ever, and the urban mainstem of the river recovered sufficiently to host the Rivers International Fly Fishing Championship in 2009.

Pointing towards the gaping culvert under the concrete wasteland where the largest colliery in south Wales once stood, Tony permits himself a moment of self-congratulation. "When the pits were running and all the coal washings came out at night, that used to be one of our main sources of pollution. I even wrote a letter to the chairman of Welsh Water, telling him I thought it would be nice to see the fish coming up the Taff with miners' lamps, because that was the only way they'd have got through the coal dust in the water. But look at the riverbed today – it's spotlessly clean and even the otters are returning."

End of trout season: rosehips redden on the banks of the Taff, while autumn mists hang over the hills above Merthyr Vale station (bottom left)

Merthyr Vale: River Taff

Who's looking after the river?

Since 2001, Merthyr Tydfil Angling Association has been restoring the Taff's headwaters on the Taf Fechan as a wild trout fishery, recreating spawning and juvenile habitat with soft bank revetments, flow deflectors, skylighting and gravel riffles. As part of the South East Wales Rivers Trust, the club is involved in educational initiatives, including the *Taff Salmon Home Coming Project* and developing riverside nature reserves.

In partnership with the Environment Agency, Merthyr Tydfil County Borough Council, the Wild Trout Trust and other community groups, working parties and clean-ups are regularly held on the main river. Keep Wales Tidy is also instrumental in clearing rubbish from the river and its surroundings.

For the latest information, visit:
www.mtaa.co.uk
www.keepwalestidy.org
www.ffisw.com

Getting there

The Taff is 2 minutes' walk downhill from Merthyr Vale station, but the railway follows the river along the valley, and access is possible at many other points.

Maps are available from the Tourist Information Centre on Glebeland Street, Merthyr Tydfil CF48 2AB: OS Explorer 166 is also recommended.

Seasons and permits

Brown trout season runs from 3 March to 30 September.

Merthyr Tydfil Angling Association controls about 8 miles of the upper Taff from Quakers Yard upstream to Merthyr Tydfil, as well as most of the Taf Fechan and Taff Fawr headwaters, and several ponds and reservoirs. For full details and a list of day and season ticket outlets, visit: www.mtaa.co.uk

Fishing tips

When a hatch comes off on the upper Taff, it's clear that the river has recovered well from its polluted past, with an incredible density of trout averaging 8 to 10 inches, and occasional trophies to 3 or 4lbs. Grayling are gradually making their way upstream from the lower river, but at the time of publication, they have yet to reach Merthyr Tydfil Angling Association water.

For the Taff's open spaces and complex currents, a rod of 9 to 10ft is ideal, rated for a 3 to 5 weight line. Local experts like Gareth Lewis fish confidently with small and even micro-pattern dry flies, since both trout and grayling will rise freely to patterns smaller than size 24. Key hatches cover all four major families, with large dark olives, pale wateries, midges, blue winged olives and several sorts of sedge featuring prominently. Overall, a stealthy approach is often the deciding factor, and an artificial of roughly the right size and silhouette is more important than colour.

Don't miss

● Aberfan memorial garden: on the site of Pantglas junior school, a memorial to the 5 teachers and 144 children killed by a landslide of more than 150,000 cubic yards of debris from Merthyr Vale colliery's waste

38

EDINBURGH

Water of Leith

"Mention London, you think of the Thames. Mention Glasgow, you think of the Clyde. But mention Edinburgh, and most people don't think of a river at all," says John Adams, honorary high bailiff of the Water of Leith.

Unlike many other long-abandoned urban streams, and the much younger conservation organisations now looking after them, the stories of the Water of Leith and its honorary bailiffs are both relatively well known and genuinely ancient. The bailiffs themselves, *'Auld Reekie's'* original river conservation group, preside over Scotland's first and only free brown trout fishery, as they've done since time immemorial. And best of all for a wandering angler, the well-signposted Water of Leith Walkway (begun in 1971 with a government job-creation scheme that paid for riverside pathways on condition that the Council funded local transport and foremen) follows the full urban length of the river from Balerno to Leith, tracking the old valley-bottom railway line that once served more than eighty mills.

Dubbed *'a silver thread in a ribbon of green'*, the Water of Leith still tends to hide its secrets from the outside world. Rising in the peat, shales and sandstones of the Pentland Hills, it slips under Edinburgh's outskirts at Balerno, and rattles and glides its remaining 12 miles to the Firth of Forth at Leith, in what Jon Beer once described as a long, green tunnel of tranquillity, burrowing through the city. Even in the heart of Edinburgh it's hidden away, almost underground, and never more so than the entrance to the Dene's classical municipal gardens, where Thomas Telford's Dean Bridge soars 106ft above the river's gorge, just ten minutes' stroll from the commercial chaos of Princes' Street.

But the din and clatter of commerce once defined the Water of Leith, and continue to fragment its tannin-stained waters with weirs and lades impassable to fish. The power of the river sawed and shaped wood, processed hides for glue, and 'waulked' (washed and softened) wool and linen. At various times, its mills ground snuff, oats, barley, peas, spices and pepper. After 1595, several mills were adapted for paper-making, some of which found its way into Bank of Scotland banknotes, and created an industry of national importance, with major mills at Juniper Green, Currie and Balerno working well into the twentieth century.

With a just-perceptible grin, temporary volunteers officer Nickol Stewardson

Looking down from Dean Street bridge, white-water rapids show how fast the river's gradient falls at this point

is clearly enjoying the educational part of his job description as he tells me about the end of the milling industry on the Water of Leith. "Bells Mill was the very last working mill on the river. It was still grinding wood flour for linoleum in 1972 when a spark caught the fine powder and blew the whole building to smithereens. They're still rebuilding it now for housing!"

In due course, commercial necessity created the river's honorary bailiffs, who trace their history back to fourteenth century *'bailies'* collecting taxes from the millers and ship-owners at the port of Leith. In 1893, the City of Edinburgh Council began stocking the Water of Leith, creating a trout fishery with four full-time river-keepers. Today, all 15 bailiffs are voluntary, with lorry drivers, company directors, and Scotland's most senior wildlife police officer among their number. They patrol the banks checking the thousand-plus free permits issued each year, kick-sample 12 sites along the river to monitor its invertebrate populations, and rake gravels every September in preparation for trout spawning. They also create pools in the torrential upper reaches, each around 3ft deep and 30ft long, to boost natural fry and invertebrate survival.

The Water of Leith in Dean Village

As a result, the river supports a very visible population of otters, and no fewer than six species of fish-eating birds: kingfishers, herons, mergansers, goosanders, bitterns, and cormorants in winter. Songbirds abound, and the population of raptors in the valley has dramatically increased.

Mindful of predation and a daily anglers' bag limit of two trout over ten inches, the bailiffs arrange supplementary stocking of around 1,000 trout each year, although according to limited statistics a good proportion of fish are safely released, and some local fly-fishers question the need to stock at all. They also organise fishing courses for local children chosen by the Lothian and Borders Police, with equipment donated by local tackle shops: if the kids attend all three days, learning the basics of responsible fishing and watercraft, they can keep their kit afterwards.

As you might expect, these activities are designed to complement those of the Water of Leith Conservation Trust, founded by the bailiffs in 1988. Less than ten years later, the Trust won Millennium Commission funding to complete the Water of Leith Walkway, finally linking up the full 12 miles of the urban river for local people with a £5 million capital project match-funded mainly by the City of Edinburgh Council and LEEL. One of the Trust's founding Trustees, Graham Priestly, is commemorated with a plaque on the wall of the enviable visitor centre he helped to create in the shelter of Slateford's junction of railway arches and aqueducts. With easy access from public transport, this is now the co-ordinating hub for more than

100 volunteers, who dedicate thousands of hours every year to keeping their river clear of litter. Recent finds include a surf board, a grand piano, a police car, and an historic millstone since set into the wall below the Priestley memorial plaque. Annual sponsored duck races and other events organised by community and volunteers officer Charlotte Neary boost funds from the Council, which has also paid for advice from Fraser Somerville, erstwhile honorary secretary to the bailiffs, on controlling invasive species.

With such successes already achieved, it's almost inevitable that John, Fraser, Nickol and their colleagues still see storm-clouds on the horizon. Seventy per cent of rain that falls on Edinburgh eventually runs into the river with its solution of sediment and heavy metals; flood defence schemes in the Balerno area threaten spawning beds

A grayling from the Water of Leith

The Water of Leith Trust's visitor centre at Slateford. Only fly-fishing with barbless hooks is permitted

with siltation; and the balance between natural recruitment and supplementary stocking in this heavily-pressured fishery may soon be upset by the Scottish Parliament's freshwater fisheries management legislation.

In over 400 years of their history, the bailiffs of the Water of Leith have shown how long-term fishing and conservation interests can work hand in hand, and how a river can evolve over time.

"Sixty years ago," John recalls, "fly life on the river used to be prolific, with diverse hatches of February reds, March browns, olives through the summer, and blizzards of iron blue duns whenever it rained."

Now, with much more silt and urban run-off in the river, midges are spreading, and local wisdom suggests fishing very fine, with small flies. Whilst visiting the city that gave us *Trainspotting*, I spend several golden early-autumn hours pottering downstream

from the visitor centre, picking up a brace of beautiful wild brownies to 11 inches on tiny Griffiths Gnats almost under the walls of Edinburgh's prison.

Next day, I work up the Walkway from Dean Bridge under a dreich and drizzling sky, finally finding a hatch of minuscule stoneflies alongside the Bells Mill redevelopment, and releasing eight trout and a perfect steely grayling in front of a friendly, photo-snapping audience of dog-walkers.

So will we ever have to pay for this wonderful fishing on the Water of Leith? "There'd be no point," John and Fraser conclude. "It's much more important to give people the chance to get out and go fishing... as well as recreational, the social benefits are so enormous!"

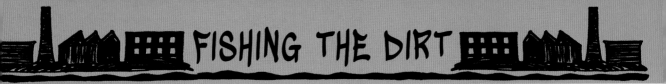

Edinburgh: Water of Leith

Who's looking after the river?

The Water of Leith Conservation Trust was founded in 1988 as Scotland's first community river charity, and now works with the bailiffs of the Water of Leith to promote biodiversity, raise awareness of the river as Edinburgh's key environmental asset, and deliver over 50 river clean-ups and habitat improvement tasks annually with more than 100 volunteers.

The Trust's state-of-the-art visitor centre at Slateford is the clear first port of call for anyone visiting the river.

For the latest information, visit: www.waterofleith.org.uk

Getting there

The Water of Leith is 5 minutes' walk from Slateford station, or 10 minutes by bus from Princes Street. The river is also easily accessible at Dean Bridge and Stockbridge, and the well-signposted Water of Leith Walkway runs the full 12-mile length of the fishery

By foot from Princes Street or Queen Street, an easy 10-minute walk will bring you to the river at Dean Bridge or Stockbridge. From Haymarket station it's an equally short walk to the Bells Mill stretch.

Maps are available from the visitor centre on Lanark Road, EH14 1TQ: OS Explorer 350 is also recommended.

Seasons and permits

Brown trout and grayling season runs from 1 April to 30 September. The City of Edinburgh Council does not allow fishing for salmon or sea trout, which in any case are largely blocked by the weirs.

Fishing rights are managed by the honorary bailiffs of the Water of Leith on behalf of the council, so fishing for trout and grayling on the urban Water of Leith is free with a no-cost permit, available from the visitor centre and tackle shops across the city. Spinning and fixed line fishing are completely prohibited, and only fly-fishing with barbless hooks is permitted between Slateford Bridge and Balerno. Please send the catch return on your permit back to the bailiffs at the end of the season to help calculate future stocking levels.

Fishing tips

Trout to 4lbs have recently been recorded in the Water of Leith, with most much smaller. Grayling up to ½ lb have also been present in the lower reaches since the 1980s: an excellent indication of high water quality.

A rod of 7 to 8ft is ideal, rated for a 1 to 4 weight line. The river gets fished hard, and the fish respond best to relatively sophisticated techniques: fine nylon, and small dries and nymphs. According to John Adams, black spiders work well in early season, with dry Grey Dusters effective from June, together with other midge and small general patterns.

Don't miss

- The Water of Leith Conservation Trust's visitor centre at Slateford: complete with river-related films and interactive water installations
- Saughton Mains allotments: urban gardening as an art form
- Antony Gormley's '6 Times' series of statues in and around the Water of Leith

39

GLASGOW

Rivers Kelvin and Glazert

As I clatter up the escalator from Kelvin-bridge subway station, Alistair Stewart is already waiting for me at the top. "Top marks for coming round the Clockwork Orange in waders," chuckles the vice chairman of the River Kelvin Angling Association. "You've had the full urban fishing experience already... I used to wear mine all the time on the buses between Anniestown and Partick, but it's amazing how rarely you get trouble from anyone. All dressed up in fishing kit, you look even more deviant than they are, and they just leave you alone!"

It's not every day that you get to fish with one of the UK's original fly-fishing bloggers: an urban angling pioneer whose wryly-recorded adventures on Glasgow's second river helped to define the international 'brownlining' genre with a *Wall Street Journal* interview in 2009. So I've been looking forward to this meeting for months, not least because reading his blog all those years ago helped to validate my own early efforts on the Wandle, 350 miles to the south.

"When I started fishing the Kelvin in the 1900s," Alistair tells me, "you'd never meet another soul with a rod. Back then, it really was a dirty river: the turning point

came in 2003, when they closed the old sewage treatment works and replaced them with the Kelvin Valley Sewer. The blogging began about the same time... I thought of keeping a diary, then decided I might as well do it online, and called it *Fly-fishing the Kelvin*, which later became *The Urban Fly Fisher*. I was amazed by the number of people reading it, not just from Glasgow, but expats all over the world. A lot of them seemed pretty amazed too that there was this mad bloke catching trout in the river they remembered running blue, green and red from the factories upstream."

Today, as we hop over wrought-iron railings in Kelvingrove Park to fish idyllic pocket water and clear glides lined with willow sweepers, the river's dirty reputation already feels like ancient history, but hanging from the branches just around the corner there's evidence to the contrary.

"We've named this the Sanitary Towel Pool for obvious reasons," Alistair grimaces. "Nobody can work out where they all come from, just like no-one knows why the Petrol Pool near the Botanic Gardens always smells of oil." The trout take their cue from the hard-boiled place names, and we frequently find ourselves searching the darker corners of our fly boxes

··

for something to tempt these belligerent Weegie browns. But we finally crack the code: Alistair with olive emergers, myself with tiny beadhead nymphs and sparsely-hackled partridge and orange spiders, well ginked to float in the surface film of the rippling runs and pools.

There's no doubt that this is a quirky little river. Whereas most streams are steepest and rockiest in their headwaters, the Kelvin reverses the usual structure over its twenty-mile length: rising in a bog at Dullutur on the side of the Campsie Fells, meandering slowly to Killermont past its confluence with the Glazert, then turning south and dropping steeply to the Clyde through a rocky, wooded gorge that once formed Glasgow's eastern boundary. For today's urban fly-fishers, this implies textbook trouting in the shadow of a succession of dignified bridges and viaducts carrying roads, railways and the Forth and Clyde Canal. But from the early Middle Ages onwards it meant easily-accessible power for the mills that dotted the river from Killermont downstream.

Most of these have now been demolished, but you can still detect their absence by ruined weirs, blocked sluices and the negative space now occupied by public gardens and car parks. From the late eighteenth century, Glasgow's west coast location helped it to capture much of Britain's trade with North America and the West Indies, and Clydebank became a global byword for ship-building and heavy engineering. Although the city's grain mills had traditionally been located on the Molindinar Burn near the cathedral, Glasgow Bakers' Mills moved to this stretch of the Kelvin

Glasgow skyline, local tipple

in the 1570s, and continued to grind flour here for a full 400 years. Partick became dominated by flour and other forms of milling, including the Slit Mill which used eight water wheels to mechanise traditional blacksmithing processes: hammering, stamping, grinding, using water-powered rollers to flatten iron bars, and then cutting them with water-operated shears to make tools for export across the British empire.

Upstream, the Kelvin's output included cotton, paper, snuff, malt for brewing, and softening flax for weaving, whilst Lennoxtown was purpose-built as accommodation for the cotton, alum and nail-making industries. The area in front of Kelvingrove Museum was once occupied by the Clayslaps milling complex, whose owner gradually built his weir so high that the flat water behind it stretched more than half a mile upstream and swamped the wheel-pool of Woodside Mill at Kelvinbridge, itself a cotton mill with more than 8,000 spindles powered by the Kelvin. The flint mill at North Woodside made powdered glaze for ironstone pottery and sanitary ware by roasting flints for three days, then dumping the hot ash and chippings in the river, and pulverising the remaining good flints with hard chert blocks. Steam boilers had begun to replace the need for water power in Glasgow as early as 1799, but the flint mill only ground to a halt in 1959.

As the mills closed and disappeared, the Kelvin scoured itself clean, and local resident Mark Eden-Bushell remembers the exact moment when he realised the river was coming back to life. "I was walking across one of the bridges with my wife, and we saw a cormorant – that was our impetus for founding the Friends of the River Kelvin in 1991. I'm not a fisherman, and we do things differently from Edinburgh, but they've had their bailiffs on the Water of Leith for many years, and I thought we could benefit from a similar river-focused group here.

"Very shortly afterwards, we also set up the River Kelvin Angling Association, because the salmon and sea trout were starting to come back, and I wanted to stop the city boys from buying bits of the river for lots of money. There are many unemployed people who fish the Kelvin, just as their parents fished it before them, and their grandparents before that – most of them were appalled at the idea of paying even £5, but it's kept the fishing open to all-comers, and that's a good thing."

Since then, the river's recovery has generated interest from more than fifty groups catchment-wide, one of these being the Clyde River Foundation whose flagship *Trout in the Classroom* programme added 14 Kelvin valley primary schools to the 300 already visited by the scheme between 2001 and 2011. "The point was to take a well-tested project and give it a whole new dimension, introducing kids to real scientists with microscopes and electro-

Cracked it! A Kelvin trout

fishing equipment on their local feeder burn, sometimes just across the road from their school playground," says co-ordinator Willie Yeomans. "And the feedback has been absolutely amazing!"

Back in Glasgow's city centre, the Kelvin has one more surprise in store. Across the river from the subway station the buddleia bushes are full of frantic grannom, the air smells of petrol and pigeons, and a long slow swirl in the water shows us where the rarely-spotted Kelvin otter is lounging in the shadows of the next bridge downstream.

"He's probably swigging dregs of Irn Bru and munching discarded takeaway pizzas," snorts Alistair affectionately. "Classic delinquent city otter, but legendary PR for the river!"

What every urban angler wants to hear...

Another good haul of rubbish collected by the Friends of the River Kelvin

Glasgow: Rivers Kelvin and Glazert

Who's looking after the rivers?

Formed in 1991 and 1992 respectively, the Friends of the River Kelvin and River Kelvin Angling Association have championed the river's recovery in partnership with Glasgow City Council, SEPA and Kelvin Clyde Greens-pace, organising volunteer river clean-ups on the first Saturday of every month, and improving access to the river.

In 2010, the Clyde River Foundation launched the *Kelvin in the Classroom* programme with funding from LEADER: future plans include establishing an environmental network to co-ordinate the efforts of more than 50 voluntary groups across the catchment, including habitat improvement work by the Wild Trout Trust and Campsie Angling Association on the Glazert tributary as part of the *Trout in the Town* programme.

For the latest information, visit:
www.fork.org.uk
www.fishkelvin.com
www.urbanflyfisher.com
www.clyderiverfoundation.org
www.wildtrout.org

Getting there

Via Glasgow's subway system (known locally as the Clockwork Orange), Kelvinbridge station is 30 seconds' walk from the river. The Kelvin Walkway is well signposted from the Clyde all the way upstream to Killermont and Milngavie. Just a little further out of the city, the Glazert at Lennoxtown is about 5 miles from the nearest station at Lenzie.

Maps of Glasgow are available from the Visit Scotland Information Centre on George Square, G2 1DY: OS Explorer 342 and 348 are also recommended.

Seasons and permits

Brown trout season runs from 15 March to 6 October; salmon and sea trout from 11 February to 31 October.

The River Kelvin Angling Association controls all fishing on the Kelvin except the Glazert and Luggie waters: up to 10 miles of water within Glasgow. Fly-fishing is the only method allowed on Sundays. The Glazert is controlled by Campsie Angling Association.

For full rules and details of how to apply for membership, visit: www.fishkelvin.com and http://campsieaa.blogspot.com

Fishing tips

The River Kelvin Angling Association stopped stocking the river in 2011, so populations may take a few years to stabilise. In the meantime, the river holds a good head of wild trout averaging 10 inches, with a few up to 1 and occasionally 2lbs. Runs of salmon and sea trout are improving, and still absorb much of the local angling effort.

For both rivers, a rod of 7 to 8ft is ideal, rated for a 2 to 4 weight line. Large dark olives, grannom, blue-winged olives, iron blue duns, yellow may duns and caddis have all repopulated the river by drifting down from unpolluted headwaters: Alistair Stewart suggests imitating them with Comparaduns, F-flies, Wyatt-style Deer Hair Emergers, little Pheasant Tail nymphs, and the modern classic CDC and Elk in very small sizes.

Don't miss

● Glasgow School of Art's building on Garnethill: designed in Art Nouveau style by Charles Rennie Mackintosh

● Glasgow's drumlins: elongated hills of debris left behind by the glaciers after the last Ice Age

40

COOKSTOWN

....

River Ballinderry

Anywhere else in the world, Britain's largest freshwater lake and its night-running dollaghan trout would be internationally iconic. A few miles outside Belfast, ten rivers flow from all points of the compass into a vast fertile saucer more than 150 miles square, where this unique strain of salmonids grow to ten pounds or more before returning to the rivers to spawn.

But Ulster's years of violent conflict left a legacy of damaged perceptions as well as environmental degradation, and for many years Lough Neagh and its rivers suffered on the wrong side of history.

Rising at Camlough in the Sperrin mountains, and flowing through thirty miles of County Tyrone to the shores of the Lough, one of those rivers was the Ballinderry. With bomb blasts and gunfire echoing down the streets of Cookstown, in a catchment encompassing some of the most hostile 'bandit country' in Northern Ireland, the river's sustainability came last in most people's minds. Miles of the Ballinderry's banks became infested with giant hogweed whose photo-activated sap can cause third-degree burns on bare skin, fertilisers and slurry from dairy farms poured down into the Lough and nearly killed it with eutrophication, and the runs

of dollaghan dwindled and almost died.

But a few local fishermen noticed, and decided to act. For some, like third-generation Cookstown angler Henry Noble, fishing had been the best way for a young man to keep his head down during the Troubles and stay safely unnoticed by both sides. Now he joined Alan Keys, a fellow angler who would later serve as a prominent honest broker of the Good Friday Agreement, in a desperate attempt to save the dollaghan's unique genetic code by electrofishing broodstock from a tributary of the river that had never been stocked with farmed trout. "I remember running blue dye over those eggs every day to keep them alive and healthy," Henry says as we fish up the river he's known all his life, "and by the end of it, we managed to hatch enough of them to save the Ballinderry dollaghan. Not many... but enough."

Today that early hatchery has grown into the Ballinderry River Enhancement Association: Northern Ireland's first Rivers Trust, an organisation based on the clear understanding that the river's future needs to be secured by the communities living around it. Up to one and a half million native Ballinderry dollaghan, salmon and brown trout fry are now stocked each year,

Before the Ballinderry River Enhancement Association breached the weir behind the Glenavon House hotel, this was a major poaching hotspot

and the Association has received financial support from WWF-UK and the Heritage Lottery Fund to develop and implement a collective vision and action plan for the river and its catchment.

Under the acronym of *RIPPLE* (*Rivers Involving People, Places and Leading by Example*) project officer Mark Horton took a year to consult more than 300 Tyrone residents and distil their aspirations for their river. "We think the *RIPPLE* process was unique in the way it brought scientists and the community together," he confides. "People don't like scientists just telling them what to do, and scientists don't know all the ground-truth details that local people know. This way, we reduced conflict within the catchment, and got the best out of everyone."

With a third of the local population living around the mid-point of the river in Cookstown, Mark's consultation also

generated a vital resource for delivering the 115 different actions needed to turn residents' vision for the Ballinderry into reality: volunteer time and effort, which added up to 11,500 hours in the first year alone.

A typical volunteer-led project is *CURE* (*Clean Up the River Environment*) which removes tyres, bottles, agricultural litter and discarded kitchen appliances from the river corridor with help from local scout groups. Invasive giant hogweed, Himalayan balsam and Japanese knotweed are being progressively sprayed by trained teams, and ark sites and conservation plans have been established for threatened native crayfish and freshwater pearl mussels in the upper river's Area of Special Scientific Interest and Special Area of Conservation.

The Ballinderry's recovery will also be tracked by a riverfly monitoring group, with protocols and trigger levels closely

Henry Noble casts a long line across a pool which he personally restored with a digger

Juvenile dollaghan can be identified by their slightly snub-nosed profile

agreed with the Northern Ireland Environment Agency, but much work remains to be done. Like many other Ulster rivers, the Ballinderry was aggressively dredged in the 1960s, and the catchment's connectivity is fragmented by many weirs, relics of the area's past as a centre of the linen-weaving industry, which continue to form convenient snatching points for poachers.

So much habitat diversity needs to be restored that opinions still differ on the river's ability to support heavy stocking of dollaghan and other fry when the fly-life and channel profile may be insufficient to sustain them. Water quality is affected by seepage from septic tanks, and black market fuel-launderers sometimes dump tonnes of diesel-saturated cat litter on the banks after using it to strip red dye from agricultural fuel.

And then there's Lough Neagh itself, which also poses problems for the survival of the Ballinderry's migratory salmonids.

"Despite being designated as a RAMSAR site, ASSI and SAC," says Mark, "the Lough has never had a fishery survey, so there's no baseline of data for us to work from, and licensing takes no account of cumulative effects.

"Like salmon, dollaghan tend to move in pods, which means it's very easy to catch whole runs in modern monofilament nets, and there are miles of these nets in the Lough picking up trout, salmon and dollaghan as a by-catch of the roach fishery which supplies the zoo trade with food for sea-lions and so on. Even while we've been improving the productivity of the Ballinderry, dollaghan catches have been steadily falling in the rivers all round the Lough in correlation to the roach fishery's operations. There's a lot of unregulated fishing too, and we're asking the Department of Culture, Arts and Leisure to patrol more and pick up boats that are out there at funny times of night. But it's quite politically contentious, and Lough Neagh also supports Northern Ireland's last remaining eel fishery, which many families depend on, so that's another reason we can't come down too hard on the whole situation."

Even so, significant victories have already been won. Around the turn of the millennium, as founder of Kingsbridge Angling Club on the water just below

Tied by Henry Noble, a reliable range of flies for adult dollaghan returning from Lough Neagh

Cookstown, Henry made it his personal objective to get the town's sewage treatment works upgraded: built for a population of no more than 5,000, they were at least eight times overloaded, and the famous spawning gravels at Killymoon were clogged with gelatinous grey sewage fungus.

By 2005, thanks to Henry's campaigning efforts, one of the worst-performing treatment works in Europe had become one of the best, and salmon and dollaghan have been seen spawning again under the windows of Killymoon Castle.

On this early summer morning, snub-nosed baby dollaghan are boiling after black gnats in the deep far run of Benson's Pool, resculpted by Henry himself with a digger, and there's a faraway look in his eyes as he gazes downstream to the castle and the pool where he caught his own biggest dollaghan (two ounces short of twelve pounds), remembering what the river looked like before the dredgers came.

"Old Albert Montgomery used to say *'if you can't catch six or seven dollaghan a night at Killymoon, you're not a fisherman'*, but that was when a good dark flood off the peat would be fishable for four days at a time. Now you'll be lucky if it lasts just one day… but maybe we'll get it all back, maybe we will!"

Cookstown: River Ballinderry

Who's looking after the river?

The Ballinderry River Enhancement Association was formed in 1984 as an alliance of 7 local angling clubs in response to the dwindling numbers of native dollaghan trout in the Ballinderry River, and problems of pollution and habitat loss across the catchment.

Supported by WWF-UK and the Ballinderry Fish Hatchery community business, BREA's RIPPLE (*Rivers Involving People, Places and Leading by Example*) project is placing the river's fortunes back into the hands of local people. Volunteer champions are now leading actions including river clean-ups, riverfly monitoring, eradicating invasive species, improving access and conserving iconic native species like dollaghan, white-clawed crayfish, freshwater pearl mussel and ranunculus.

For the latest information, visit:
www.ballinderryriver.org
www.wwf.org.uk/ripple

Getting there

Although 2 different railways once terminated at Cookstown, it's now impossible to reach the town by train, but there's plenty of parking along the wide, tree-lined streets.

Maps of Cookstown are available from the Burnavon Arts and Cultural Centre on Burnavon Road, BT80 8DN: OSNI Discoverer 13 and 14 are also recomended.

Seasons and permits

Brown trout, dollaghan and salmon seasons run from 1 March to 30 October.

Department of Culture, Arts and Leisure game fishing licences are available from the Burnavon Centre. Kings Bridge Angling Club controls around half a mile of fishing alongside the Cabin Wood walk on the south side of Cookstown. For full details, visit: www.ballinderryriver.org

Fishing tips

The Ballinderry holds increasing numbers of resident brown trout to ¾ lb, as well as juvenile dollaghan and salmon parr. Between July and October, mature dollaghan return from Lough Neagh weighing 6 to 10lbs, with occasional specimens even larger.

For stalking the smaller resident trout, a lightweight rod of 7 to 8ft is ideal, rated for a 1 to 4 weight line. The river has always been renowned for its hawthorn fishing, and many locals favour falls of terrestrials like black gnats and aphids, despite growing populations of olives, caddis and small pale shrimp.

At the back end of the season, dollaghan fishing demands a more robust approach, with a rod of 9 to 10ft for a 6 to 8 weight line. For anglers like Henry and James Noble, Irish shrimp patterns on double hooks have proved their worth over many years. Muddler Minnows twitched across the surface can also provoke explosive, predatory takes.

Don't miss

● Killymoon Castle: visible from the Kings Bridge Angling Club water, built in 1803 to a design by John Nash, architect of London's Regent Street

● The National Trust's Wellbrook Beetling Mill: the last working water-powered linen mill in Northern Ireland

● The annual Banks of the Ballinderry Fair at Wellbrook Beetling Mill

Urban fly-fishing techniques

Stealth, observation and matching the hatch: fly-fishing is fly-fishing, and many of the skills and principles you'd normally apply to more rural waters can easily be transferred to city streams.

But whilst you're getting your strategies in order, it's also worth thinking about a few tried and tested ways you can contribute directly to making your urban fishing truly sustainable for the future.

Best of all, they'll even help you make the most of your sport today.

Fish stealthy

Rules like fishing upstream nymph and dry flies only are rare in the edgelands, so you're usually free to try any method that takes your fancy, and each chapter includes details of locally-recommended flies and techniques. The vast majority of the fish photographed in these pages

Stealth in the city: the author's standby one-weight rod and fly box

were caught and safely released on outfits rated for a 4 weight line or lighter. Delicate lines fall gently on the water, and offer less resistance when a trout or grayling takes your fly: light rods are also very good at cushioning the fine tippets you may need to adopt for clear water, tiny flies and streetwise fish.

Travel light

One of the biggest bonuses of fishing in the urban jungle is that you're rarely far from a supermarket, pub, café or petrol station. So you can afford to travel light, picking up food and drink on the way. With a map, a small rucksack, a travel rod, a couple of fly boxes, and a few tools on a lanyard over breathable waist or chest waders, you're all set to blend into your surroundings, and move fast and far.

Go by public transport

Why worry about parking your car in the badlands when you can often get to the riverside faster by bus, train or tram? Public transport can give you a whole new angle on the city, and cuts your carbon footprint too. Travel and fishery information is included at the end of every chapter (although this may change, so check online before you go) and it's always worth investing in the relevant Ordnance Survey Explorer maps for your chosen urban streams.

Catch and release

Recovering rivers and their growing populations of wild trout and grayling can easily be damaged by human predation. If in doubt, most of the organisations in this book would strongly advocate returning all your fish to the water. Practising catch and release is simplest with flies tied on barbless or debarbed hooks: these penetrate well, commonly fall out in the net, and are easier to remove from clothing, trees and bushes. Try to touch fish with wetted hands only, in order to preserve their protective layer of slime: an important defence mechanism in a hostile urban environment where heavy metals, sewage and other contaminants abound.

Check, clean, dry

If you fish different waters, it's becoming more and more important not to spread invasive non-native species from one to another on wet or dirty kit. Wash any mud or silt off your boots and waders before you leave the river, then check your clothing and tackle for bugs or fragments of vegetation which might want to hitch a lift. If possible, dry everything overnight or longer before visiting your next fishery: in damp conditions, some species like the killer shrimp can survive for five days, and crayfish plague spores remain viable for up to two weeks.

Avoid hotspotting

Leave only footprints, take only photos (and maybe a bag of litter you've picked up on the way), and try not to be too specific about exact locations if you write or blog about your inner-city adventures. Urban fisheries are vulnerable to poaching, so why tell the whole world about that productive pool you've discovered?

Report any pollution

If you find dead fish or discover any evidence of pollution, including strange smells or oily blooms on the water, report your suspicions immediately to the Environment Agency's incident hotline on 0800 80 70 60, or go to your NIEA or SEPA equivalent. The faster the authorities find out about a problem, the sooner they can stop it damaging one of our precious urban streams.

Getting involved

Why you're needed

No matter how well an urban river is looked after, there's always more to do, and any of the people and organisations profiled in this book would be immensely grateful for your help. From invertebrate monitoring to river clean-ups – or even making a small contribution to core running costs – you'll find plenty of ways to get involved. Even statutory bodies like the Environment Agency can do their work far more effectively with active collaboration from anglers and others who care about the health of our rivers. Contact your chosen group via the website details at the end of each chapter... or buy a map, check out your own local river, and contact the Wild Trout Trust to set up a *Trout in the Town* chapter of your own!

Restoring an urban river can be hard work, but it's very satisfying and can be great fun

Staying safe

Exploring the steel and concrete canyons of urban rivers can sometimes feel like an extreme sport. No-one designed these raw, uncompromising surroundings to provide an angling experience that's manicured or even safe: they can offer world-class fishing and a real sense of adventure, but it's wise to take some of the possible risks into account.

Treat this list of suggestions as your starting point, and remember that when you want to get out alive, there's no substitute for common sense.

Watch the water levels

Many post-industrial rivers are located in V-shaped valleys where mill owners could maximise the kinetic energy of steeply-falling water. Today, rain running off acres of roads, roofs and other hard surfaces makes these rivers even flashier, raising water levels within hours or minutes if there's a storm further up the catchment. Check your escape routes, and don't think twice about using them.

Fish with a friend

Experienced urban fly-fishers sometimes go solo on well-known rivers, but if you're investigating a new stream it's often advisable to make the trip with a fishing pal. Two's company if you need to deter an opportunistic mugger on a lonely bank, and it's also much easier to get up and over obstacles with a helping hand.

Beware of silty, sharp and steep

Vast quantities of silt accumulate behind structures like weirs, and any part of the river can conceal sharp or slippery debris. If you find yourself sinking into deep silt, walk back out the way you came. Consider using a wading staff as well as steel-shanked or toecapped boots, and don't jump into water where you can't

see the bottom or a reliable way to climb out again. Watch out for dangerous plants like giant hogweed, with its hairy stems and huge, jagged leaves: each hair holds a droplet of photo-activated sap which can cause recurring third-degree burns for years.

Treat culverts with caution

Wade upstream into culverts if you must, never down. You don't know what's in there, and if you're working against the current in the first place, you can partly rely on it to help you get out again, rather than force you further into trouble.

Wash your hands

Water quality in most urban rivers has improved dramatically in the last twenty years, but many still suffer from sewer misconnections, CSOs and the legacy of years of industrial pollution. Areas of slow-flowing or stagnant water may also harbour leptospirosis (Weil's disease): a bacterial infection transmitted in rats' urine which can prove fatal if not treated quickly. Consider carrying a first aid kit, cover any cuts or grazes with waterproof plasters before fishing, and wash your hands before eating, drinking or smoking. If you develop flu-like symptoms within three weeks of fishing an urban river, it's probably worth visiting your doctor and mentioning the possibility of leptospirosis.

Well, sometimes...

Beware River

Acknowledgements

More than most research and writing projects, a book of this scope would have been impossible to put together without generous assistance from literally hundreds of experts and professionals.

In the best copywriting tradition of art directors everywhere, my old advertising pal Andy Bullock provided me with a title, and my visionary publishers Merlin and Karen Unwin have offered encouragement and support at every step of the way Needless to say, I'm eternally grateful to…

John Abraham, John Adams, Mike Adams, Malcolm Anderson, Denise Ashton, Richard Aylard, Jo Aylwin, Chris Bainger, Jenni Balmer, Allen Beechey, Mike Beeson, Cyril Bennett, Adrian Bicknell, Robert Blackett, John Blewitt, Tony Bostock, Rick Bossons, Mark Bowler, Tim Boycott, Dave Brown, Christina Bryant, Matt Buck, Nicole Caetano, Rod Calbrade, Andrew Caldwell, Fran Cambridge, Nick Carter, Paul Carter, Katherine Causer, Roy Christie, Bekka Close, Paul Cole, Ray Collier, John Connolly, Danny Connor, Ian Cook, Graham Counsell, Andy Coyne, Greg Cracknell, William Daniel, Bella Davies, Tom Davis, Derrick Dennis, Mike Denny, Sandra Dodkins, Tom Donnai, Richard Doran, Rob Doyle, Mike Duddy, Ivan Dunn, Andy Eaves, Mark Eden-Bushell, Peter Ehmann, Fiona Ellwood, Erica Evans, Simon Evans, Mark Everard, Peter Evoy, Martin Fenn, Rachel Fielding, Ian Finylas, Chris Firth, Allan Frake, Dave French, Stephen Frye, Dominic Garnett, Alison Graham-Smith, Kevin Gregson, Sarah Guest, Nick Hart, Matthew Hawkins, Ian Hayes, Tony Hayter, Colin Hides, David Holland, Diane Holland, Mark Horton, Tanya Houston, Kathy Hughes, Ashe Hurst, David Hyde, Alex Inman, Neil Ireland, Tim Jacklin, Nick James, Tim James, Paul Jennings, Simon Johnson, Seth Johnson-Marshall, David Jones, Jason Jones, Kirsty Jones, Morgan Jones, Dick Kew, Alan Keys, Raif Killips, Louis Kitchen, John Knowles, Mick Krupa, Gareth Lewis, Vaughan Lewis, Peter Lapsley, Shaun Leonard, John Leyland, Paul Lidgett, Martin Limbert, Mark Lloyd, Ray Lockyer, Chris Longsdon, Philip Lord, Jenny Mant, Neil Marfell, Christine Marsh, Mick Martin, Burnie Maurins, Pete McParlin, Owain Mealing, Toby Merigan, Patrick Mileham, Sally Mitchell, John Morgan, Tony Murphy, Kevin Nash, Charlotte Neary, Malcolm Newson, Henry Noble, James Noble, Tony Norman, Ian Oates, John O'Brien, Simon Ogden, Steve Ormerod, Andrew Parker, Rob Parnell, Donald Patterson, Neil Patterson, John Pawlica, Bridget Peacock, Bob Pearce, John Pearson, Jon Petterssen, Alan Poulton, Andy Pritchard, Vicky Pudner, Charles Rangeley-Wilson, Ian Rees, Tony Rees, Gideon Reeve, Paul Rendell, John Rennie, Tom Richards, Arlin Rickard, Stacey Riley, Dai Roberts, Sir John Roberts, Martin Ross, Roger Round, Steve Rowe, Archie Ruggles-Brise, William Rundle, Mark Rylands, Paul St Pierre, Matthew Schofield, Graham Scholey, Steve Skuce, Warren Slaney, Fraser Sommerville, Roger Smith, Will Smith, Jim Stanford, Colin Stanley, Nickol Stewardson, Alistair Stewart, John Sutton, Lawrence Talks, William Tall, Andy Thomas, Rose Timlett, Andreas Topintzis, Neil Trudgill, Bill Turner, Pete Tyjas, Herman Wagler, Geoff Waites, Andrew Wallace, Tim Walmsley, Mike Weaver, Dave Webb, Stephen Webster, Tom Whitehead, Andy Wigley, Sarah Williams, Simon Withey, Henry Wood, Dave Woodhead, John Woods, Pete Worrall and Willie Yeomans…

… for years of hard work on restoring urban rivers so that trout and grayling can thrive, and the rest of us can chase them. And then for gifting me with endless wisdom, time, advice, flies, and hospitality whilst I've tried to understand the intricacies of their catchments.

In particular, I'd also like to thank my own fishing pals (and fearless co-conspirators in urban exploration and river-mending) from the Wandle and the Wild Trout Trust: Richard Baker, Stuart Crofts, Paul Gaskell, Adrian Grose-Hodge, Jez Mallinson and Duncan Soar. Left to my own devices, without their heron-like ability to read rivers and catch fish, there wouldn't be nearly so many portraits of trophy trout and grayling in these pages.

But my very biggest thanks must go to my wife Sally, who bakes great cake for the Wandle's volunteers, swings a mean river-restoration sledgehammer… and hasn't objected once as I've headed out to catch trout in dirty places, and then locked myself away with Winnie the cocker spaniel to write about them.

Finally, to anyone who may have been inadvertently omitted from this list, I offer my heartfelt thanks and apologies. Any omissions or inaccuracies within the text are entirely my own.

253

Index

About the author

Theo Pike is an angling, environmental and marketing writer. As Chairman of the Wandle Trust, he has been instrumental in starting to restore South London's River Wandle to its historic status as a world-famous chalkstream fishery. This project's success inspired the Wild Trout Trust to establish a national *Trout in the Town* programme, with the Wandle as its flagship initiative.

As a result of his experience in urban river restoration, Theo has done much work advising other groups on mobilising local support, motivating volunteers, best practice for river clean-ups, and promoting positive links between angling and conservation. He was awarded the Wild Trout Trust's *Bernard Venables Award* for services to wild trout conservation in 2008, and internationally honoured as a Sage Conservation Hero in 2009.

He lives, with his wife Sally, in south London.

Photo credits

The author thanks the following for permission to use their photos:
- Adrian Grose-Hodge: back cover plus page 164
- Dominic Garnett: front cover plus pages 5, 9, 28, 30, 31, 256
- Duncan Soar: pages 69, 206
- Matt Buck: page 109
- Merlin Unwin: page 126
- Mick Martin: page 121
- Paul Gaskell: pages 186, 192, 204
- Tim Longstaff: page 68 (bottom)